# NATIONS OF THE MODERN WORLD

AUSTRALIA     O. H. K. Spate
*Director, Research School of Pacific Studies,*
*Australian National University, Canberra*

CEYLON     S. A. Pakeman
*Formerly Professor of Modern History, Ceylon*
*University College; Appointed Member, House of*
*Representatives, Ceylon, 1947–52*

MODERN EGYPT Tom Little
*Managing Director and General Manager of*
*Regional News Services (Middle East), Ltd., London*

ENGLAND     John Bowle
   A Portrait     *Professor of Political Theory, Collège d'Europe,*
*Bruges*

MODERN INDIA Sir Percival Griffiths
*President of the India, Pakistan and Burma*
*Association*

MODERN IRAN    Peter Avery
*Lecturer in Persian and Fellow of King's College,*
*Cambridge*

ITALY     Muriel Grindrod
*Formerly Editor of* International Affairs *and*
The World Today
*Assistant Editor of* The Annual Register

JAPAN     Sir Esler Dening
*H.M. Ambassador to Japan, 1952–57*

KENYA     A. Marshall MacPhee
*Formerly Managing Editor of* The East African
Standard Group; *producer with British Broadcasting*
*Corporation*

MALAYA     J. M. Gullick
*Formerly of the Malayan Civil Service*

MOROCCO        Mark I. Cohen
               and
               Lorna Hahn

NIGERIA        Sir Rex Niven
               *Colonial Service, Nigeria, 1921–59; Member of
               Northern House of Assembly, 1947–59*

NEW ZEALAND    James W. Rowe
               *Director of New Zealand Institute of Economic
               Research, Inc.*
               Margaret A. Rowe
               *Tutor in English, Victoria University, Wellington*

PAKISTAN       Ian Stephens
               *Formerly Editor of* The Statesman *Calcutta and
               Delhi, 1942–51; Fellow of King's College,
               Cambridge, 1952–58*

SOUTH AFRICA   John Cope
               *Formerly Editor-in-Chief of* The Forum; *South
               African Correspondent of* The Guardian

SUDAN
  REPUBLIC     K. D. D. Henderson
               *Formerly of the Sudan Political Service; Governor of
               Darfur Province, 1949–53*

TURKEY         Geoffrey Lewis
               *Senior Lecturer in Islamic Studies, Oxford*

THE UNITED     H. C. Allen
STATES OF      *Commonwealth Fund Professor of American History,*
AMERICA        *University College, London*

WEST           Michael Balfour
GERMANY        *Reader in European History, University of
               East Anglia*

YUGOSLAVIA     Muriel Heppell
               and
               F. B. Singleton

NATIONS OF THE MODERN WORLD

---

# KENYA

# KENYA

*By*

## A. MARSHALL MACPHEE

**FREDERICK A. PRAEGER,** *Publishers*

New York · Washington

BOOKS THAT MATTER

Published in the United States of America in 1968
by Frederick A. Praeger, Inc., Publishers
111 Fourth Avenue, New York, N.Y. 10003

© 1968 in London, England, by A. Marshall MacPhee

Library of Congress Catalog Card Number: 68–21161

Printed in Great Britain

To

J.D.T. with memories of

happy years, and for R.T.G.

a reminder of where he

was born

# Preface

To PUT on record in a single, comprehensive and factual account the story of Kenya from earliest times to the position it holds today among the nations of the world has been a challenging task. The country has such wide contrasts in people, land and climate and it is still, as Winston Churchill once described it, a world in miniature, a place where the social, racial and economic stresses which rack modern society can be seen at work. That Kenya has been able to survive as an independent nation despite these stresses and the anxious years of the 1950s when it was a land of violence and a battleground for the African, European and Asian, makes it a fascinating, if complex, subject for the student of African affairs.

In creating this account I have consulted many authentic works, a list of which appears in the Bibliography, and I readily acknowledge their value in any study of Kenya and its history. But I have also been fortunate enough to be able to use the knowledge and understanding that can only come from living happily in a country for a number of years and knowing its people.

*The Monk's House*  A. MARSHALL MACPHEE
*Withyham*
*Sussex*
*December 1967*

# Contents

# Map

# List of Illustrations

(All are inserted between pages 96 and 97)

1 Fort Jesus, the seventeenth-century stronghold on Mombasa Island

2 Arab dhows, the type of ships that have been sailing along the monsoon trade routes to eastern Africa since the dawn of history

3 Kikuyu herd boys on the Limuru escarpment overlooking the Great Rift Valley

4 An African farmer and his family picking pyrethrum on his new farm in the former 'White' Highlands of Kenya

5 The heart of Kenya's soda industry at Lake Magadi on the floor of the Great Rift Valley

6 Old Mombasa, *Mvita*, the Island of War

7 Modern Nairobi, Kenya's capital city

8 Harry Thuku, pictured in retirement

9 Sir Philip Mitchell, Governor of Kenya from 1944 to 1952

10 Jomo Kenyatta, in middle age

11 Sir Evelyn Baring (later Lord Howick), Governor of Kenya from 1952 to 1959

12 Mr D. N. Pritt, Q.C., who led the defence in the Kenyatta trial

13 Kikuyu tribesmen, suspected of Mau Mau activities, await screening in a fortified police post at Nyeri

14 Mau Mau detainees at the Thomson's Falls detention camp with temporary gallows in the background

15 A young Kikuyu, ragged follower of Mau Mau, arrested by security forces in a forest action

16 Forest fighters of the Kenya Land Freedom Army after their surrender under the 1963 amnesty

13

# Acknowledgements

ACKNOWLEDGEMENT for kind permission to reproduce illustrations is made to the following, to whom the copyright of the illustrations belongs:

Barnaby's Picture Library: 1, 6, 7, 16

United Press International (UK) Ltd: 2, 4, 5, 8, 14, 17, 18, 20, 21, 22, 24, 25, 26, 28, 29

Paul Popper Ltd: 3, 10, 12, 13, 15, 19, 23, 27

Keystone Press Agency Ltd: 9, 11

Acknowledgement is also made to the Hutchinson Publishing Group Ltd for permission to quote extracts from *African Afterthoughts* by Sir Philip Mitchell.

# Part One

# EARLY HISTORY

## Chapter 1

# The Lands of Azania and Zinj

## I

LONG BEFORE the Bantu people appeared on the Kenya scene, lapping the areas of Nilo-Hamitic occupation in their northward and eastward migrations, there existed between the Stone Age and medieval times a civilisation which has been called Azanian — after Azania, the name given by the ancient Greeks to East Africa south-west of Cape Guardafui. The Azanians occupied a large part of the Kenya Highlands and remains found there show that they lived in substantially-built enclosures of stone, dug hut-circles, re-vetted walls, made properly-engineered roads and possessed the art of irrigation. It is thought that they may have been part of a Hamitic civilisation that flourished in the Horn of Africa, now the state of Somalia, during the first 700 years A.D. and was destroyed by Islam, its makers retreating southwards through Kenya.[1] But in the ebb and flow of migration and warfare, of conquest and settlement which covered a period of five hundred years before the nineteenth century, the Azanian civilisation disappeared and little of its culture has survived.

The Azanians must have found the Kenya hinterland, with its temperate climate, a veritable paradise after the deserts of the north-east. Set high on the African tableland, the greater part of the country lies behind a range of natural barriers and it is separated from the coastal plain by the *nyika*, a stretch of steeply-rising ground, over a hundred miles in length, waterless and covered with thick forest and thorn. The *nyika* follows the 300-mile length of the coast-line deep into Tanzania in the south and its northern limit merges with yet another barrier, the desert province along the border with Somalia, Ethiopia, the Sudan and Uganda. There is a river, the River Tana, which runs between these two arid lands but never at

[1] *Antiquity*, G. W. B. Huntingford, *The Azanian Civilisation of Kenya*, p. 164.

any time has it provided a practical route to the interior as rapids
soon develop where it cuts through the foothills guarding the approaches to the Highlands. In the south there is the savannah
country of the Tanzania border with its immense distances and
scant water supplies and only in the west in the region of the great
lakes, the gateway to the Congo, the 'hot wild core of Africa' which
has still to emerge completely from its primitive state, did geography in the past offer any kind of reasonable access. But this
centre of Africa was isolated behind its own natural barriers and any
contacts with Kenya from the outside had to come from the East
Coast; and thus the hinterland was virtually isolated from developments in the western world till the middle of the nineteenth century.

Yet at one time the Kenya hinterland was the scene of those early
race migrations that determined the distribution of historical mankind. They took place most probably along the route of the Great
Rift Valley. This gigantic fault in the earth's outer crust – in effect a
system of rifts and lakes – runs for three thousand miles down a
sinuous, meridian line from the Red Sea to the Zambesi. The Kenya
branch is the Valley at its most spectacular and splits the country
into two, almost equal but environmentally different, parts. Apart
from the scenery it is a window on the prehistory of the world, for
there is ample evidence of man's primeval movements in the number
of different hand-axe cultures found along its route. One of them,
the Oldowan culture, is the oldest evidence yet found of man's tool-
making capacities and is known to have spread from Africa into the
peripheral areas of Europe and Asia.[1] The fossils and prehistoric
camping sites uncovered along the Kenya and Tanzania section of
the Great Rift Valley by Dr L. S. B. Leakey and other antiquarians
since the 1930s also give credibility to the theory that the human
race originated in Africa, though the exact dating is still in dispute.[2]
They have shown that Kenya, being within the ice-free equatorial
belt, was a haven for many kinds of plants, beasts and men during
the world glaciations of the Pleistocene period.

The early Stone Age Kenya people were hunters, great travellers, and a trace of them can be seen today among the last remnants of the Dorobo people who live around the Mau forests on the

[1] *History of East Africa*, Vol. I: S. Cole, *The Stone Age*, p. 27.
[2] 'Although the theory is still open to scientific question, the balance of
opinion suggests that the African continent now has the first claim to pre-
eminence as the cradle of mankind.' *History of Mankind*: Jacquetta Hawkes,
*Evolution of Man*, p. 34.

western shoulder of the Rift Valley and who at one time occupied much of eastern Africa. Although over the last 300 years the Dorobo have adopted the cultures of their neighbours, the Nilo-Hamitic Nandi people, and are often indistinguishable from them outwardly, they still retain the characteristics of symbiotic hunters. They are accorded the local distinction of being the original inhabitants of the world, a legend well-recorded in tribal lore and supported to a certain extent by the scientific observation that they are survivals of one of the early stocks which have contributed to the rest of the modern peoples of East Africa.[1]

The ancient Dorobo might well have shared the occupation of early Kenya with another stock, a strange race of tall, long-headed people with fine features and pronounced European-type characteristics. These Caucasoid or Upper Kenya Capsian types lived in settlements by the Rift Valley lakes and possibly came from a cradle-land in south-west Asia, crossing the land bridges that at one time spanned the Red Sea.[2] They led a fairly sedentary and sophisticated life for their times and relied more on fishing than on hunting for their existence. They worked pottery, bone, leather and wood, and for their stone tools they used obsidian, the black volcanic glass which they mined close to their settlements and traded over great distances. They buried their dead ceremoniously and adorned themselves with red ochre and beads of tortoiseshell.

The Upper Kenya Capsians have persisted as a type right up to the present day as they were reinforced, or more likely absorbed, by succeeding migratory waves of the related Hamites who began to appear in north-east Africa during the late Stone Age. These Hamites, also from south-west Asia, have had a strong influence on the racial characteristics of the present peoples of Kenya, as strong as their influence on the peoples who inhabit the cradle of civilisation round the Mediterranean.[3] To the ancient Greeks they were the

[1] *History of East Africa*, Vol. I: G. W. B. Huntingford, *The Peoples*, p. 63.
[2] These individuals of the Caucasian race had no negroid characteristics. They were a mesolithic people and gave rise to the Upper Capsian culture which is estimated to have lasted from about 10,000 B.C. to 4,000 B.C. Cole, op. cit., p. 34.
[3] In the 1957 revised edition of Seligman's *Races of Africa*, p. 84, the Hamites are described as Europeans, i.e. belonging to the same great branch of mankind as the whites. Seligman says the Eastern Hamites comprise the ancient and modern Egyptians (in the latter case recognising the infusion of foreign blood in the upper classes), the Berberines (Nubians), the Galla, the Somali and, though mixed with Semites and Negroes, most Ethiopians.

Troglodytes, one of the four great races of man living to the south
of Egypt.[1]

The Negro, though appearing later on the historic scene, has had
by far the greatest racial influence in Africa. Yet the negro influence
is less marked north of the so-called Bantu line, the irregular, ethno-
graphical boundary running across the continent from Cape Verde
in the west to Mount Kenya in the east. There is no evidence of
Negroes being in eastern Africa before the beginning of historical
time about five thousand years ago, and negro blood does not exist
among the various Kenya peoples in any kind of purity.

Exactly where the Negroes came from has still to be firmly
established; one theory is that they came from Central India where
there are aborigines with negroid characteristics; but more likely
they developed from the negrillos or pygmies of the thick forests near
the headwaters of the River Congo in a cradle-land somewhere in
southern Sudan. It was in this part of Africa, along the banks of the
Nile in an area between Khartoum and Lake Victoria, that a mixed
group of peoples developed from the meeting between the Negroes
and the Hamites. Known as the Nile Valley peoples they spread deep
into Kenya in two major divisions: the Nilotes, the Luo of Victoria
Nyanza, and the Nilo-Hamites, the Nandi and Masai of the Highlands. All of them have negro blood in various degrees – the Luo the
most – the Nandi and Masai the least.[2]

The foundation stocks of the Kenya people are present in separate
distinctive forms; but they also come together as a racial mixture in
the Bantu, the widely-spread congeries of peoples who occupy three-
quarters of the African continent south of the Sahara and who also
make up most of the population of Kenya. They have been formed,
through centuries of migration, intermarriage and conquest, into
tribes which vary in size from a few hundreds to many thousands
of members. There is an enormous variation in racial characteristics:
skin colour ranges from coal-black to golden brown; and stature
from tall and muscular to small and wiry. But the Bantu are clearly
identified by two positive links – their black, crinkly hair and their

---

[1] The first attempt at classifying the peoples of north-east Africa was made
by Agatharchidus of Cnidus in 130 B.C. Huntingford describes it as a remark-
ably acute classification for so early a period. *History of East Africa*, Vol. I:
*The Peoples*, p. 60.

[2] The sickle-shaped blood cell, the distinctive feature of Negroes, is used by
anthropologists to determine the amount of negro blood in an ethnic group.
Huntingford, op. cit., p. 58.

language. All the Bantu languages are basically the same and the group description was taken from *Abantu*, the typical common word which means people.

The Bantu reached their present homes in East Africa in a series of movements, possibly from the north under pressure of the successive Hamitic invasions. There were two migratory waves into Kenya. One came round the north side of Lake Victoria from the west and settled in the Kavirondo district between the lake shore and the Nandi uplands. Out of this migration developed the Luhya group of peoples known as the Bantu Kavirondo – not to be confused with the Nyanza Luo. The other wave came south of the lake, across what is now Tanzania and then northwards up the Kenya Coast to the legendary dispersal area of Shungwaya situated between the Tana and Juba rivers at the north-eastern end of the Bantu line. These Bantu split up into a number of major tribes: the Pokomo of the Tana, the Nyika and Taita of the coastland, the Kamba of the eastern plains, and the Kikuyu, Embu and Meru of Mount Kenya.

By the nineteenth century a third of Kenya was occupied by Bantu peoples, the rest by Nilo-Hamitics and a sprinkling of pure Hamitics, akin to the present Somali and Boran, who lived along the northern boundary, and a settlement of Nilotes, the Luo, round the shores of Lake Victoria. All these peoples were in clearly defined tribal communities, each with its own area of influence; but during the middle part of the century, when Dr Johann Ludwig Krapf[1] was opening up the interior to the outside world, the Nilo-Hamitic Masai dominated all other tribes, spreading their orbit wherever there were plains and good pasture lands. The Masai, whose ruling passions were cattle and warfare, had come in the late sixteenth century

---

[1] Dr Krapf was the first European to record his impressions of the Kenya interior. He reported in 1849, much to the scepticism of geographers, the existence of a snow-capped mountain on the Equator and surrounded by cool, highland country. This mountain, a glimpse of which he caught from the Kamba village of Kitui, he called *Kima ja Kegnia* which he said was the Kamba name for Mount of Whiteness. But Krapf seems to have misunderstood the local dialect for there is no such word as Kegnia in the Kamba vocabulary. However, the name Kegnia has persisted and developed by common usage into Kenya which is similar to *Erukenya*, the Masai description of a mountain shrouded in mist. The Kikuyu name for Mount Kenya is *Kere-Nyaga*, the Mountain of Mystery. One theory of the misunderstanding by Krapf of the Kamba description of the mountain is that the Kamba have neither the letter R nor the letter G standing alone in their language and therefore they pronounce *Kere-Nyaga* as *Kiinyaa*. The Kamba of course are closely related to the Kikuyu and their vernacular is similar.

from a homeland in the far north round the basin of Lake Rudolph, and a rapid southward movement had taken them down the Rift Valley and into what is now Tanzania. They had displaced on the way their fellow Nilo-Hamites, the Nandi, who were forced back to their hills overlooking Lake Victoria.

Masai warfare, to which their young men, the morans, were submitted by rigid discipline, was rarely directed to the conquest of territory or subjects. Its sole objective was the procurement of cattle and the proving of Masai manhood, and warriors raided indiscriminately leaving behind them a trail of terror. Unlike the Zulu, the Masai never fought as a single, compact army; but their warrior bands were very effective in open combat. They would form a solid phalanx of buffalo-hide shields and in two lines surge forward in a rush and hurl their broad-bladed spears with deadly accuracy. This, however, was for war on the plains and it was not quite so effective in the forests and on the rocky slopes of the uplands. The other more peacefully-disposed tribes, who occupied the higher ground in greater numbers, were therefore able to keep the Masai at bay. While the Masai were the masters of the plains, the Kikuyu in their forests and the Taita, Kamba, Nandi and others in their hills were able to develop in numbers and prosperity in the higher, more fertile and productive land.

There was a broad equilibrium in the pattern of early Kenya life, disturbed only by internecine strife and the toll of disease, both human and animal. By the nineteenth century there was a certain amount of inter-tribal trade and the Masai, for instance, traded hides with the Kikuyu for grain and other crops to augment their blood and milk diet.

For the Kamba trading was a major occupation. Related closely to the Taita of south-east Kenya and to the peoples round Kilimanjaro, they had friendly connections over a wide area of East Africa and when Dr Krapf first visited them in 1849 he recorded that they were in active trade with the Coast on the other side of the *nyika*, selling hides, ivory and slaves in return for cotton goods, beads, copper wire and salt. They were the collectors and transporters for the entrepreneurs of the Coast and their trading caravans travelled through most parts of the interior free from the Masai.

But during the second half of the century it was the Arabs from Zanzibar, the Zanzibaris, who fully exploited what trade there was with the interior. Their activities were part of a wider penetration of East Africa, their objective a route to Lake Victoria and to the country of the Nile that was shorter and more direct than the other trading routes which had struck inland from Zanzibar and already covered the western side of the lake and Uganda.

## II

The Arabs have been trading to East Africa since the dawn of history. Their ancient biographers knew it as the land of Zinj, the Negro Coast, and for centuries its islands and lagoons behind their protective, coral reefs have been used as staging posts in the great Indian Ocean trade between Asia and Africa. The maritime belt, separated from the rest of Kenya by the *nyika*, has, therefore, a distinct history of its own.

Kenya by the sea is tropical and influenced both climatically and historically by the Indian Ocean monsoons. From May to September these winds blow as moderate to strong south-east trades along the Coast, changing direction to the south-west as north of the Equator they are caught up in the oceanic monsoon. From November to March they are replaced by the steady, light wind of the north-east trades which in character and direction fit into the continental monsoon of Asia.[1] They are the main source of Kenya's rainfall and over the centuries they have provided the propellant power for the trading ships of Asia, blowing them south to the East African Coast from November to March, and conveniently back again to Arabia and beyond from May to September. They are one of nature's great aids to man and still play a vital part in the traditional dhow trade between the ports of Kenya and the Persian Gulf.

Hippalus the voyager informed the civilised world about the monsoon trade winds in A.D. 67 and by the end of the first century Graeco-Roman ships were trading down the East African Coast from the ancient Red Sea port of Berenice, bringing with them dyed cloaks and tunics, copper and tin, and returning with frankincense, tortoiseshell and ivory.[2] This trade lasted till the late fourth century when Persian sea-power became dominant in the Indian Ocean and the Aksum empire, the forerunner of modern Ethiopia, extended its own trade routes into Kenya. The Aksumites in turn lost the

[1] *History of East Africa*, Vol. I: S. J. Baker, *The East Africa Environment*, p. 9.
[2] W. H. Schoff, *Periplus of the Erythrean Sea*, 1912.

coastlands to the Muslims in the eighth century and from then on the Kenya Coast came under the influence of Islam.

There were also contacts with the Far East and by the tenth century Chinese geographers had a detailed knowledge of *Po Pa Li*, the country bordering the north-east coast, and knew about the customs of the 'black and ferocious' inhabitants of *Mo Lin*, present-day Malindi.[1] Most of the wealthy merchants in Canton had African slaves who, together with ivory, rhino-horn for the manufacture of love potions, and ambergris, were known to China as the products of the Land of Zinj. The Chinese probably bought these from the Indonesians of Sumatra who introduced the outrigger canoe and the banana to East Africa. Traders came, too, from the Chola kingdom of south-east India and by the fourteenth century the Indian system of weights and the Maldive cowrie-shell currency were widespread in the coastal regions.

During the fourteenth century, the great Islamic states of Egypt, Arabia, India and Indonesia were all-powerful in the Indian Ocean. They controlled the trade between the East and medieval Europe, a trade in which East Africa with its ivory and gold played an important part. But by far the greatest value of East Africa to the Islamic states themselves was the market it provided in the slaves who were considered essential to the Muslim way of life.

The vast hinterland of primitive peoples was an inexhaustible reservoir of slaves, and by the fifteenth century the Arabs had established along the Coast a number of trading ports which had grown prosperous through the possession of local catchments. These ports were, in effect, autonomous city states and being Arab were often at feud and bitter enemies. It was this fact that no doubt prevented any extensive colonisation – though in time the Arabs were to become absorbed, losing their characteristics as invaders and, by interbreeding with the local people, creating the Swahili whose language, part Arabic and part Bantu, is now spread over most of eastern and central Africa.

Arab prosperity was at its peak in 1497 when the Portuguese sea-explorer Vasco da Gama rounded the southern tip of Africa and made his way up the Coast to Mombasa. The Portuguese were searching for some means to reach the fabulous markets of the East by outflanking the strong forces of Islam who dominated the Mediterranean and land approaches farther north, and when they reached

[1] *History of East Africa*, Vol. I: G. Mathew, *The Coast*, p. 107.

Mombasa they found it packed with ships bound for Arabia and the Far East and heavily laden with slaves, ivory and gold from the southern trading centres of Sofala, Kilwa and Zanzibar. Eight years later the covetous Portuguese were able to claim the whole of the Coast and the trade route to India and beyond, for the East African Arabs of the sultanate ports – in effect 'city states' – were divided among themselves and unable to deal with a common enemy.

But the Portuguese occupation of East Africa, if it could be called that, was a tenuous affair – the establishment on Mombasa Island never numbered more than 200 soldiers and customs officers, and the figure for the whole of the Coast was only nine hundred. Throughout the period, the Afro-Arab inhabitants were in a continual state of revolt and a policy of non co-operation, combined with smuggling on a considerable scale, robbed the Portuguese of the treasures they had hoped for.

Portugal never made a profit out of her East Africa dominion. Nevertheless, though fully occupied developing more profitable interests in the south-east at Mozambique and across the ocean on the Indian coast, her conquistadores were tenacious in their efforts to keep a foothold in Mombasa. Their first setback was in 1588 when the Mombasa Arabs with the help of the Turks from Aden rose in revolt and massacred the settlers and the local people who were friendly to them. A Portuguese fleet was then despatched from India and drove the Arabs and Turks into the Island's walled town. Unfortunately for the rebels, this event coincided with the arrival of the Zimba on the mainland opposite.

The Zimba, a militant Bantu tribe, had broken northwards from their home in the neighbourhood of modern Zululand and swept up the whole eastern coast of Africa laying waste the countryside and indiscriminately killing all before them in a period of terror and cannibalism. They found the Portuguese besieging Mombasa from the sea too strong for them and asked to be allowed to invade the Island. The Portuguese agreed and then happened the bloodiest incident in Mombasa's turbulent history.[1] The Zimba combed out the town and the whole island with their spears and nobody was spared from the resultant slaughter. It was an effective revenge and left the Portuguese once again masters at Mombasa.

The Zimba were allowed to carry on up the Coast laying bare the country like a plague of locusts until they were halted at Malindi by

[1] The Swahili name for Mombasa is *Mvita*, meaning war.

the Sergeju, a tribe from the hinterland who were equally warlike. After being beaten in open battle and suffering heavy losses, they retreated southwards never to be heard of again; their only contribution to the history of East Africa being a massive depopulation of the coastal regions.

The Portuguese re-established their suzerainty over Mombasa by building a fort overlooking the harbour. Solidly built of stone in an impregnable position, Fort Jesus, as it was called in recognition of the piety of the invaders, still stands today; but it did not prevent another Arab revolt in 1631. Again a fleet was sent from India and after two attempts the Portuguese regained occupation of Mombasa and its fort. It was not before time as 2,000 miles to the north where they occupied key points on the Arabian coast they were facing attack by the Omani Arabs of Muscat. These attacks were so successful that in 1650 the Portuguese were thrown out of Arabia. Flushed with this success, the Omanis sent a raiding party to the Kenya island of Pate and then on to Zanzibar. They drove the Portuguese from there and in 1660 returned and took the town of Mombasa, but not the fort. The last act in the drama of Portuguese decline and the intervention of the powerful Omani Arabs in East Africa had begun.

For the next twenty years the European and Asiatic invaders struggled for power in East Africa, and despite their reverses, the Portuguese set out from India with a strong fleet in 1678 to deal once and for all with the Arabs in the coastal towns. This they did successfully; but the ferocity of the punishment they exacted was a sign of failing strength. The beheading of all the Arab rulers, the heavy indemnities and the vast amount of loot taken away were in vain, for the Arab squadrons from Muscat had become the superior fighting force in the Indian Ocean. In 1698 after nearly three years of siege the red flag of Oman was flying over Fort Jesus.

Successive expeditions for the recapture of Mombasa and the northern ports were despatched from Lisbon and Goa but all were fruitless. Though they seized a chance in 1728 and briefly recovered Mombasa when both the coastal Arabs and Oman were crippled by internal feuds, the Portuguese were finally expelled from Kenya by the people they had sought to replace as invaders.

The Portuguese conquest was an unhappy affair for all concerned. The only tangible evidence of the two and a half centuries of occupation is Fort Jesus and the maize seed which the Portuguese intro-

duced from South America and which in time has spread far inland
from the Coast to become the staple food of countless Africans.
Cassava, cashew, cucumber, avocado, guava and African-grown
tobacco also have Portuguese origins. So do some sixty words in-
corporated in the Swahili language. But apart from this the Portuguese had little effect on the way of life of the local inhabitants.

### III

The Omanis – in the middle of the eighteenth century the strongest
power in the west Indian Ocean – were no less grasping than the
Portuguese. For a hundred years and more they asserted their economic and political dominion of East Africa. But in 1741 the Mazrui
family, who were the rulers of Mombasa, renounced allegiance to
their overlords. They had welcomed the Arabs of Oman only as
deliverers from the Portuguese, not as masters; and in a feud which
lasted eighty-five years they fought bitterly for control of the Kenya
Coast.

It was the famous Seyidd Said Ibn Sultan, the Imam of Muscat,
who in the early nineteenth century finally broke the power of the
Mazrui and banished them from Mombasa. With the help of the
British, Said had established his authority over Oman, and East
Africa was his most important and lucrative dominion. In Zanzibar, the trading centre for the whole of the East African Coast, his
agents extorted large sums of money from the Indian *banyans* who
administered the trade for the local Arab landowners. The sultans of
the coastal towns offered him substantial tribute and so too did the
French slave traders who were active along the Coast recruiting
slaves for the sugar plantations on the Mascarenes, the islands south
of Madagascar colonised by France. Slaves were by far the biggest
element of East African trade in the early years of Said's dominion
and up to 10,000, who had been shipped to the Zanzibar market
from ports on the mainland, were exported annually to Muscat and
beyond to feed the insatiable demand of Islam; for the followers of
the faith, slavery was still an institution sanctioned not only by im-
memorial usage but also by the specific injunctions of the Koran.[1]

Under Seyidd Said, Zanzibar became the commercial and strategic
base for Arab expansion in East Africa. And for this expansion, control of Mombasa was vital to Said, not because of its contribution to

[1] R. Coupland, *East Africa and its Invaders*, p. 207.

the slave and ivory trade of the Coast, which was substantial, but
because it dominated the lines of communication to the Arab north
and the monsoon trading routes. The Mazrui of Mombasa were
always a thorn in Said's flesh and never more so than in 1823 when
they appealed to the British for protection. For their part, the
British showed no desire to take possession of what to them was an
unimportant town on the African coast; it offered neither commercial nor strategic advantages, and its occupation would be offensive to Said who, in Muscat, held the gateway to the Persian Gulf
and whose friendship was necessary for the safe passage of British
ships through the Arabian Sea to India.

It was therefore a period of embarrassment to Britain when in
1824 Captain William Owen, R.N., the leader of a British naval
expedition surveying the East African coastline, acceded to the
demand of the Mazrui rulers of Mombasa and hoisted the Union
Jack over Fort Jesus. Owen's intentions were honourable for he
thought Britain might use Mombasa for attacks on the slave trade,
which she had declared illegal. But as it turned out, his Protectorate
was short-lived and lasted only two years. The British Government
could not concede that Mombasa was worth the disruption of
relations with the Imam of Muscat. In any case, it was of doubtful
value as the Mazrui continued to support the slave trade and only
wanted the British flag to protect them from Said.

The transfer of Said's court from Muscat to Zanzibar in 1840
marked the beginning of an era that brought East Africa into permanent contact with the West. In order to achieve the power and
prestige he wanted for his East African dominion, Said had to increase trade. Zanzibar was the natural entrepot for the Coast and he
set out to stimulate the export of the chief products – ivory, cloves,
gum opal, coconuts, copra and palm oil. He found when he arrived
to settle permanently on the island that this trade was limited
to the lands round the fringe of the Arabian Sea; but it soon
began to reach out, as it did in the old days, to the rest of India and
beyond.

Not only in Bombay and Calcutta, but also in the Dutch East
Indies, and even in China, agents of Arab trade were installed once
more. There was, moreover, a growing market for East Africa's
products in Europe and North America, with the added advantage
that the white traders came to Zanzibar in their own ships. Said
welcomed them and willingly negotiated commercial treaties with

their governments; with the United States in 1833;[1] Britain in 1839; and France in 1844. He must, however, have been aware that these new economic interests with the West might one day lead to political interference. He certainly knew that in so far as the British were concerned they would mean pressure to reduce the scope of the slave trade, his main source of revenue. But for Said's own life, and for a generation after, the risks were justified and at his death in 1856 the markets of Europe and America were absorbing a large proportion of the products of East Africa passing through the hands of the Zanzibaris.

Slaves were no part of the growing trade between Zanzibar and the West. Nevertheless, the slave trade had, indirectly, the greatest influence in the development of East Africa for it laid the foundations of British involvement and eventual domination. Throughout the eighteenth century the British were the greatest culprits among the sea-going peoples of Europe in the export of slaves from Africa to the transatlantic colonies. But as a nation they were the first to recognise their guilt and mend their ways. Slave trading was made illegal for British subjects in 1807. Four years later it was made a felony punishable by transportation, and the law was so rigorously enforced that British 'slavers' ceased to exist. The French and the Portuguese, who were among the European powers most active along the East African Coast in the slave trade, followed Britain in making the practice illegal. On the other hand, the Arab nations continued to supply a market for slaves and to provide the traders.

Despite his dependence on slavery Seyidd Said, in the complicated state of Indian Ocean politics at the time, was anxious to retain the support of his powerful friends the British and in 1822 signed an agreement with the British naval captain Moresby declaring that 'all external traffic in slaves from his dominions and dependencies should be abolished and that the sale of slaves of any of his subjects to Christians of every description was prohibited'. The agreement also provided for the appointment of a British agent at Zanzibar, or on the East African Coast, 'for the purpose of having intelligence

---

[1] Charles Millet of Salem was the first American trading captain to visit the East African Coast. He called at Mombasa in 1827 in the brig *Ann* and from then until 1859 when the trade was at its peak the Americans had a virtual monopoly of the Coast. A relic of this trade is *Merikani*, the Swahili name for the coarse, unbleached cotton cloth woven in the mills of Massachusetts and which came into universal use in Africa and Arabia. Coupland, op. cit., p. 379.

and watching the traffic in slaves with Christian nations'.[1] It gave
Britain the legal right to begin her fifty-year war against the Arab
slave trade, though it was limited in scope and internal trading in
slaves between ports under Said's rule or overlordship was allowed.
African slaves from Zanzibar and Mombasa continued to be sold all
over Arabia and in the great slave markets of Bussora and Baghdad.

A system of naval patrols achieved little success in suppressing
the trade under the conditions of the Moresby agreement and in
1845 another treaty was signed banning the export of slaves. Nevertheless, it was not until 1897, when the legal status of slavery was
abolished in the Sultanate of Zanzibar, that all the loopholes were
sealed and the people of East Africa were freed from the threat of
deportation under the most inhuman of conditions and for the monetary gain of Islam. No longer were the unwary inhabitants of the
hinterland pressed into slavery by the heavily armed Arab caravans
that ranged deep into their territory: no longer was the full in-
humanity seen in the bestial conditions of the sailing ships the Arabs
used to break the British blockade.

An eyewitness account by a British naval officer of the capture of
a large Arab dhow in the sea lane between Zanzibar and Mombasa
conveys all the horrors of slavery:

'She was just a huge open boat filled practically to the last chink
of space with black humanity; men, women, some children and
infants in arms; but no old people. Old slaves like horses are not
marketable. The sun cooked the closely-packed mass of people
and the smell was awful. We had tried once or twice to give the
poor creatures some relief from burning thirst and hunger, particularly the women with small infants, but the attempt caused
such a fierce fighting scramble in which everything was spilt or
scattered and nobody profited that we gave up.'[2]

The abolition of the slave trade was the virtual end of Arab domination in East Africa for it removed a vast source of revenue and
cheap labour. By the end of the nineteenth century Seyidd Said's
one-time realm had shrunk to Zanzibar, with its neighbouring island
of Pemba, and the narrow coastal strip—even this remnant was a
British Protectorate. All the rest had been partitioned between
Britain, Germany and Italy. So ended the epoch of Arab control

[1] Coupland, op. cit., p. 215.
[2] Admiral Sir Richard Cresswell, *Close to the Wind*, p. 171.

which, broken only by the period of the Portuguese conquistadores, lasted in one form or another for a thousand years. The Europeans had taken over and in less than half a century they in turn would give way to that 'great black background to the comings and goings of the brown men and white men on the coast'; but not before they had brought a degree of prosperity and enlightenment to the East African peoples, thereby giving them the chance to lead their lives in their own way and for their own ends as independent nations.

## IV

The evangelical revival in Britain, that led to the great missionary and humanitarian movements of the nineteenth century and also to the abolition of slavery, stimulated a wider extension of the trade and political control developed by the Arabs in East Africa; for leaders of the advance into the hinterland during the second half of the century were the white missionaries and explorers. These men, with the highest motives, blazed a trail through the thorn jungle of the Coast and across the East African plateaux: the missionaries to 'bring enlightenment to the heathen peoples'; and the explorers to find a direct route to the Nile. Johann Ludwig Krapf, the German-born missionary; the British army lieutenant John Speke and the explorer Joseph Thomson, if they did nothing else at least put Kenya on the map.[1] They were followed by others and what they found on their travels they reported back to their sponsors at length and in great detail, so that in 1869 when the Suez Canal was opened and eastern Africa was brought 2,000 miles closer to Britain by sea the commercial possibilities could not be ignored. British trade increased while that of other nations declined or remained stationary.[2]

This commercial expansion did not, however, lead to the establishment of British rule as a matter of course. The British Government still felt that the main task in East Africa was to create conditions necessary for Christianity and legitimate commerce to expand without the establishment of colonial rule and through the existing authority of the Sultan of Zanzibar.

[1] Krapf compiled the first Swahili dictionary; Speke is credited with the 'discovery' of Lake Victoria and the source of the Nile, and Thomson was the first European to travel through Kenya, or Masailand as it was known at the time.
[2] History of East Africa, Vol. II: C. C. Wrigley, Kenya Patterns of Economic Life, p. 242.

In 1877, Sir William Mackinnon, the Scots shipping magnate and humanitarian who had begun running the ships of his British India Steam Navigation Company to Zanzibar on a regular monthly service, put forward the idea of a commercial company to develop the mainland under a lease from Sultan Barghash, Said's son and successor. Though it fitted in well enough with Britain's policy the scheme was doomed to failure. It was opposed by the Conservative Foreign Secretary Lord Salisbury who, preoccupied with the complications of Egyptian and Middle East politics, was personally convinced that involvement on the East African mainland, even through a respectable enterprise which had the support of the Sultan of Zanzibar, had to be avoided at all costs. Mackinnon, the mainspring of British enterprise in East Africa in the latter part of the century through his schemes for the economic penetration and development of the interior, had to wait another ten years for his concession.

Other powers were not quite so reluctant as Britain to become involved in the exploitation of the African continent. At the time of Mackinnon's first scheme the scramble for Africa had begun. France, Germany, Belgium and Italy had pressed their claims and established colonies by rights of occupation and through the simple method of declaring Protectorates.

Britain's eventual, though unwilling, involvement in East Africa came through the actions of Germany, her greatest rival in Europe, which under Bismarck embarked on a colonial career after the British occupation of Egypt in 1882. When the Cameroons and south-west Africa were safely annexed, the Germans moved their attention to the East Coast. Dr Carl Peters, leader of an extreme group within the German colonial movement, secured treaties with a number of chiefs in what is now Tanzania and brought a large area of the interior under German 'protection'. A chartered company was set up in 1885 to exploit these treaties, but even more serious for Britain was the acceptance by the rebel Swahili Sultan of Witu of a German Protectorate over his territory and the neighbouring lands of the Tana River basin. The Germans were now in a strategic position on the Somalia border and too near to the Middle East and India shipping routes for Britain's comfort.

It was, however, left to Sultan Barghash to protest strongly at Germany's moves against his 'dominions'; but his protests were in vain. Germany had never recognised his sovereignty over the East

African coastlands and reinforced this view by sending a naval
squadron to Zanzibar to impel the Sultan to accept the concessions
given to the German colonialists. Barghash capitulated while his
friends the British stood by, silent spectators of another blow against
their prestige in Africa.

It was an extraordinary situation. The British, with the Middle
East and India firmly in their grasp and with their powerful navy
now in control of the Indian Ocean, were, of all the European powers
concerned in the scramble for Africa, in the strongest position to
enforce their rule along the eastern shores of the continent. But
Britain, under a Liberal Government at the time, shrank from any
expansion on a warlike basis. Her Ministers were concerned, moreover, with the chessboard of European politics and the ever-present
threat of Russian intervention in the Middle East and India. They
were unwilling to offend the Germans and certainly did not wish to
become involved in a naval war in the Indian Ocean and no counter-
move was made against the demonstration of German power to the
defenceless Sultan of Zanzibar.

The threat of German expansion was not lost on some influential
people in Britain and the idea of a private concession was revived in
1885 when the British Consul in Zanzibar, Frederick Holmewood,
prepared a memorandum with the object of persuading politicians
and commercial interests to take a closer look at East Africa. He
described in glowing terms the economic prospects of the region
between Mombasa and the Great Lakes. And he bespoke the existence of 'an immediately profitable trade especially in ivory, infinite
possibilities for export crops, and the prospects of a near paradise in
Kenya for European settlers with abundant African labour'.[1]

The persuasive tone of Holmewood's memorandum encouraged
Mackinnon, together with a group of wealthy Manchester merchants, to put forward a second scheme for a concession to develop
the regions not occupied by Germany. Mackinnon was successful in
obtaining support from the British Government but first Germany
had to be consulted. Negotiations between the two powers followed
to determine the extent of the Sultan of Zanzibar's mainland possessions and to define the British and German 'spheres of influence'. The Anglo-German partition of East Africa had begun.

In November 1886 an agreement was signed in London defining
the German sphere as south of a line from the Umba River to Lake

[1] *History of East Africa*, Vol. I: John Flint, *Background to Partition*, p. 372.

Victoria (the present Kenya and Tanzania border) and the British
sphere as north of this line to the Tana River, but with the exception
of the Witu Protectorate. Sultan Barghash was allowed the islands
of Zanzibar, Pemba, Mafia and Lamu, together with a ten-mile-wide
coastal strip of the mainland and including the port of Mombasa
and the town of Malindi. Mackinnon and his associates then went
ahead and formed the British East African Association to operate in
the British sphere. But Britain was yet again reluctant to become too
closely involved despite the recommendation of Colonel (later Lord)
Kitchener, the British member of the Anglo-German delimitation
commission, who urged that Mombasa was of vital strategic importance to British sea-power in the Indian Ocean and should be
acquired to counteract the German possession of Dar-es-Salaam.

It was not until September 1888 that Mackinnon was able to
obtain a royal charter for his company, thus giving it the might of
British protection. His Association was renamed the Imperial
British East Africa Company. The sum of £250,000 was subscribed
as the initial capital and the names of Mackinnon and leading merchant and philanthropic interests in Britain featured prominently
in the list of subscribers. The prospectus of the new Company enabled it to act both as a trading and development agency and as an
administration. Headquarters were established at Mombasa; an
advance post set up at Machakos in the Kamba country; treaties
concluded with the Nyika, Kamba and Teita tribes; and preparations
made for the 'effective occupation of the interior'.[1]

In the years that followed, British interest was concentrated on
Uganda and the 'populous surroundings' of Lake Victoria. Under
the Heligoland Treaty of 1890 Germany recognised Uganda as a
British sphere of influence, abandoned all claims to Witu and accepted a British Protectorate over Zanzibar. Britain in return recognised German rights over the Tanganyika (now Tanzania) section of
the coastal strip and ceded the strategic island of Heligoland.

It may seem strange that Germany should have given up so much
potential territory in East Africa for a small island in the North Sea,
but it was all part of the international bargaining that marked the
struggle between the Great Powers for stakes in Africa. Furthermore,
Germany was never a compulsive colonial power and was more concerned in the late 1890s with making herself the leading nation in
Europe. Heligoland was essential to her programme of naval expan-

[1] R. Coupland, *The Exploitation of East Africa*, p. 482.

sion and so Uganda, which controlled Lake Victoria and the head-waters of the Nile, was 'sacrificed' to Britain.

But while Uganda was important to Britain's overlordship of the Sudan and Egypt, there was yet once again that traditional reluctance to become too closely involved in eastern Africa on a government level. As a result, the Imperial British East Africa Company was asked to extend its activities to Uganda. Captain Frederick (later Lord) Lugard, an employee of the Company at Mombasa and later a distinguished pro-consul, set off on an expedition to Uganda after the signing of the Heligoland Treaty. On his way he added to the Company posts he had already established fifty miles apart along the Kenya route to the lake, the main one being at Dagoretti on the edge of the Kikuyu country and a few miles from the present city of Nairobi. Lugard went on to lay the foundations of British influence in Uganda, but only after protracted negotiations with rival kingdoms and religious factions had culminated in the short but sharp war at Kampala against Mwanga, the Kabaka of Buganda, who preferred the French and the Germans to the British but who eventually found himself on the losing side.

The cost of maintaining British influence in Uganda was £40,000 a year, an intolerable burden in those days for a private, commercial concern with limited resources. By 1891, it was clear that the commercial occupation of Uganda could not continue and plans were made for the Imperial British East Africa Company to withdraw to Kenya and make Dagoretti their farthest outpost. But these plans to abandon a key point in Africa created a public outcry. On 28 September 1891 *The Times* said:

'Such a withdrawal would be nothing short of a national calamity. It would mean not only the loss of a great amount of capital already expended, but the destruction of our influence and prestige throughout Central Africa, the practical defeat of our anti-slavery policy, the persecution of numerous missionaries labouring in Uganda, and the reconquest by Mohammedan fanatics of the only African state that has shown a disposition to accept Christianity. Whether we desire it or not the British East Africa Company must be identified for all practical purposes with national policy.'

Money was raised by Mackinnon and his friends, and also the Church Missionary Society, to enable the Company to continue its Uganda operations. Nevertheless, its days in Uganda were numbered

and in 1893 a British Protectorate was declared on the advice of Sir
Gerald Portal, the Consul-General at Zanzibar. The Company withdrew and its work in Uganda, and indeed in the rest of East Africa,
was finished.

In the five years of its existence it had spent nearly half a million
pounds trying to stave off Germany's aggressive policies and occupy
for Britain 750,000 square miles of Africa. It was an impossible task;
for the Company received only a small revenue from the collection
of duties on goods from the interior which, in the face of the British
Government's imposition of free trade on the Coast, was sufficient
only to meet the annual payment on the concession lease from the
Sultan of Zanzibar.

The Imperial British East Africa Company, unlike other chartered British companies in Africa and India, was purely administrative and did not trade on its own account. It was left with practically
no resources other than its own capital, and Sir William Mackinnon
and his fellow directors, who were forced to wind up their Company
in return for their efforts to provide Britain with an East Africa
empire, received £250,000 compensation, not from a grateful Government, but from the Sultan of Zanzibar who was made to pay the
biggest share. The British Government did, though, take over responsibility for paying the annual rent to the Sultan for the lease of the
ten-mile-wide Kenya coastal strip which became an integral part of
the mainland territory. The rule of the Company, at its best a make-
shift affair, ended unhappily for its founders who had entered into
the original Association with such high hopes.[1] But as Mackinnon
himself wrote afterwards: 'With all its faults it has been an honest
concern, not a money-making one, and but for its work we should
not now possess a footing in East Africa.'

The administration of the Imperial British East Africa Company
was taken over by the Foreign Office and what is now Kenya became
the British East Africa Protectorate on 15 June 1895. A sub-com-
missioner responsible to the Consul-General in Zanzibar was appointed and the whole of the British sphere of influence was at last
under direct, governmental control.

British administration had, however, come to East Africa in name
only. Some years were to pass before it was a reality and this tardi-
ness of Britain in accepting her responsibilities was typical of the

---

[1] At one time it was suggested that the territory over which the Company
ruled should be named 'Ibea', the initials of its title.

attitude that prompted her intervention in eastern Africa. Little interest continued to be shown in the acquisition of a territory which, in the British view, had always rested on strategic considerations and the need to preserve a dominant position in the Middle East. In 1895 Kenya was economically valueless and the British Government was in no hurry to cover the country with a network of administrative stations or to pour capital into its development.

## Chapter 2

# Protectorate Government
# 1895–1920

## I

K ENYA WAS KNOWN as the British East Africa Protectorate for
twenty-five years. The country developed in that period from
an unwanted liability into a land where, if self-government as
an independent and economically viable state was still some years
away, independence from outside control was at least a possibility.
Nevertheless, the early years of the Protectorate, in the expressed
view of the British Foreign Office a 'sterile region', gave little
promise of things to come. There were no centres of population to
compare with the country round Lake Victoria. The Nilo-Hamitic
tribes, the lords of the plateauland, were spread thinly over a wide
area, while the Kikuyu and their fellow Bantu were still locked in
the fastness of the forests round Mount Kenya. Disease, famine and
civil war had swept across the land creating devastation among the
people and their livestock. It was a beautiful but bare land and even
the vast herds of wild game that roamed the plains and forests were
reduced to insignificant numbers by the great rinderpest epidemic of
the 1890s.

Kenya was little more than a highway to Uganda and a difficult
country to cross. The caravans, which had increased in numbers and
scope to include Indian and European traders as well as Arab, took
six weeks to march from Mombasa to Dagoretti, the half-way post
on the edge of Kikuyuland, and at that time on the Protectorate
boundary with Uganda. Loads were carried on the backs of porters
and the cost for the full journey from the Coast to the lake was
about £250 a ton. Only ivory could make a commercial profit at
this figure and in the days of the Imperial British East Africa Company various attempts had been made to find a substitute for the
porters, many of them former slaves from Zanzibar. Donkeys, camels

and ox-carts were used without success and there was even an attempt to introduce a steamship service on the River Tana from the sea to the foothills of Mount Kenya. The only answer, of course, was a railway.

But several years were to pass before a rail link between Mombasa and Lake Victoria became a reality. And the decision by the British Government to lend its financial support was not based entirely on commercial considerations, though it had been painfully obvious to the Company's administrators that the value of possession of the East African Coast lay in the commerce of the distant interior.

The guiding light of Britain's peaceful penetration of the interior, if it could be called that, was the General Act of the Brussels Conference called in 1889 by King Leopold of the Belgians at the suggestion of the British Government. Three years later, by an Order in Council, the Act became, in effect, a suppression of the slave-trade treaty to which all the major powers with an interest in the African continent were parties. And it stressed the need for the construction of railways as one of the measures to put an end to 'the crimes and devastations engendered by the traffic in African slaves and ensuring for that vast continent the benefits of peace and civilisation'.[1]

In the opinion of one Liberal member of the House of Commons, Henry Labouchere, who was a constant critic of the Conservative Government's East African policy, the railway was the first step along the path of jingoism.[2] It would do nothing to stop the slave trade and was a waste of the taxpayers' money which could be better spent in England. Mr Labouchere argued that the proposal was of doubtful legality for the Government had no right to drive a railway through country belonging to the Masai. And he condemned as 'wholly fantastic' the popular picture of vast numbers of Englishmen going to this 'tropical region' as colonists with their wives and children in order to support a railway.

But regardless of the Liberal Opposition's arguments, a Bill was passed in 1896 providing a Government loan of £3 million to construct a railway between Mombasa and Lake Victoria. Six years later the first locomotive was run through, although a further three years were to follow before the line was in full operation as a per-

[1] M. F. Hill, *Permanent Way*, p. 46.
[2] Jingoism was an expression of boastful pride in Britain's imperial might and came from a popular song of the 1870s: 'We don't want to fight but by jingo if we do we've got the ships, we've got the men, we've got the money too!'

manent way. By that time, in September 1904, the capital cost had risen to over £5½ million – almost double the original estimate. It was, however, money well invested. While the railway, as it turned out, added little to the eclipse of the slave trade, an increasing amount of commercial traffic was being carried on the final completion date. This traffic, which was related from the beginning almost exclusively to exports and imports, turned the railway into an economic life-line and was vital to the development of Kenya and to Uganda as independent nations.

It has been said that Kenya was not conquered by force of arms but by a railway. This was to some extent true in that the railway overcame geographical obstacles and provided the means for development.[1] Nevertheless, arms were needed to enforce the rule of law in a land 'peopled by very few sparse and primitive tribes, very few of whom had any settled habitation, fighting against each other, village against village, tribe against tribe, ridge against ridge, spear against spear'.[2]

It was the Arabs of the Coast who were the first to feel the effects of the new order. In a dispute between the Mazrui Chief Mubarak-Bin-Rashid and the Commissioner for the Protectorate, Sir Arthur Hardinge, over the succession to a minor shaikhdom north of Mombasa, the Mazrui revolted. Mubarak was encouraged in his defiance of the authority of the Protectorate, in what he considered was a matter for the Mazrui to decide for themselves, by fellow Arabs who were life-long opponents of Britain's anti-slavery policy. Hardinge, on his part, was not reluctant to use force to make it plain that for the British there could be 'no question as to our being the masters'.[3]

For several months, Mubarak terrorised the countryside round Mombasa and Malindi in his revolt against the Protectorate; but a British gunboat, together with a naval landing party and regiment of soldiers from India, effectively suppressed the rebellion. As Hardinge said in his despatch to the British Government on the affair, it had not been an unmixed evil. Once and for all the power of the influential Arab potentates at the Coast had been broken. Supporters of the slave trade, they had never subjugated themselves

---

[1] The line was 572 miles long and on its way across the Great Rift Valley and the wooded slopes of the escarpments rose from sea level to a height of 9,000 feet.

[2] Sir Edward Grigg, a former Kenya Governor, to the Africa Society, London, 1927.

[3] *History of East Africa*, Vol. II: D. A. Low, *British Rule*, p. 6.

either to the Sultan of Zanzibar or to the Imperial British East Africa Company and sooner or later they would have involved the Protectorate administration in trouble. They would never have submitted without a trial of strength and it was as well that the dispute was on a mere family issue on which local opinion itself was divided. The trouble with the Arabs had to come and it was fortunate that it arose in the infancy of the Protectorate and before commercial interests had sprung up which would have been jeopardised or destroyed by civil war.[1]

The outcome of the Arab rebellion marked the substitution of European for Arab influence throughout the Protectorate.[2] Inland, the first of the indigenous people to be shown the effectiveness of modern rule when backed up by force of arms were the Masai who, paradoxically, were to become peaceful allies of the alien intruders. But for this friendship the British penetration of the interior would have been made much more difficult, if not impossible, without a stronger element of force than was available to the new administration.

The Masai lorded it over the open country across which every caravan and the railway itself had to pass on the way to Uganda. Isolated and weakly-defended outposts set up to promote trade existed only on their goodwill and the British were not slow to recognise this. It was therefore official policy that the Masai were to be brought under control by peaceful means and not by force. Such a policy needed the utmost tact and patience, but it was most successful.

The Masai saw little to threaten their dominance of the open country; for the British made no attempts (at that time) to settle and, in any case, not being possessed of cattle—the object of most Masai raids—had little to excite cupidity. No attempt was made by the British to restrain those raids into territories over which they had as yet no jurisdiction and this, coupled with the preoccupation of

[1] Hill, op. cit., p. 143.
[2] In his recollections *From Chartered Company to Crown Colony*, p. 169, C. W. Hobley, one of the Protectorate's first administrators, writes that the Arabs with their intimate knowledge of the Kenya Coast born of centuries of trading and administration were reduced to the status of 'imposing functionaries' with little interest in the progress of their people in the Protectorate. 'Arabs whether in gorgeous burnous or in rags were all the same. A people who had destroyed without creating, who had divided when their unity would have made them great, who would have lived in theory' (R. V. C. Bodley, Arabist, traveller and writer).

the Masai with their own troubles of rinderpest, smallpox and internal strife, created a mutual tolerance that was to last throughout the period of British occupation. But to begin with, it took the Kedong massacre and brutal retaliatory measures by a solitary white man to show the Masai that the British had all the power necessary to impose their will. The massacre took place on 28 November 1895 when a large Swahili caravan returning down the Rift Valley was attacked on the Kedong escarpment by local Masai over the abduction by the caravan headman of two young Masai girls. In the resultant fight, 650 caravan porters were killed for the loss of only forty Masai warriors. Hearing news of the massacre, a passing British trader, Andrew Dick, decided to attack the Masai with the aid of three French travellers who were also near-by on a shooting expedition. Dick killed over a hundred Masai before he himself lost his life through reckless folly and the jamming of his rifle at a critical moment.[1] The Masai fled but not before they were impressed with the ability of four white men to shoot down so many of their warriors.

In the peace talks which followed, British officials repudiated the actions of Dick and his companions and accepted the fact that the Kedong massacre was a result of extreme provocation by the Swahili caravan. The Masai under their leader Lenana were reassured by this example of British justice and so the good relations between the Masai and the British were cemented. Lenana's Masai were given help to fight the outbreak of rinderpest among their cattle and numbers of their warriors found profitable employment as auxiliaries in British expeditions against other peoples.[2]

The first ten years of the Protectorate Government saw a gradual extension of its authority – as slow and as difficult in many respects as the progress of the Uganda railway across the Kenya Highlands. At the outset, the Taita in their hills one hundred miles from Mombasa objected to the new order. But a number of small punitive expeditions against them were so successful that an official report several years later described the Taita as 'the most obedient and peaceful natives in the Protectorate'. By 1900 British overlordship had spread into the modern Machakos district of the Kamba country, although again not before further military expeditions and the establishment of police posts throughout the district.

Kikuyuland or Kenya Province, as it was known at the time – it stretched from the strong administrative post of Fort Smith at

[1] Hill, op. cit., p. 143.                    [2] Low, op. cit., p. 14.

Dagoretti to the stations of Fort Hall and Nyeri in the foothills of Mount Kenya – was brought under alien rule without any great difficulty mainly because of lack of resistance among the Kikuyu people, ravaged by disease and famine in the remaining years of the nineteenth century. The same was true of the Taita and Kamba country. But the Embu and Meru tribes, who are closely related to the Kikuyu, were not quite so amenable to the British overlords. Safe and remote in their hilly, wooded country along the northern slopes of the mountain, they could afford to be hostile and it took several years and more punitive expeditions to bring them within the orbit of Protectorate administration.

Until 1902, the region west of the Rift Valley from Lake Naivasha to Lake Victoria was part of Uganda and in order to ensure that Masailand lay within one Protectorate and that the railway would be the responsibility of one administration, the British East Africa Protectorate now became the governing power for all the upland areas that lay between the sea and Victoria Nyanza. Here again, in this western region, the progress of British authority was slow though effective nonetheless.

Mumias, the trading post on the main land route to the Uganda Protectorate headquarters at Entebbe, was made the control centre for the Luhya and Luo peoples of the modern Nyanza province. It was from here in north-west Kavirondo and from sub-stations at Kakamega, Kericho and Karingu that the noted administrator C. W. Hobley and his colleagues brought a large and important sector of what became the East Africa Protectorate under firm government. With the help of Baganda and Masai levies, Hobley's Sudanese troops forcibly stamped out any opposition among the medley of tribes in the province – the Wanga, Ketosh, Elgumi, Bugusu, Luo, Kipsigis, Nandi, Gusii, Sotik and Buret – and so effectively that thirty years later he was able to boast that not since 1895 had a shot been fired in anger between Mumias and Mount Elgon.

Hobley maintained that once the Kavirondo were beaten they readily made peace, and, once they made peace, it was peace. Within a few hours the women were in camp selling food, and one had no anxiety about a subsequent treacherous attack.[1] But his success in bringing law and order to Kavirondo aggravated relations with the neighbouring Nandi who, in the fastness of their grassy hills in the

[1] C. W. Hobley, *Kenya: From Chartered Company to Crown Colony*, p. 88.

plateau country between Lake Victoria and the Rift Valley, had never accepted alien rule. Despite several fierce and bloody military campaigns the warlike Nandi were destined to give the Protectorate Government a great deal of trouble for a number of years and were always a threat to the new railway as it passed in its final stages close to their territory.

When the railway did eventually reach the lake at Kisumu — established in 1899 as the terminus and the main trading port of the lake — the pattern of modern Kenya was laid down. Uganda's eastern region was now the Kisumu and Naivasha provinces of the Protectorate. A trunk road as well as a railway stretched across the country from Mombasa to Kisumu and a chain of administrative stations, the nucleus of towns, lay on either side of the route: Voi, Taveta, Kitui, Machakos, Nairobi (the future capital city in the swamplands between the Kikuyu escarpment and the Athi Plains), Narok, Naivasha, Eldama Ravine, Fort Hall, Nyeri, Kericho, Kapsabet, Kakamega and Mumias. In the wild country north of Mount Kenya and the Tana River — three times the size of the already occupied Protectorate — the stations Archer's Post, Moyale and Baringo were established to watch the frontier with Somaliland and Ethiopia, and to act as nominal control points for the nomadic desert tribes, the Pokot, Samburu, Turkana, Rendile, Boran and Somali, and to protect them from armed Ethiopian ivory- and cattle-raiders. It was, however, only a pattern — a system of names with which to draw the map of Kenya.

Nowhere in the Protectorate during the early years of the twentieth century was government control anything but tenuous, though the sharp and severe lessons imposed by British military expeditions had brought peace to the warring and raiding tribes. As a result many of the peaceful tribes had expanded outside their protected areas in the hills to the no-man's-land of the plains and open country and there were even attempts by Protectorate officials to develop agriculture on an organised basis. But unlike northern Nigeria and southern Uganda where native political institutions and feudal 'kingdoms' abounded and provided the elements of government by indirect rule — the Dual Mandate system of Lugard — through hereditary or nominated chiefs, Kenya had little on which to build authoritative government.[1]

[1] In the introduction to the second volume of the *History of East Africa*, Margery Perham notes that Lugard's system of indirect rule in West Africa

The native population was about 2 million in a country with some 75,000 square miles of habitable land, and the various tribes, the Nilo-Hamitic, Kavirondo and Bantu, were split up into numerous clans and small family groups with a certain amount of control induced by a warrior system, but on military not social matters. Among the Nilo-Hamites, leadership was provided by *laibons* or *orikoiyots*, personalities with priestly or ritualistic authority — more like prophets than chiefs; and among the Bantu, by men with distinctive personal powers, such as warlike abilities and skill in witchcraft, trade and debate. These leaders of Kenya's tribes had, for instance, none of the traditional, political authority of the Anglo-Saxon tribal kings and resembled in their functions the feuding clan leaders of the Irish and Highland Scots. Nevertheless, they were the main points of contact with Protectorate officials and provided the essential links with the country's new administration.

## II

In 1890, the centre of Protectorate government was moved from Zanzibar to Mombasa and seven years later to Nairobi. By 1903 the administration had followed a bureaucratic course and had grown to fifteen distinctive Government departments: Judicial, Military, Police, Medical, Trade and Customs, Transport, Audit, Public Works, Post Office, Telegraphs, Port Office, Police, Agricultural, Forestry and Veterinary. There was little economic foundation for this new administration and the pattern of trade had changed little from the days of the Kamba and Arab caravans.

The railway with its massive capital cost involving a first loan from Britain was also a burden for the new country to carry and the administrators had to look for other means to support the economy and wipe out the continuing indebtedness to the British treasury. Mineral resources had been shown to be practically non-existent because of the huge lava cap covering the country and the only natural resource that could be exploited was the land. So a quick remedy to Kenya's initial poverty appeared to be the agricultural

(F. D. Lugard, *The Dual Mandate in British Tropical Africa*, London, 3rd edn., 1926) was strikingly successful but was not applicable to Kenya. When Sir Percy Girouard, Lugard's successor in northern Nigeria, came to Kenya as Governor in 1909 full of enthusiasm for the system he had inherited he found the Protectorate sterile ground for any administrative transplanting.

colonisation of the empty, but potentially productive, lands along the track of the railway as it passed through the Kenya Highlands above the five-thousand-foot contour in country 'suitable in all respects for the alien white man'.

The idea of white settlement was not new for it had come up in the British Parliament during the long debate on the railway and at the time of the controversy over the retention of Uganda as a British possession. Lugard was also an advocate of white settlement and in his own words maintained: 'It is possible that British Central and East Africa will be the embryo empires already dawning – empires which in the zenith of their growth and development will rival those dependencies which are the pride of the Anglo-Saxon race.'[1] It was a vision of a White Africa that was to come right in part but historically it disregarded that 'great black background' to the comings and goings in Africa of brown men and white men.[2]

Various colonisation schemes were put forward. One which attracted considerable attention and controversy in Europe was the settlement of Zionists in the Uasin Gishu plateau west of the Rift Valley. It appeared to the British imperialist Joseph Chamberlain, the promoter of the scheme, to be a means of introducing capital to the Protectorate and at the same time satisfying the demands of world Jewry for a national home. But the area was not considered large enough to accommodate the Israelites from the ghettoes of eastern Europe.

Another scheme would have made East Africa 'Brown Africa' if it had got past the report stage. Sir Harry Johnston, a British Foreign Office man, and Special Commissioner for Uganda, considered that the Uganda and East Africa Protectorates were only necessary to Britain because of their geographical position astride the headwaters of the Nile. Whoever controlled the Nile controlled Egypt – over which Britain had a peculiar interest in that the Egyptian posts were an important stage on the way to India. By a roundabout logic Johnston reported that as Britain was compelled to reserve control of a large portion of East Africa on account of the Indian Empire and regard for its political future, East Africa was a suitable outlet for Indian trade, enterprise and emigration. 'East

[1] F. D. Lugard, *The Rise of our East African Empire*.
[2] 'The life of the invaders, Arab sheikh, Indian trader or European farmer, has been maintained from first to last on a basis of African labour, and it is broadly true to say that nothing can be done in tropical Africa unless Africans help to do it.' R. Coupland, *E.A. and its Invaders*, p. 14.

Africa should be from every point of view the America of the Hindu.'[1]

Johnston certainly had historic grounds for his views. Contacts between India and the East African Coast were centuries old. Trade was in the hands of the Indian *banyans*, many of whom had supplanted the leading Arab families as landlords. Whenever a call went out for troops it was to India that Britain looked for reinforcements. The currency was the Indian rupee and the railway, because of a lack of inducement to the indigenous peoples and the absence of time to train them in the ways of modern labour, had been constructed by Indian coolies, a number of whom remained behind afterwards as petty traders.

But in his special report on East Africa Johnston reserved the Highlands as being suitable for European settlers and was probably the first man to coin the phrase 'White Man's Country'. And while his idea of East Africa as an 'America' of India with massive, Government-backed immigration was rejected, Indians were not discouraged from settling as market gardeners and planters around Kisumu by the torrid shores of the Kavirondo Gulf. Neither were they discouraged from moving into the embryo towns and up-country stations as traders and middlemen. It was that tract of country 'almost without parallel in tropical Africa, a region of 12,000 square miles, admirably well-watered with a fertile soil, cool and perfectly healthy climate covered with noble forests and, to a very great extent, uninhabited by any native race' from which the brown man was debarred – the White Highlands which in time were to become the reserve of a vociferous minority of Europeans, hardworking, adventurous, politically acute, and who were to provide Kenya with the social and economic foundations without which it would never have become an independent nation.

The man credited with giving the initial boost to white settlement in Kenya was Sir Charles Eliot, the Protectorate Commissioner from 1903 to 1904. It was Eliot who actively discouraged all acquisition of land by Indians except in the vicinity of towns. He was convinced that Kenya was a white man's country and that the land along and near the railway was suitable for European cultivation alone. The indigenous up-country peoples, their numbers greatly reduced by the famine and disease epidemics of the 1890s, were concentrated round the eastern shores of the lake in Kavirondo

[1] Hill, op. cit., p. 220.

from Mount Elgon to the Nandi Hills; in the foothills of Mount
Kenya and in the Ukambani, districts where there was always a
high density of population. The Masai as pastoralists roamed at
will over the rest of the country and the only inhabitants of the
forest glades were the few, fleeting Dorobo hunters.

It was to this extensive, apparently empty, virgin land that Sir
Charles Eliot, with the support of the British Foreign Office, who
were the Protectorate Government's overlords at the time, introduced his white settlers. Most of the land settled, the Kapiti Plains
south of Nairobi, Donyo Sabuk on the borders of Ukambani, the
central Rift Valley, the Mau, the Laikipia Plains between Mount
Kenya and the Aberdares, and the Uasin Gishu plateau, was formerly
occupied, if somewhat sparsely and tenuously, by the Masai; but
there were other pockets of land, notably Kiambu in Kikuyuland
and parts of Nandi and Lumbwa, which were alienated. Therefore,
almost all the peoples between Lake Victoria and the sea were able
to point to some portion of their ancestral lands which had fallen
under European occupation.

Lord Delamere, the 'father' of white settlement, and the leader of
agricultural progress, was given 100,000 acres on the western flanks
of the Rift Valley in return for a rent of £200 a year and a pledge
to spend £5,000 on development within five years. A group of
London and Johannesburg financiers who called themselves the
East African Syndicate and who had been prospecting in the Protectorate for minerals, but without success, were given a direct lease
by the Foreign Office on 300,000 acres of land to the east of the Rift
Valley in an area where the Masai were concentrated – an award
which led to the resignation of Sir Charles Eliot on the grounds that
he had not been consulted.

But it was to South Africa that the local administration looked to
provide the bulk of the new settlers and the response to a 'sales'
tour by a Protectorate official was unexpectedly rapid, for the mission coincided with the period of depression after the Boer War.
Shiploads of Boer farmers arrived in search of empty, untamed acres
and, to begin with, most of them settled outside Nairobi in the
Kiambu district, in an unplanned, hurried operation which sowed
the seeds of the acrimonious land dispute between the Government
and the Kikuyu. Later, however, the South African settlers moved
to the Uasin Gishu plateau where they formed an island of Afri-
kaners in the heart of Kenya.

The Masai held the key to white settlement for it was their land, the Masailand of the early geographers, that the settlers occupied. After two formal agreements, one completed in 1904 and the other in 1913, they were given, as compensation, treaty rights over a vast expanse of land along the southern boundary with German East Africa. The first agreement gave them two separate reserves, one of 4,500 square miles north of the railway in Laikipia, and the other 4,350 square miles along the border south of the railway.

In the minds of the Protectorate Government, under its new Commissioner, Sir Donald Stewart, the total area for an estimated 45,000 Masai and their livestock was a generous award. But in other minds it was eviction thinly veiled by the cloak of formal agreement. The first agreement was never really enforced and under the second agreement the Masai were induced, after legal protests and a series of administrative muddles, to remove themselves from Laikipia and join together in one great extended reserve along the border. Laikipia was then thrown open to white settlement and the Kenya Masai were at last united in proximity to their brethren in German East Africa. Their new reserve covered a total of 15,000 square miles and gave one and a half square miles to each family – a generous enough allocation and one which has enabled the Masai to continue their traditional way of life virtually undisturbed.

The Masai agreements had an important effect on Kenya's land policy and political history. They laid down a pattern for the demarcation of other tribal areas into reserves and in doing so created the White Highlands reserve for exclusive European colonisation.[1]

In 1905 the Protectorate came under the aegis of the British Colonial Office and the Commissioner was renamed Governor with an Executive Council and a Legislative Council to advise him. Kenya was henceforth a colony in all but name. The granting of land in the Highlands to Europeans proceeded – but slowly, because

[1] Low goes so far as to conclude that the interminable muddles of the Masai agreements and the first awards of their land to settlers – coincident with the resignation of Sir Charles Eliot and a later Governor, Sir Percy Girouard, which received extensive publicity – quickened the suspicions of liberal and humanitarian elements in Britain that the European settlers were being given an unwarrantably free rein. This, he maintains, was not the least of the reasons why the settlers in Kenya, unlike the settlers in Southern Rhodesia, failed a decade or so later to procure responsible government for themselves and with it control of the territory's internal affairs. Op. cit., p. 38.

of difficulties over land regulations, and it was not until 1915 that
an Ordinance was passed into law giving 999-year leases and individual rights over occupied land. There was no specific racial bar to
the ownership of land in the 'settled areas', though the Governor
had the right – of which he availed himself – to veto any transfer of
land between members of different races. This veto offended the
small but growing Indian community and later, in the 1920s, it gave
rise to the vexed Indian question that nearly put an end to European
dominance in Kenya. As long as the Governor was sympathetic to
the cause of European settlement and recognised the Highlands as
their particular reserve there was no possibility of an Indian or an
African owning land there outside the townships.

But in the first years of British colonial rule it was the controversy
over the supply of labour to work the newly settled farms and to
service the embryo urban areas that caused the most friction. The
settlers argued that if they were expected to take a leading part in
developing the country then it was the Protectorate Government's
responsibility to see that there was sufficient labour available from
the populated African reserves. On the other hand, the Government
was understandably reluctant to prejudice future relationships with
the indigenous peoples by using anything but indirect influence to
improve the supply of labour. It was undoubtedly sensitive to outside liberal opinion which saw in the settlers' demands the makings
of a forced labour policy.

The Protectorate administration had, therefore, to tread warily,
though labour was also needed for the railway and the Government
services, and it was obvious that by encouraging Africans to work
for wages they would have the cash with which to pay taxes and
support the cost of running the country. District officers were neither
encouraged nor forbidden to induce Africans in their care to leave
the reserves and go out to work for the Europeans, the railway or
the Government.

By 1907 the shortage of farm labour had become acute and many
Europeans had given up their land. Small in numbers, but powerful
through the influence of its leader Lord Delamere, the newly formed
Colonists' Association protested to the Governor, Sir James Hayes-
Sadler, at the lack of a firm Government policy on African labour.
As a compromise, a board of officials and settlers was set up to
review the situation and for a time there was some improvement in
the flow of Africans to the Highland farms and to Government

employ—mainly on the railway. All kinds of pressures were used by officials, the African chiefs newly nominated by the administration, and the settlers themselves, to force the tribal Africans out to work, many of whom were, for the first time, enjoying freedom from Masai raids and already spreading out from the primitive life of the forests and hills to the flatter and more easily worked agricultural lands on the plains. And so resentment against the land and taxation policies of the Government was increased by a distrust of the migrant labour system which not only upset traditional, tribal ways of life but also replaced the freedom of idleness with the 'dignity of labour'.[1]

Notwithstanding land regulation and labour difficulties the Protectorate made swift economic progress in the six years from 1908 to the outbreak of the First World War, when East Africa provided a tropical battleground for the warring nations. Sir Percy Girouard, who had succeeded Sir James Hayes-Sadler—'Old Flannelfoot' of settler derision—as Governor, had served in Egypt and South Africa as well as Nigeria. He was an active man and a good administrator, and though his term of office was brief he is credited with having taken the first steps towards laying the foundation of Kenya's economy.

Trade in 1908 was still based on 'ivory, beeswax, hides and skins'. There was a substantial deficit of expenditure over revenue; insufficient funds to provide for the cost of running the Protectorate's administration, and the British Treasury had to give £130,000 a year of grant-in-aid. With the final eclipse of the slave trade and the breakdown of free labour the old coastal economy had collapsed and the trading links with the Near and Far East were only slightly in evidence. The products of European settlement—coffee, sisal, tea, wheat, wattle, maize, butter and wool—had yet to have an appreciable effect on the country's export trade. But four years later the economy was in such a sound position that the grant-in-aid was discontinued voluntarily and Kenya was able to taste the first fruits of economic freedom. There were two reasons for this: a

[1] An official minute C.O. 533/43 of 1908 noted: 'In the E.A.P. of all Protectorates the presence of a European population of *bona fide* settlers and the desire to develop its rich natural resources greatly increases the risk of improper pressures being brought to bear on the natives in order to fit them into the vacant place in the economic system, which requires their immediate co-operation. It leads to questionable methods of inducing them to work and to undue haste in screwing Hut Tax out of them.' Low, op. cit., p. 53.

welcome period of good rains after years of semi-drought and a big
expansion of British overseas investment. The immediate success
of Uganda's new cotton crop as an export revenue earner for the
railway also helped – the net profit to the controlling authority, the
East Africa Protectorate, was £134,000 a year. But it was Girouard's
reorganisation of the management of Kenya's finances that possibly
did most to consolidate the quick economic advance.

When Girouard resigned in 1912 because of a dispute with the
British Colonial Office over the proposals to move the Masai from
Laikipia, the Protectorate was set fair for a period of stable government and prosperity. Road and rail communications, vital to such an
expansive country as Kenya, were improved. Branch railways were
built, one to Lake Magadi where the soda deposits were being
exploited and the other from Nairobi to Thika where the coffee and
sisal plantations on the boundary of Kikuyuland were at last bearing fruit. The shipping berths at Kilindini, the Port of Mombasa,
were extended and deepened to deal with the rising volume of imports and exports which had more than doubled in combined value
from £1½ million in 1909 to £3½ million in 1912. More settlers were
coming in and, in the African areas where the cessation of tribal
wars and disease epidemics had resulted in a rising population, the
products of the soil – principally maize – were increasing both in
quantity and value. A full exchange economy was in being. Nairobi
had grown out of the pioneer town stage and had the makings of a
capital city. Nakuru, Eldoret and Kisumu were becoming sizeable
market towns and townships were springing up around the headquarters of district administrations. The population, however, was
not large: fewer than three million, of whom only 3,000 were European and 20,000 Indian.

On the political front, the Europeans with their Convention of
Associations – an amalgamation of the Colonists' Association and
the Pastoralist Association known as the 'settlers' parliament' –
demanded elected representatives on the Protectorate's Legislative
Council. The Council, formed of leading officials with the addition
of two nominated settlers, was already marked by 'an almost continuous atmosphere of political controversy' on the part of the two
immigrant races. Winston Churchill who, as Liberal Under-Secretary of State for the Colonies, had been critical of the Protectorate's
political developments, was sent to Kenya in 1907 and summed
up the situation after only a few days in the country: 'Every

man in Nairobi is a politician and most of them are leaders of parties!'

Their scant numbers did not deter the Europeans from being vociferous in their demands for political freedom. Unlike the colonists who had pioneered other parts of the British Empire, they had arrived in the country in the wake of a Government administration. And from the beginning they found themselves struggling continually against the bureaucratic machine which, bearing heavily on their task of taming an undeveloped country and earning a living, they considered to be an intolerable burden. To them the only answer was self-government and freedom from bureaucracy, but this even to the outsider was a hopeless quest, as from the very beginning the Protectorate was under State control and ownership.[1]

Perhaps the root of all the political controversies that raged in Kenya for more than half a century lay in the instructions given by the British Foreign Office to Sir Donald Stewart when he succeeded Sir Charles Eliot as Protectorate Commissioner in 1904. Stewart was told, in writing, that it was only by a 'most careful insistence' on the protection of native rights that His Majesty's Government could justify their presence in Africa. This clear indication of British policy was never published, and, until the declaration twenty years later that Kenya was primarily an African territory and that the interests of the Africans must be paramount, the settlers were led to believe that Eliot's view of Kenya as a white man's country where European interests were paramount was official policy.

In the record of his journey to Kenya in 1907, the young Winston Churchill saw the future clearly. To him it was impossible that Kenya should ever be a white man's country 'inhabited wholly by white people and subsisting upon an economic basis of white unskilled labour'.[2] Colour was the dominant question, but there was room for all – the white man and the brown man. For the 'dark folk' there was room too – after all it was their country!

[1] 'The Government held the land; they owned the railway; they held the key to the flow of labour; they issued laws and regulations and imposed taxes by decree. Justice was largely a function of the executive. Minerals and forests were owned by the State. Transport except by ox or mule wagon was a state monopoly. The settler had to acquire land from the State and he could only sell land with the State's permission. He could not cut timber on his land, nor draw water from a river flowing through his land without the State's consent. The East Africa Protectorate was practically an estate belonging to His Majesty's Government.' Hill, op. cit., p. 296.
[2] W. S. Churchill, *My African Journey*, p. 45.

It was Churchill who supported the presence of Indians in East
Africa because of their contribution to the country's economy. He
queried their omission from the unofficial side of the newly formed
Legislative Council, and A. M. Jevanjee, a wealthy Indian who had
made a fortune as a railway contractor and was the leader of his
community, became the first of his race to be appointed to the
Council. But the 'dark folk' had to wait another twenty-seven years
before their first representative was appointed, though when the Hut
Tax was introduced in 1903 they were the first to pay taxes and
give financial support to the Protectorate administration. For them it
was 'taxation without representation'.

However, one of Girouard's last acts, before he left Kenya in
1912,[1] was to introduce the idea of local government in the African
tribal areas through nominated chiefs and councils of elders. This
was not indirect rule on the Nigerian model – though there was a
semblance of self-government over matters of tax collection, public
works and tribal courts in the African reserves – and it was not
until 1924 that legally constituted Local Native Councils were set
up.

In the meantime, the European settlers made all the political running. By 1914 they had so advanced their position under the influential leadership of Lord Delamere that they were on the verge of
achieving their ambition of holding elections for the appointment of
representatives to the Legislative Council, and they were well on the
way to Delamere's objective of ultimate self-government for the
white community and of Kenya itself. The British Colonial Secretary, Mr Lewis Harcourt, had pronounced himself sympathetic to
the settlers' demands after a long interview in London with Delamere. He had also expressed himself willing, on behalf of the British
Government, to grant a loan of £3 million to the country's development. But this, together with the proposals for European political
advancement, was submerged by the outbreak of the First World
War.

## III

The war in East Africa played only a small role in the world-wide
conflict caused by the unexpected turn of political events in Europe.
It was essentially an African war, in that most of the troops engaged

[1] Girouard later became managing director of Vickers, the armament
makers.

in it were African and the country over which it was fought was
uncharted, waterless bush, disease-ridden and infested with man-
eating lions and teeming herds of wild game. It was not in terrain
or climate suitable for a war of large entrenched armies. The campaign, just as long drawn out and bloody as in Europe though on a
much smaller scale, had to be thought of in terms of 'bushcraft,
human transport and quinine rather than guns, lorries and aero-
planes'. And like everything else in Africa it could not have been
waged without the active participation of the 'dark folk'. Such a
situation had been taken into account in 1885 when the framers of
the Berlin Act, in order to avoid 'conflicts between the handful of
Europeans charged with the control of millions of Africans', inserted clauses to provide for neutrality in Africa in the event of war
elsewhere. However, these clauses proved ineffective as by the time
attempts were made to invoke them hostilities between the two main
signatories, Germany and Britain, had already taken place.[1]

The Germans and the British faced each other in East Africa in a
thin line along a frontier that stretched for over four hundred miles
from the Indian Ocean to Lake Victoria. Within fifty miles of the
frontier, on the Kenya side, ran the Uganda railway: in the east and
west were the vital ports of Mombasa and Kisumu. These were the
targets for the Germans who at the outbreak of the war had, with
their 3,000 white officers and N.C.O.'s, and 8,000 African troops, the
advantage of overwhelming military superiority.

There were, however, no great actions. It was mainly a war of
marauding patrols, though casualties whenever the two sides met
were heavy. Thousands of miles from their homeland and with supplies so severely restricted by the sea blockade that they were
practically non-existent, the Germans had to look elsewhere for reinforcements. But skilful use of local resources and strict training of
their African troops made them, under the able leadership of their
commander, General von Lettow-Vorbeck, a formidable enemy to
the British throughout the four years of the campaign.

At first, the British did not expect the war in East Africa to be any
different from that in Europe and to last more than a few months;
but it was obvious from the initial success of the Germans in the
frontier skirmishes that local troops by themselves would be unable
to defend the railway and the approaches to Mombasa and Kisumu

[1] H. Moyse-Bartlett, *The King's African Rifles: A study in the military
history of East and Central Africa 1890–1945*, p. 262.

for any length of time. The King's African Rifles, formed twelve years previously to establish British authority in the Protectorate, and the East African Mounted Rifles, the settler volunteer force, were therefore reinforced with troops from India and Britain.

By the end of 1915, as the war dragged on and it seemed that the Germans would be a permanent running threat to Kenya's security, it was decided to launch a major offensive against them. More troops were called in from Britain, India, South, West and Central Africa, and, under the command of the South African General Smuts, the British invaded German East Africa. Endurance on both sides was the keynote of this stage of the campaign, for it lasted three years and the chase of von Lettow's forces took the British through the length and breadth of German and Portuguese East Africa. It ended with the cessation of hostilities in Europe in November 1918. When von Lettow surrendered on receipt of the news of the armistice, his force of 155 Europeans, 1,168 African troops and 1,522 African porters was in excellent condition and in effect unbeaten.

If it had little bearing on the general course of the war the campaign in East Africa did at least show – on both sides – that the African soldier, well trained and led, could march and fight to a standstill.[1] It also showed – and this was to be proved again twenty-one years later – that Kenya as a strategic base for men and materials could support a war far removed from its own boundaries.[2]

The war in East Africa, while it disrupted the country's economic development, provided only a temporary lull in the politics which were a constant feature of life in the Protectorate. Under pressure through lack of manpower and resources, the government machine was unable to cope with the demands of the British military command and the settlers found themselves sharing the criticisms that East Africa was not pulling its weight in the war. It is true that during the first flush of enthusiasm at the outbreak of war the majority of the 3,000 settlers volunteered for the armed forces. But their farms

[1] A British army staff officer remarked: 'The conclusion is the same that every thinking soldier in the force has arrived at after a year in British East Africa, namely that only the best and most highly-trained troops, British and Indian, are, or can hope to be, a match for the trained Africans of a fighting tribe in the bush.' Moyse-Bartlett, op. cit., Part II.

[2] Excluding Allied and naval forces, about 114,000 troops and 494,936 non-combatants were engaged in the East African campaign. Of the 18,000 casualties, 7,000 were African troops: 40,000 African porters, most of them from Kenya, are also said to have died from disease and illness contracted during the campaign.

ran down as a result and in 1915, when the campaign entered a more positive phase, they were persuaded by the Government that they should return to their farms and fight the war by producing food instead of patrolling the frontier.

When the settlers, on their return, found the country in what they felt was a state of disorganisation, a mass meeting, that panacea of all political ills in Kenya, was held in Nairobi. The meeting was highly critical and outspoken and called on the Government for a 'more vigorous and effective policy to organise the country's resources for war'. Allegations originally made by the British military command were repeated: first, that the Government seemed to have washed its hands of the war and secondly that the settlers were shirking their duty by remaining on their farms. But Lt.-Colonel Ewart Grogan, before and afterwards the stormy petrel of Kenya politics, accused the meeting of being destructive and defeatist.[1] He urged them to decide on the policy they wanted and then to force it upon the Government. The outcome of a meeting which began as a mass protest was a unanimous resolution placing the entire European community and their resources unreservedly at the Governor's disposal for military service and demanding immediate steps for the introduction of conscription.

In the face of this expression of public opinion the Government, as Grogan said it would be, was forced to act. The Governor, Sir Henry Belfield, appointed a War Council almost immediately under the chairmanship of his Chief Secretary, Sir Charles Bowring, and composed of two officials, three settlers and a military representative. The influence of the European community on the Government at the time was such that at its first meeting the Council resolved that its membership be increased by three more settlers and elected by popular vote. The Protectorate was then divided into three electoral areas and from each a representative of the settlers was elected, thereby winning for the settlers the principle of electoral representation.

Theoretically, the Kenya War Council was an advisory body but in practice it acquired powers and influence which made it virtually an executive – a device employed many years later during the pre-independence Emergency. Within weeks of its formation, conscrip-

---

[1] Grogan was a member of the Kenya Legislative Council for many years. As a young man, between 1898 and 1900, he walked the length of Africa from Cape Town to Cairo. He was active in Kenya politics until the granting of independence.

tion of Europeans to the armed forces was introduced and a survey undertaken of the country's resources in manpower and materials. A scheme was also put forward for the settlement of white ex-soldiers in the Highlands in order to 'ensure internal security by increasing the number of settlers'. Not for the first time was the fear that because African troops had been trained for war and might employ their fighting skills when they returned to their own country, used in the interests of internal security to consolidate the position of Europeans in Kenya. There is no denying, however, that four years of war conditions at a critical stage in its development left Kenya a weary and impoverished country. The administration, the railway, the roads and the land had all suffered. Rinderpest had reappeared and there was hunger, too, for 1918 was a year of drought and famine. Kenya needed strong government to repair the ravages of war and to undertake the tasks of reconstruction. Here again the settlers were to seize the opportunity and take the lead.[1]

Sir Charles Bowring had acted as Governor after the retirement of Sir Henry Belfield in 1917, but before the end of the war the European Convention of Associations decided that a Governor selected from the ranks of the British Colonial Service was not the type of person able to deal with the country's post-war problems. They demanded, and got, from the British Government a military Governor in the person of Major-General Sir Edward Northey, who had commanded the Rhodesian and Nyasaland forces in the last two years of the East African campaign.

From the European point of view Northey was, of course, a good choice, especially when in the course of his first address to the Legislative Council, shortly after his arrival in January 1919, he announced that on the dissolution of the War Council two unofficial European members would be nominated to his Executive Council and that a Bill to implement the grant of the franchise to Europeans would be introduced immediately. Thus Northey gave effect to the British Government's formal recognition in 1916 of the settlers' claim to elect their own representatives to the Legislative Council. Further, within two months of his arrival, a revised soldier settlement scheme was introduced and 4,560 square miles of the Highlands were alienated for the settlement of European ex-servicemen. Later, in 1919, an Ordinance was enacted establishing eleven European electoral areas and the official Colonial Service member-

[1] Hill, op. cit., p. 378.

ship of the Legislative Council was increased to give a Government majority. Elections were held in January 1920, the total European population, strengthened by the soldier settlement scheme, having risen to 9,000.

The African population of two million were silent spectators of this constitutional development, but not so the Indians whose population now numbered 22,000. They had been told by Northey that 'European interests must be paramount'. The report of the Economic Commission, set up in 1917 and composed of official and unofficial members, had gone even further. It said that the African must be defended against the Indian economically and from the 'antagonistic influence of Asiatic, as distinct from European philosophy'; that white settlement should be encouraged to carry out the trust and to expose the 'natives' to Western civilisation.[1]

The Indian community was indignant. Although before the war few of them had taken an interest in politics, and as an industrious people were more concerned with developing their standing as middlemen in the economy, the situation was now quite different. After a war in which India had contributed greatly to the Allied cause both in Africa and in Europe, Indian nationals had become conscious of their position and their potential political power. The nationalist movement for self-determination in India had also gained momentum and this, together with the other problems facing them in the 'great' dominion, made the British Government listen with more attention to the demand of the Indians for political recognition in Kenya where they had been told by Northey that 'universal suffrage for the Asiatics in this Protectorate on equality with the whites is out of the question'.[2]

But the Kenya Indians did not want merely equal representation with Europeans on the Legislative Council: they wanted the end of segregation in townships, the right to hold land in the Highlands, and promotion on merit, not race, to the highest posts in the police, army and civil service. This was the core of the Indian question, a controversy which was to be the bane of Kenya politics until the time when the African people themselves began to voice their demands.

The Europeans, outnumbered as they were, proved too strong politically for their Indian adversaries right to the end. Paradoxi-

[1] G. Bennett, *Kenya: a Political History*, p. 43.
[2] Z. Marsh and G. W. Kingsnorth, *East Africa History*, p. 194.

cally, this battle between the two immigrant races may have done more than anything to safeguard African interests. It provoked the British Government to maintain, as a compromise and a way out of a difficult situation, that the interests of the African people were paramount in any conflict between the three races. So, without the Indian question, Kenya might well have followed Southern Rhodesia and become a self-governing colony ruled by a white minority.

Full status as a Crown Colony under direct rule from the British Colonial Office in London was given in July 1920, but this had little to do with the political situation, though the settlers, under the impression that their position would be further strengthened, had long pressed for such a change. The reasons for the change were, however, financial, as development loans – much needed because of the state of the economy at the time – could not be raised under the Colonial Stock Act by a Protectorate. The British East Africa Protectorate was, therefore, formally annexed as a Crown Colony and named Kenya, after its highest mountain. Only the ten-mile coastal strip, because of its past history, was left with Protectorate status under the nominal sovereignty of the Sultan of Zanzibar.

As the newest addition to Britain's colonial dominions, Kenya was faced with the gravest difficulties. The railway, on which it depended for much of its livelihood, was virtually bankrupt after the strain of the war years. The country was still not producing enough in the way of agricultural exports. Commodity prices on the world markets were falling. There was an acute labour shortage. Government expenditure was soaring and there was every prospect of alarming deficits in the Budget. On top of this, a disastrous currency change was in process. But as Kenya entered the 1920s as a colonial dependency there was the first glimmer of the awakening of the 'dark folk' from their unknown past: a foretaste of the changes that would sweep Africa during the next forty years.

# Part Two

## THE MIDDLE YEARS

*Chapter 3*

# Outside Interference

T HE CURRENCY in the new Crown Colony of Kenya was based on the silver rupee, the standard coin in East Africa from the earliest days of trade with India. However, since the turn of the century and the development of the railway and European settlement, trade had moved away from India to Britain and there was a natural desire on the part of the Protectorate to deal in shillings and pence instead of rupees and anna pieces. An Order in Council was made, therefore, in 1914 to change the currency; but because of the war this was shelved till 1920. By then, international movements in trade and the high price of silver had caused the value of the rupee to rise steeply. The rupee in East African currency had been fixed in 1905 at 1s 4d in terms of sterling and this was the basis on which all financial business was conducted. In 1920, when the rupee rose and fluctuated around 2s 4d, it became obvious that drastic action was needed. Two courses of action were open to the Kenya authorities. The rupee could be stabilised at a higher rate on the assumption that the rise in its sterling value was permanent and, though hard on the settlers and businessmen who were in debt to the banks, could be achieved without any violent dislocation of the money market. Alternatively, the rupee could be stabilised at the old rate of 1s 4d – despite the practical difficulties – in the belief that it would return to this level on which all debts in the colony had been contracted. The British Colonial Secretary and the creditor-financier forces in London favoured the first course: the Governor and the debtor-producer forces in Nairobi favoured the second course.

International monetary considerations weighed heavily in favour of stabilising the East African rupee at a higher rate after the Indian rupee went up to 2s 9d, and the Colonial Secretary, who had the final say in the matter, announced his decision in a statement to the House of Commons on 25 February 1920:

'The dependence of East Africa on the United Kingdom both for its market and for the capital required for development has

65

made it desirable to stabilise the East African exchange on a
sterling basis. In deciding to prevent the East African rupee from
being forced up to above 2s 4d by the recent action of the Government of India in respect of the Indian exchange, and to fix it
eventually at 2s, the most careful consideration was given to the
interests, not only of the settlers, who have been seriously affected
by the appreciation of the rupee, but also of those persons Indians
and others, who have commitments in, or dealings with, India and
of the native wage-earners.'

Although the Colonial Secretary said the decision to stabilise the
East African rupee at the 2s rate was only taken after the actions of
the Government of India had made it clear that 'the sterling value
of the rupee could never fall below 2s 9d except for possible temporary fluctuations of exchange', the Indian rupee fell within six
months to its original parity of 1s 4d and settled at 1s 6d where it
remained for many years. The East African rupee was left high and
dry, thus creating a double blow for the local debtor-producer
forces. When the rupee first jumped to a high rate in 1919 a producer selling his produce in London, and being paid in sterling,
received about half as many rupees as before: he also had to sell
half as much more coffee or maize to pay the interest on his over-
draft. Now with the East African rupee valued higher in sterling
than the Indian rupee his local debts were increased almost over-
night and by a decision in which he had no say and which brought
the colony to the verge of financial collapse. The Kenya settlers and
local mercantile interests never forgave the British Colonial Office
for taking the decision against local advice. They were disillusioned
by the apparent mishandling of the currency situation and their opposition to 'outside interference from Whitehall' was therefore
strengthened.

Controversy over the currency did not, however, end with stabilisa-
tion. There remained the conversion of the East African rupee to
sterling. This was done on 26 April 1920 when an Order in Council
established the florin, valued at two shillings, as the standard coin.
The practical difficulties in the adoption of a standard coin of such
high sterling value soon became apparent and once again the
British Colonial Office was at odds with the Kenya authorities on
the best ways in which to achieve a stable currency. There were
further arguments and counter-arguments. Not till January 1922

was agreement reached and a second Order in Council made for the introduction of an East African shilling, at the rate of 20 shillings to the East African pound and pound sterling, as the standard coin in Kenya, Uganda and Tanganyika.

The long wrangle over the introduction of a stable currency in Kenya undoubtedly hampered the country's development and there were many repercussions. Falling world prices for primary products coming on top of the economic difficulties caused by the currency changes forced the settlers to cut their costs of production. Wages were the first target. In 1919, before the conversion of the rupee to sterling, the average wage of an unskilled African labourer on a European farm was six rupees (valued at eight shillings) a month plus food and housing: in 1920, the average wage had risen to the equivalent of twelve shillings a month. Now, in 1921, the settlers through their Convention of Associations imposed a cut of 33 per cent on the wages of unskilled labourers and the African farm worker was back where he started two years previously. In the long run, he neither gained nor lost by the currency changes; but suspicions were aroused which did little to help a worsening labour situation.

The acute shortage of labour in the immediate post-war years created yet another threat to Kenya's economic development. Exports were badly needed to pay for the work of reconstruction and to meet the rise in Government expenditure on better communications, hospitals, schools, land improvement, public works and so on. The African areas were barely self-sufficient and so it was left to the land settled by European farmers to provide products which could be exported and earn foreign exchange to pay for essential imports. This increase in production was possible only through a steady supply of labour and the Government, whose financial problems were aggravated by the currency crisis, was forced into a position where it had to take positive action and, short of a policy of forced labour, induce Africans to come out and work for the settlers.

After the original controversy over the supply of labour to settler farms, a Masters and Servants Ordinance was introduced in 1910 to regulate conditions under which African labour could be employed. This provided for labour inspectors to see that good conditions in housing, rations and health were maintained on European farms. A Resident Native Ordinance was also passed in the same year to regulate the growing custom by which Africans voluntarily left their reserves with their wives and families, together with their possessions and livestock, to settle as 'squatters' on the uncultivated parts of the farms and in return for the use of half an acre of land, grazing rights, firewood and water, contract to work for so many days in the year for the farmer. Five years later, in 1915, another labour law, the Native Registration Ordinance, was passed which laid down that every adult male African who left his reserve to work should have a certificate of identification that recorded his fingerprints and periods of employment. This certificate, which came to be known as the *kipandé*, provided yet another source of irritation in the relations between the African worker and his employer.

The Ordinances were not, however, rigidly enforced until 1919 when Northey authorised his Chief Commissioner, Mr John Ainsworth, to circulate to all Government offices the official view on the supply of labour:

'His Excellency trusts that those Officers who are in charge of what is termed labour-supplying districts are doing what they can to induce an augmentation of the supply of labour for the various farms and plantations ... and he feels assured that all officers will agree with him that the larger and more continuous the flow of labour is from the Reserves the more satisfactory will be the relations as between the native people and the Settlers and between the latter and the Government. The necessity for an increased supply of labour cannot be brought too frequently before the various native authorities, nor can they be too often reminded that it is in their own interests to see that their young men become wage-earners and do not remain idle for the greater part of the year.'[1]

The Ainsworth circular provoked an immediate outburst of indignation both in Kenya and in Britain. It was interpreted as the outline of a forced labour policy regardless of the Government's protestations that it would take measures to ensure that the three labour laws passed in previous years would be made to work in order to prevent exploitation by employers. The timing of the circular was opportune but the wording was too 'pro-settler' and offensive to those liberal forces awakened by the disputes over the Masai agreements.

[1] Labour Circular No. 1, 23 October 1919. (W. M. Ross, *Kenya from Within*, p. 104.)

The controversy over the Ainsworth circular was complicated by an amendment to the Native Authority Ordinance of 1912 which enabled the Government to call out young Africans to do communal work for six days in each quarter. The amendment legalised a traditional tribal custom and was enforced only once, in 1925, when because of an acute shortage of labour the State had to recruit 4,000 men for the building of extensions to the railway; but despite the ruling that the previous consent of the Secretary of State for the Colonies had to be obtained before any compulsory labour was called out, it added strength to the accusations of forced labour from such bodies as the Aborigines Protection Society and the Conference of Missionary Societies. The Archbishop of Canterbury launched a fierce attack in the House of Lords; and in East Africa the Bishop of Zanzibar, the Right Rev. Frank Weston, declared that forced labour, except in war, was immoral and that forcing Africans to work in the interests of European civilisation was a betrayal of the weaker to the financial interests of the stronger race. Moderate missionary opinion was more receptive to the proposals contained in the Ainsworth circular. In a joint memorandum, the Bishops of the Church of England in East Africa and senior representatives of the Church of Scotland in East Africa declared that while believing that ideally all labour should be voluntary they recognised that at present this was impossible and that some form of pressure must be exerted if an adequate supply of labour necessary for the development of the country was to be secured. They felt, though, that the Government's labour policy placed 'far too great a power in the hands of native chiefs and headmen and they, therefore, desired to see it modified'.

To some extent, public opinion was reassured by a despatch from Lord Milner, the Colonial Secretary of State, who denied in strong terms that the Ainsworth circular sanctioned forced labour for private employers. He wrote that in his opinion the Government would be failing in its duties if it did not use all lawful and reasonable means to encourage the supply of labour for the settlers 'who have embarked on enterprises calculated to assist, not only the Protectorate itself, but also this country and other parts of the Empire, by the production of raw materials which are in urgent demand'. He wrote further and maintained that the interests of the native labourers were well protected by the Masters and Servants Ordinance and it would be hard to find a more comprehensive set of regulations to secure the well-being of natives employed outside their reserves.[1] In 1921, Mr Winston Churchill succeeded Lord Milner as Colonial Secretary and contributed the final, official word on the subject. His despatch, published as a White Paper, instructed the Government of Kenya to 'inculcate habits of industry both inside and outside the Reserves' and directed District Officers to give information as to where labour might be secured and obtained; but to take no further part in recruiting.

[1] Lord Milner to Sir Edward Northey, *Cmnd. 873* (1920).

## Chapter 4

# Riot and Rebellion

W HILE THE DISPUTE over the supply of labour in Kenya was being brought to a close there were indications of an awakening in African public opinion. The strict enforcement of the *kipandé* law, the doubling of Hut and Poll Tax from five to ten rupees, and the decision of the Convention of Associations to cut farm wages had not passed unnoticed by the people most affected, and a young mission-trained African named Harry Thuku provided the spark which led to the Nairobi 'Riot'. Thuku had founded the Young Kikuyu Association in 1921 as a primitive kind of trade union for the growing number of Kikuyu workers in Nairobi. He was Kenya's first militant trade union leader and his anti-Government and anti-European speeches were used not only to increase membership of the Young Kikuyu Association but also to further his own political ambitions. His main platform was a complaint that the Africans had helped the Europeans in their war and all they had got as a reward was an increase in tax, wage-cuts and a pass law. At one meeting, attended by 4,000 people, he suggested that they should hire motor lorries, fill them with the new *kipandé* certificates and dump them in the drive of the Governor's residence. This was too much for the Government to accept and on 15 March 1922 Harry Thuku was arrested and detained in the Nairobi Police Lines. Next day, there was a general strike among African workers in Nairobi. Picketing was well organised and a large crowd followed Thuku's supporters to the Police Lines where the guards had been reinforced by a detachment of the King's African Rifles. There were inflammatory speeches; but the crowd remained good-tempered and the whole affair might have been resolved peaceably if a nervous African policeman had not pulled the trigger of his rifle. Firing became general and the crowd immediately dispersed leaving behind twenty-five dead and mortally wounded.[1] The organisers of the strike were arrested and Harry

[1] Ross, op. cit., p. 232.

71

Thuku exiled to the distant Northern Frontier province. So ended
the first organised attempt by Kenya Africans to express their views
on Government policies.

On all accounts 1922 was not an easy year for the Kenya Government. Indian demands for a Common Roll with Europeans and the
right to acquire land in the White Highlands were receiving powerful support in Britain and in India. The settlers, on the other hand,
declared that they were prepared to go to any lengths to conserve
their position and rejected any suggestion of a multi-racial legislature and land policy. Churchill made the first move in what came to
be known as the 'Indian Question' when he recalled Northey, who
had never concealed his support for the paramountcy of European
interests in Kenya, and replaced him by Sir Robert Coryndon, the
Governor of Uganda. Then followed an agreement in London between the Under-Secretary for the Colonies, Mr Edward Wood,
and the Under-Secretary for India, Lord Winterton: it proposed a
common electoral roll for all British subjects; seats in the Legislative
Council to be divided between the Indians and Europeans on a four
to seven basis; and segregation in the colony to be abolished. On the
rights of Indians to acquire land in the White Highlands, the agreement proposed that this should be left open for further discussion.

The settlers in their militant mood reacted to the Wood-Winterton
proposals violently. Although only a tenth of the Indian community
would be enfranchised under the proposed common electoral roll,
this to them was the thin end of the wedge and that there should
be any doubts at all about the White Highlands was a violation of
previous assurances from the British Government. The new Governor, after consulting his Executive Council, informed the Secretary of
State, therefore, that the terms of the settlement between the Colonial
and India Offices were 'entirely unacceptable' to Europeans and
probably could not be implemented except by force. Churchill
replied that the Wood-Winterton agreement was only provisional
and was 'intended to meet difficulties in India' without departing
from the spirit of his previous pronouncements. These had included
a categorical statement at the annual East African Dinner in London that the British Government did not contemplate any settlement
or system which would prevent Kenya from becoming a 'char-
acteristically and distinctly British colony, looking forward in the
full fruition of time to responsible self-government'. In November
1922 the Duke of Devonshire replaced Churchill as Colonial Secre-

tary in yet another change of government and four months passed before there was any further move on the Indian Question. During this period, tempers had begun to cool; but they were roused again by a despatch to Coryndon pressing him to secure local agreement on the Wood-Winterton proposals and authorising the extension of the life of the existing Legislative Council so that settlement could be reached before the next election. The Vigilance Committee, set up by the Convention of Associations earlier in the year to fight for settler interests, prepared to put into operation a plan to seize control of the Government by force: the Governor was to be kidnapped and taken to a lonely farm 60 miles from Nairobi; there were to be surprise raids to take over the railway, postal and telegraphic systems; and messages were to be broadcast 'all over the Empire' stating the settlers' case and appealing to the British and Dominion publics for support. This plan for a Unilateral Declaration of Independence in early colonial Kenya, and the enforcement of minority rule by a few thousand Europeans, could have succeeded. The settlers were well armed and most of them had military experience; but although the Vigilance Committee had wide support, loyalty to the Crown and constitutional government made them hesitate to take the final step.

The British Government, thoroughly alarmed by the threatened settler revolt, proposed a truce and invited all the parties involved in the dispute to a conference in London under the chairmanship of the Duke of Devonshire. At this first of the Kenya constitutional conferences to be held in London, the Africans, the third but so far neglected party to the dispute, were represented by the Rev. J. W. Arthur, a Church of Scotland missionary. Lord Delamere headed the European delegation with a mandate to 'accept no compromise over the Indian Question', but in the long-drawn-out conference — it lasted three months — he was forced to retreat and base his case on British responsibility for the development of African interests and the 'rightful duty' of the settlers to share in this responsibility. The result of this involuntary statesmanship was, of course, compromise and an opportunity to the British Government to lay down in the White Paper on the Conference a policy for the next thirty years:

'Primarily Kenya is an African territory, and His Majesty's Government think it necessary definitely to record their considered opinion that the interests of the African natives must be paramount and that if, and when, those interests and the interests of the immigrant races should conflict, the former should prevail. Obviously the interests of the other communities, European, Indian or Arab, must severally be safeguarded. Whatever the circumstances in which members of these communities have entered Kenya, there will be no drastic action or reversal of measures already introduced, such as may have been contemplated in some quarters, the result of which might be to destroy or impair the existing interest of those who have already settled in Kenya. But in the administration of Kenya, His Majesty's Government regard themselves as exercising a trust on behalf of the African population, and they are unable to delegate or share this trust, the object of which may be defined as the protection and advancement of the native races.'

The White Paper dealt specifically with the controversy between the European and Asian communities. It decided that the official majority in the Legislative Council should be maintained: that there should be eleven European, five Indian and one Arab elected members; and one nominated unofficial member to represent African interests. The composition of the Governor's Executive Council was to be left unchanged except for the addition of a nominated unofficial member to represent African interests. Reservation of the Highlands for Europeans was to be maintained; but outside the area racial segregation as between Indians and Europeans would be abolished. On immigration, the White Paper stated that 'only in extreme circumstances could His Majesty's Government contemplate legislation designed to exclude from a British Colony immigrants from any other part of the British Empire. Such racial discrimination in immigration regulations, whether specific or implied could not be in accord with the general policy of His Majesty's Government, and they cannot countenance the introduction of any such legislation in Kenya.' First reactions of the settlers to the Devonshire White Paper were hostile and the Kenya Indians considered it a 'gross betrayal'. However, by the time the various delegations had returned to Kenya moderate opinion had taken over and there was little strength left in the rebellious threats from the two communities. Extremely heavy rains, and their effect on the crops, together with the severe economic problems facing the country overshadowed all political controversy.

*Chapter 5*

# Gilded Years

K ENYA HAD JUST PASSED through another financial crisis in which Government expenditure was drastically cut in order to avoid a Budget deficit. An Economic and Finance Committee under the chairmanship of the Chief Secretary, Sir Charles Bowring, and including representatives of the Government, the settlers and commerce, was set up to straighten the country's finances. Like many such committees in Kenya it had wide references which enabled it to consider every aspect of economic policy. Its main task, however, was to increase exports and curb imports. The annual value of exports was only about £900,000, which made up most of the total trade, while Government estimates of expenditure amounted to £2,750,000. Increased production of maize, a crop which grew well in the African areas and over a large part of the Highlands, was therefore selected as a quick way of boosting exports. It was a necessary expedient at the time and had the desired result, but the exhaustive effect on soil fertility was felt later when the slump of the thirties, combined with falling yields, brought agricultural production almost to a standstill. The Economic Committee also suggested easier railway rates for exports; a 30 per cent protective duty for wheat growing and flour milling; and aids to encourage the production of timber, rice and dairy products – important recommendations for a country whose future development lay in an expanding agricultural industry. Export duties were abolished and import duties revised to bring in more revenue. By 1924, the policies of the Economic and Finance Committee were showing results: Government expenditure had been brought down to realistic levels and with the increase in exports there was a surplus of a quarter of a million pounds in the Budget – the first for some years.

In the next five years, which have been described as the 'gilded years', Kenya made a rapid recovery from the general uncertainty and political controversies of the immediate post-war period. The country had a popular Governor in Coryndon who had wide experi-

75

ence in ruling African territories and in dealing with the 'overlords' of the British Colonial Office. Under his rule, the differences between the opposing political factions in Kenya became secondary to the country's economic development. Capital began to flow in at the rate of £1 million a year. More settlers were also coming in and with the better prices on the world commodity markets revenue continued to increase. Yet Coryndon, who being South African-born had natural sympathies for the white settlers, did not confine his interests to the development of the export-producing Highland areas. He laid down a policy of active encouragement for agricultural production in the African areas and instituted training schools. He brought to fruition Girouard's scheme for self-government in these areas in the introduction of Local Native Councils to raise rates and control public works, schools and agriculture; and he made arrangements for the 'final demarcation' of the tribal areas. His policy on African development was, in effect, an interpretation of Lugard's dual policy system, though underwritten by the Devonshire declaration of the 'paramountcy of native interests'. If he had not died suddenly in 1925 Coryndon might well have brought a lasting balance between the conflicting parties in colonial Kenya. His place as Governor was taken by Sir Edward Grigg (later Lord Altrincham), a journalist, soldier, courtier and Liberal politician with wide experience of governments but new to administration in Africa.

Grigg firmly believed in the idea of closer union between Kenya, Uganda and Tanganyika, and viewed his new appointment as a preliminary step to the post of Governor-General of an East Africa Federation. 'Almost at once the distinguished architect Sir Herbert Baker began to build, what by East African standards could only be regarded as Vice-Regal, a palace at Nairobi and another large residence at Mombasa.'[1] The British Government had first given serious thought to closer union shortly after the war when the Secretary of State, Lord Milner, directed the Governors of the three territories to examine the possibilities of co-ordination between the respective governments. Although the matter was shelved for some time, controversy over proposals for the development of the Kenya and Uganda railway drew attention to the need for some common, controlling authority. An extension of the railway across the Uasin Gishu plateau in the White Highlands to the cotton-growing areas of Uganda, and the taking over of the branch line from Voi on the

[1] Sir Philip Mitchell, *African Afterthoughts*, p. 107.

Kenya border to Kahe, a station on the German-built railway runing from the port of Tanga to the Highlands of Kilimanjaro, had clashed with the plans of the Tanganyika Government to build a railway of its own to the southern shores of Lake Victoria. There was every prospect of a freight war in competing for traffic, and the economic disadvantage of developing two rival railway systems where one was sufficient became obvious and resulted in a strong demand for the unification of all the railway systems in the East African territories.

The issue of closer union had also been officially recognised in the drafting of Tanganyika's mandate when Britain took over responsibility for German East Africa and was authorised to constitute the territory into a 'customs, fiscal and administrative union or federation with the adjacent territories'. In 1924, the report of a Royal Commission, set up by Mr J. H. Thomas, Secretary of State for the Colonies in the first Labour Government, to examine social and economic developments in East Africa, noted that there was little support for the idea of federation, and definite hostility from various quarters, including the European community in Kenya, the African Government in Buganda, various Indian associations and all shades of opinion in Zanzibar.[1] The Commission, under the chairmanship of Mr W. G. Ormsby-Gore and representative of all three main political parties in Britain, finally rejected the idea of federation on the grounds that lack of communications would be a serious obstacle and that federal government would be cumbrous, but they recommended regular conferences between the three territory Governors to discuss 'matters of general policy which presented common problems such as native administration, communications, taxation, land and labour'.

By the time the Ormsby-Gore Commission's report was published, there had been a change of Government in Britain. Mr Leopold Amery, the new Colonial Secretary, who had worked together with Grigg under Lord Milner and was also a supporter of closer union, authorised Grigg to pursue the idea of an East Africa Federation and to produce a plan in agreement with his fellow Governors in Uganda and Tanganyika. Yet Grigg, 'a politician reared in the Parliamentary tradition', failed in his appointed mission. Although the Governor of Uganda, Sir William Gowers, was amenable to some form of union of his group of self-governing African states with

[1] Report of the East Africa Commission, *Cmnd. 2387* (1925).

Kenya and Tanganyika, the Governor of the latter territory, Sir
Donald Cameron, was implacably opposed to any political association of his unitary African state with settler-dominated Kenya.
Interpreting his instructions to produce a plan as one that should be
agreed by everybody, Grigg also found that Delamere could not
harmonise his fixed ideas of a white-controlled East Africa with the
policy of dual control and independent development necessary as a
basis for agreement between the conflicting interests of the three
territories. To Grigg, the gulf between official and unofficial opinion
on closer union was unbridgeable and there was no answer to the
'ultimate question' of European or African supremacy.[1] He therefore reconciled himself to deadlock and chose to stress the economic advantage of closer union while leaving the political problems
unsolved. His detailed scheme for a Central Authority to control
economic matters, the main transport services, the customs system,
all land and air communications, defence and research was, however, accepted in principle by the British Government in 1927. It
was left to Amery to cover the wider political field and this he did in
a White Paper on Future Policy in Eastern Africa which stated that
while the responsibility for trusteeship was still that of the Imperial
Government they desired 'to associate more closely in this high and
honourable task those who, as colonists or residents, have identified
their interests with the prosperity of the country'.[2] Speaking on the
White Paper in the House of Commons, Mr Amery said that progress of the white community towards self-government meant an association with the British Government in the sense of trusteeship to
the weaker and more numerous part of the population. The Government wanted to ensure that the white settlers were 'conscious of the
destiny of East Africa as a great country which they are called on to
lead and inspire; that they should be equally conscious of responsibility towards other communities and should desire to bring those
communities in the fullness of time into association with themselves
on every matter affecting the development of the country'.

The White Paper and Amery's statement helped to reassure the
Kenya Europeans on their role in an East African federation; but
the British Cabinet, feeling as trustees that more information was
needed on the problems of closer union, appointed a Special Commission in 1928. The Commission, under the chairmanship of Sir

[1] Lord Altrincham, *Kenya's Opportunity*, p. 207.
[2] *Cmnd. 2907* (1927).

Hilton Young, was instructed to recommend whether federation between the three East African territories was desirable and how it could be brought about. It had as members a financial expert, Sir George Schuster, who was about to take up an appointment with the India Office; a civil servant from India, Sir Reginald Mant; and a missionary, Mr J. H. Oldham, Secretary of the International Missionary Council. Amery could not have had chosen for him Commissioners more likely to reject his concept of federation. This they did in a majority report published in January 1929.[1] While accepting the principle of closer union, the three members thought that the main task should be to direct a common native policy on the basis of paramountcy of African interests. They considered that until the the native population were able to take part in a representative system, the Imperial Government must retain, through a High Commissioner, the right to intervene in all the business of government in the three territories; and they went outside the terms of their appointment in recommending a common electoral roll in Kenya for Europeans, Indians and detribalised Africans subject to property and educational qualifications. The Chairman, in a minority report, recorded that he was unable to join in the opinion of the three members that till African interests were adequately represented responsible government through a majority of unofficial representation in the legislature must be ruled out as a suitable form of government in Kenya in the foreseeable future. He considered that as long as there was a Central Authority empowered to intervene on any racial issue, there could be no objection to responsible government.

The Special Commission's majority report caused dismay both in London and in Nairobi. It was criticised as having gone off at a political tangent and that it failed to recognise the importance of federation to the economic development of the three territories. Amery, therefore, made a final bid to make his idea of closer union work and to overcome the doubts raised by the report. In the April following the report's publication, he sent out his Permanent Under-Secretary Sir Samuel Wilson to seek some basis on which the agreement of the different communities could be secured on the question of federation. Wilson reported back that the Kenya Europeans had turned against any idea of closer union because it would mean the abandonment of Coryndon's dual policy and the sacrifice of their interests so that Kenya could be brought into line with Tanganyika

[1] *Cmnd. 3378* (1929).

and Uganda. He said the Indians, who had embarked on a policy of political non co-operation since the Devonshire proposals in 1923, were unlikely to agree to the principle of closer union unless the common electoral roll recommended by the Hilton Young Commission was introduced. African political opinion in Kenya was still practically non-existent, but in Uganda Wilson found that the African kingdoms were strongly opposed to federation because they feared it would entail control of their destinies being transferred to Kenya. Wilson, nevertheless, secured a measure of agreement for some form of economic co-ordination in which a High Commissioner would be appointed to administer the three territories with the assistance of a federal council and an official majority. However, by the time the Wilson report was published a Labour Government had come into power in Britain. Amery departed from the Colonial Office and his place was taken by Lord Passfield, better known as Sidney Webb, the social reformer and Fabian. The new Government was in no hurry to continue with the closer political and economic union of the three East African territories and waited another year before announcing its own proposals. By then the idea of federation had become submerged in the economic slump of the thirties and was virtually abandoned; but in the years ahead closer union never failed to be considered a lost opportunity by those who saw in East Africa the makings of a great multi-racial dominion.

## Chapter 6

# Depression and Tensions

HE FIRST HINT of economic troubles came with the plague of locusts which swept over East Africa in 1928, destroying crops already withered after a year of drought. The invasion was entirely unexpected as no locusts had been seen in Kenya for thirty years. They had come from breeding grounds somewhere to the north in the region of the Red Sea and it was to be some years before an adequate locust prevention policy could be established. In the meantime, Kenya, like her neighbours, had to suffer the locust blight. The Government was forced to give £200,000 for famine relief and food had to be imported. Agricultural exports, on which the country depended, fell by over £500,000 to £2,745,910, making a deficit in the Budget. Two years later, in 1931, another locust invasion swept through Kenya. Again crops were destroyed and the estimate of the damage was put at a quarter of a million pounds. An even worse attack on the Kenya economy was, however, about to happen. The great world depression of the thirties had begun and the actions of various governments to bolster their economies seriously affected the commodity markets on which Kenya depended for its agricultural exports.

Between 1928 and 1933 the value of maize fell from Shs. 11/10 a bag to Shs. 3/20 a bag; sisal from Shs. 541/– a ton to Shs. 171/– a ton; coffee from Shs. 89/50 to Shs. 46/50 a hundredweight; butter from Shs. 143/– to Shs. 58/– a hundredweight; wattlebark from Shs. 161/– to Shs. 36/– a ton.[1] Most of these export commodities were produced on settler farms although the price of African-grown produce also dropped: hides from Shs. 30/– to Shs. 6/– a frasila; ghee by 66 per cent; and pulse crops by 50 per cent. The first response to these price falls was an increase in production and with the help of a season of good rains exports mounted. In 1930 they had risen to £3,400,000; but by 1934 they were down by nearly half. The Kenya soil had proved that it was not inexhaustible and

[1] Hill, op. cit., p. 483; figures quoted are in East African shillings.

81

yields could not keep pace with the drive to increase production to offset the fall in commodity prices: it had limits as an earner of foreign exchange.

Devaluation, and the reduction of the sterling exchange value of the East African shilling to a point at which costs and prices could be brought into harmony, might have eased the strain on Kenya's economy. Yet no relief was granted by the British Government either on the question of devaluation of the currency or in any reduction of annual interest and repayment on loans which, by 1934, totalled £1 million Kenya continued to be tied to sterling and to the needs of the London money market. Economic recovery as a result was slow and not until the outbreak of the Second World War did any real measure of prosperity return to Kenya.

While the Great Depression retarded Kenya's growth at a crucial stage in its economic development, and had serious repercussions on the life of the country, there was no slackening of political tensions. The year 1930 marked the decline of European influence and the end of Delamere's dream of an independent, settler-governed state. For in the June of that year the British Labour Government published, in a series of White Papers, its views on the closer union of the three East African territories and on the future policy for Kenya.[1] The White Papers recommended the appointment of a High Commissioner with dictatorial powers to supervise Kenya, Uganda and Tanganyika and declared that the relationship of His Majesty's Government to the native population of East Africa was one of trusteeship which could not be devolved. A common electoral roll was 'the object to be aimed at and attained'; and responsible government was recognised as the goal, but by 'a Ministry representing an electorate in which every section of the population finds an effective and adequate voice'. The reaction of the settlers to what was called the 'black papers' was immediate. They sensed the introduction of an all-black policy which would submerge the European community and believed that they had been betrayed. Statements of policy by previous British Governments had always recognised that white settlement was an essential part of the colony's development and that the European community was closely associated in the 'high and honourable task' of trusteeship for the African people. Now a Labour Government had repudiated past assurances and they felt that, short of taking the law into their own hands and

[1] *Cmnd. 3573* (1930); *Cmnd. 3574* (1930).

using force, there was little left for them to do but to increase their demands for more political power in order to reassert their position.

Because of the fierce European reaction to his Government's policy, Lord Passfield agreed to a suggestion that the controversial affairs of East Africa should be referred to a Joint Select Committee of the two Houses of Parliament for final settlement. The Committee met in London and at lengthy meetings representatives of all the colony's communities were allowed to give evidence. In preliminary efforts to persuade the Labour Government to amend its policy on Kenya, the ailing Lord Delamere outlined in these words the Kenya settlers' case on the differences with the British Government:

'We ourselves did and do consider ourselves trustees for the future of the indigenous races. Our trusteeship (cannot we go back to the real meaning of the word which is responsibility?) is that of all governing peoples for the uncivilised races under their rule. It means that during the long period of time likely to elapse before they can take their place on a civilised plane, we will see that they have every chance in the state of life and the standard of civilisation to which, as a whole, they rise ... certainly that their interests should be paramount over those of all other inhabitants of East Africa.

'I think the difference between Lord Passfield's policy and ours is a definite one. His policy is that until these backward peoples are capable of taking part in the government of these countries, the whole political future of Eastern Africa is to stand still. Until that time bureaucratic rule is to hold the field and no further political advance is to be made. Our policy visualises the future as a period of native advancement in their own reserves, on their own councils, before they are capable of taking part in the central direction and government of these countries. We visualise native councils going forward gradually from the present small units to a point where over those small units is a Central Native Council, dealing with native affairs under the Central Government, but with wide powers. That is as far as we can see at present. During that long period it is impossible to stifle the rights and aspirations of the civilised community which has to develop the whole of the rest of these countries.'[1]

[1] E. Huxley, *White Man's Country*, p. 287.

Delamere's views were the basis on which the Europeans gave evidence to the Joint Select Committee; but the Africans, represented by Chief Koinange of the Kikuyu Association, and Ezekiel Apinde of the Kavirondo Taxpayers' Association, rejected any idea of political apprenticeship through Local Native Councils and asked for direct representation on the Legislative Council in equal number with the European members.

The report of the Joint Select Committee was published in 1931, the year after the London hearings. It came to the conclusion that any far-reaching step in the direction of closer union between the three East African territories would be inopportune on account of the increased financial cost at a time of economic depression. Another factor was the reluctance of African representatives from Uganda and Tanganyika to be more closely connected with Kenya. The Committee also referred to the 'lack of adequate communications and of any common consciousness in the population of the territories'.[1] However, the Committee recommended that the Governors of Kenya, Tanganyika and Uganda should meet in regular conference, and that a joint secretariat should be set up for inter-territorial conferences on technical matters. White settlement was praised as 'an important element in the progress of East Africa'; and on the statement in Devonshire's White Paper of 1923 which declared that native interests were paramount, the Committee recorded the view that 'the doctrine of paramountcy means no more than that the interests of the overwhelming majority of the indigenous populations should not be subordinated to those of a minority belonging to another race, however important in itself'. The Committee maintained that the responsibility for the trusteeship of native interests must remain 'the function of His Majesty's Government', although the assistance of the non-native communities should be encouraged to carry out this obligation. Other points from the report were that a common electoral roll for Europeans and Asiatics in Kenya was impracticable for the present, that there was a need for increased African representation in the Legislative Council, and that 'suitable Africans' should be appointed when the Governor considered they became available. The Joint Select Committee's report, while suggesting solutions to problems which had caused so much controversy, received little attention in Kenya. Yet another change of government in Britain and the continuing economic de-

[1] *Report of the Joint Select Committee on Closer Union*, H.M.S.O., 1931.

pression were sufficient to relegate the report to the background. Nevertheless, the Committee's work was not in vain, for three of its main recommendations were, in time, accepted: an annual Governors' Conference; a detailed inquiry into the land needs of the people; and an examination of the tax structure.

Sir Joseph Byrne, Governor of Sierra Leone and a former policeman, was appointed to succeed Grigg in 1931. Lord Delamere died nine months later on 13 November 1931 and without him to dominate the Kenya scene, the new Governor was able to enforce the British Government's policy in Kenya without too much interference from the settlers. The settlers had, in fact, been told by Delamere that Kenya could not afford to give so large a proportion of its time to politics and that they should 'concentrate on their work, consolidate their economic position and leave political argument for the present'. Byrne himself had said before taking up his appointment that he would seek to work with 'reasonable men in Kenya who disliked politics and publicity'.[1] While the European community turned away temporarily from politics, there were, however, strong political undercurrents in the affairs of the other communities. Not all Indians supported the policy of non co-operation in the Legislature as a continuing protest against the denial of a common electoral roll by the British Government. Divided among themselves on the wisdom of a policy which as a political weapon had failed, the Indians had split into two opposing factions which in the main followed religious lines: the Hindus supporting non co-operation, and the Muslims co-operation, with the Government. Nevertheless, in the general election of May 1931, the five Indian candidates pledged not to enter Legislative Council after their election were overwhelmingly elected and the policy of non co-operation continued. Among the African community, the foundations were being laid for the nationalist movement of the 1950s. Johnston (later Jomo) Kenyatta, the General Secretary of the Kikuyu Central Association which had replaced the Young Kikuyu Association as the platform for Kikuyu aspirations, had left for Britain and Europe to present the African case for recognition and to widen his education and political experience – he was not to return until 1946. Firm measures taken by the Kenya Government in 1922 after the agitations of Harry Thuku were still in force. They had continued to

[1] G. Bennett, *Kenya: a Political History*, p. 73.

stifle African political activity, although Thuku was allowed to return from exile on the understanding that he would only oppose the Government in a constitutional manner. This he did, first as President of the Kikuyu Central Association and later as leader of moderate African opinion in the breakaway Kikuyu Provincial Association. African political activity in the thirties was confined to the struggle between extremists of the K.C.A. and the moderates of the K.P.A. for the right to express the views of the Kikuyu people who were at that time the most advanced of the tribes. Kikuyuland was a strong African flank to the European settled area and included most of the surrounding districts of the growing capital town of Nairobi. Its inhabitants were, therefore, more conscious of the sophisticated political developments of the day, though restricted by lack of education and experience to overcome Government measures and play a full part in the political life of the country.

The financial picture of Kenya in the thirties was one of continuing depression and enforced economies. Expenditure in 1930 had risen to £3,438,878 and in five years, to the end of 1933, deficits in the Budget amounted to £673,812. Reductions in Government expenditure made little difference to the gap and although a levy on official salaries and a poll tax for Europeans and Asians was introduced in 1932 to raise revenue, it was inevitable that the Government should think in terms of income tax. An attempt had been made in 1920 to introduce such a tax, but this had failed mainly because of the difficulties in collecting it and the non co-operation of the wealthier European community who were principally concerned. Hence, the visit of Lord Moyne to Kenya in 1932 was timely. His task as financial commissioner was one of the recommendations of the Report of the Joint Select Committee and he was asked to examine and report on 'certain questions of expenditure and racial taxation'. There had in previous years been criticisms that the spread of taxation in Kenya was unfair and that the African community paid the larger share of indirect taxation for a relatively smaller share of Government expenditure. Despite the difficulties of separating Kenya's accounts on a racial basis, Lord Moyne was able to find that the European community, which then numbered 17,285, contributed about £665,781 in direct and indirect taxation, and received in purely European services about £171,247; the Indian community of 56,903 contributed £385,658 and received £46,080; the African people, who were estimated to number about 3,000,000 (although this figure was shown in a population census some years later to be on the low side) contributed £791,100 and received £33,956. Lord Moyne concluded that he could find no precise means to determine whether, in the light of their relative numbers, the respective contributions of the Europeans and Africans represented an equitable division. His opinion was that in the development of general services in Kenya the prevailing bias had been towards 'the convenience of a civilisation in which the African had so far shared little of the direct advantages'. He considered that the African could not be expected to bear any increase of taxation, and if further revenue had to be raised it must be derived from the non-native communities.

Lord Moyne's proposals were not received well by the European community who saw themselves faced with the main burden of taxation. It was not until 1936 that they agreed to accept a light income tax, and only then on conditions which they had successfully negotiated. These were that the Governor's Executive Council should be reconstituted more closely to associate the unofficial communities with the government of the country and that they should be given an assurance by the Government that it did not intend to pursue a policy of 'increasing native services, reducing native taxation, and placing the burden on the shoulders of the non-native communities'.[1]

Taxation, however vital as a revenue earner, was not the only financial problem for Kenya in the thirties. The railway, around which the country had developed, was expanding at such a rate that it had outstripped agricultural production which, in the main, it served. Lavish expenditure in the general expansion of the late 1920s had assumed that agricultural exports would increase and bring more imports and general prosperity; but the low commodity prices of the Depression years eliminated profit margins and both exports and imports fell in quantity and in value. Further, the Depression and the general political insecurity in Kenya had checked the increase in European farm settlement and the production of export crops, on which the country still depended. Kenya had borrowed £13,251,808 for its railways and harbours compared with £3,953,792 for other purposes such as public works, loans to local authorities, repayment to revenue of military expenditure and the setting up of a Land and Agricultural Bank. In addition, Kenya's

[1] Hill, op. cit., p. 495.

credit was affected by the contingent liabilities of the original loan of £5,502,292 to the railway and the claim of £1,405,016 by the British War Office for expenditure during the First World War. The Government could not itself engage directly in production and raise revenue to service all these massive loans, so reliance had to be placed on 'private enterprise and the personal endeavours of the inhabitants'.[1] Here, too, the financial problems were formidable. The Board of Agriculture, formed in 1929 to administer European farming, estimated that the total indebtedness of farmers was between £4 million and £5 million in 1932 and that loans and advances to agriculture by Kenya banks was a further £2 million. The Land and Agricultural Bank set up by the Government to help with long-term loans was considered a step in the right direction for a developing agricultural country, though its funds were insufficient and the rate of interest high. The maize industry was helped with a loan of £108,000 to bring the price of maize up to Shs. 6/– a bag, but owing to the difficulty of recovery it was never repaid. In an attempt, therefore, to help farmers with further credit to offset the effects of the Depression a Central Advances Board was introduced to finance farming operations until harvest. However, many farmers were so deeply involved in financial troubles that only about a hundred of them were able to take advantage of the scheme.

At the end of 1933, Kenya's financial position had deteriorated to such an extent that there was a cash deficiency of £196,644. From then on, strict economies and deflation by the Government were necessary to keep the country solvent. The rate of recovery was slow, although it would have been much slower but for the fortuitous development of the Kakamega gold fields. It had been known for some time that there was gold in north-west Kenya, and the 'rush' in the thirties to exploit the workable quantity in the new Kakamega field was not on the scale of the Klondike or Kalgoorlie. Nevertheless, a thriving mining industry developed to give jobs to 1,000 Europeans and 10,000 Africans, most of them from farms in the settled area. Kakamega gold provided incomes for many whose livelihood had been affected by the Depression and brought much needed revenue to the railway and to the Government.

Another factor which aided Kenya's economic recovery was the discovery that high-quality pyrethrum, the daisy-like flower which provides an effective insecticide when the flower head is dried and

[1] Report of the Economic Development Committee (1935).

processed, could be grown in the Highlands. In 1933, most of the world supply came from Yugoslavia and Japan, but the Kenya pyrethrum grown at heights of 8,000 feet and over had a high pyrethrin content and was able to earn a premium in London and in America. Yields per acre were also high and as the cultivation of the crop was profitable, so the acreage in Kenya multiplied rapidly.

While the 1930s saw Kenya struggling for economic survival, there was also the question of land, which, to the still unsophisticated African people, was the only real source of wealth and security. Another of the Joint Select Committee's recommendations was carried out when the Kenya Land Commission was set up in 1932, under the chairmanship of Sir Morris Carter, to inquire into land rights and to define the African and European Settled Areas. The Carter Commission inquiry was lengthy and detailed.[1] It endeavoured to settle once and for all African grievances over the delineation of tribal lands and the extent of the White Highlands in an elaborate 'profit and loss' scheme of land additions and offers of compensation. The existing African reserves were divided into nine land units and allocated to the major tribes; and the White Highlands area was fixed at 16,700 square miles (including 3,950 square miles of forest reserve) out of a total land area of 220,000 square miles. African opinion, especially in Kikuyuland, did not accept the Carter Commission Report, though it was accepted in its entirety by the British Government. Alienation by the Government of African land for the Kakamega gold fields without reference to the Local Native Authority was still a bitter memory. The Kikuyu, moreover, were adamant that regardless of the generous adjustments made by the Commission, only they had any rights to the land around Nairobi and in the Highlands area along their tribal boundaries.

Sir Joseph Byrne, who had proved himself to be – in so far as the settlers were concerned – a hard, uncompromising Governor, left Kenya at the end of 1936. He was succeeded by Air Chief Marshal Sir Robert Brooke-Popham whose military background proved valuable in defence matters at a time when the clouds of war were gathering to the north of Kenya's frontiers. The Italian conquest of Abyssinia and the agitation by Germany for the return of Tanganyika created threats to Kenya's security; but the country, in

[1] The Kenya Land Commission Report, *Cmnd. 4556* (1934).

better economic shape and with a Budget surplus of £200,000, was able to make plans for the defence of its frontiers.

Despite his lack of political experience, Brooke-Popham was a popular Governor with the settlers and they were able to regain the ground they had lost under the régime of Byrne, who had largely dispensed with the 'government by agreement' policy of his predecessors. Lord Francis Scott, the successor to Lord Delamere as leader of the settlers, returned, together with his colleague Major Ferdinand Cavendish-Bentinck, to the Governor's Executive Council from which they had both resigned in Byrne's last year. The Europeans' considerable influence on Government policy soon became apparent. They succeeded in securing the equivalent of the Native Lands Trust Board (recommended by the Carter Commission) to safeguard the White Highlands and make them a European 'reserve'. Once more they offended the Indians who had given up their policy of non co-operation in 1933 when their representatives were authorised to attend sessions of the Legislative Council and take their places on the relevant committees. The years of non co-operation and internal community strife had weakened the Indian case for full political recognition and although their protests against the reservation of the Highlands for Europeans had support from the Government of India, they were largely ineffective.

The years 1938 and 1939 were years of consolidation for Kenya in spite of the growing threats of war. Politically, the country was comparatively quiet, though there were signs of unrest among the African people. In a primitive display of anger against the Government 1,500 Kamba tribesmen marched on Nairobi to protest at the policy of de-stocking in their reserve. The Government had been forced in 1938 to kill thousands of head of cattle because of their effect on the land which, through years of drought and heavy rains, had become eroded and was rapidly turning into a desert. While the operation was considered essential for the good of the Kamba people, its inept handling by administrative officers caused deep resentment among the Kamba to whom, as a pastoral tribe, cattle were a currency and a source of wealth and prestige. The demonstration by a people who had loyally supported alien rule and provided many of the men needed for the army and police was a salutary lesson for the Government who, henceforth, were obliged to be more tactful in their handling of de-stocking in the African tribal areas.

In Mombasa, where the urban population had grown rapidly to

meet the needs of the developing port, more trouble awaited the Government. Conditions among the expanded labour force had been poor for some time and the situation was fomented by Makhan Singh, the Sikh organiser of the Labour Trade Union. A full-scale strike developed and, when it was over, an official inquiry into the causes revealed serious shortcomings in housing and wages. It was an effective first labour strike, and conditions improved in time for Mombasa to play a leading role in the war years ahead.

# Chapter 7

# Strategic Base

HE OUTBREAK OF the Second World War in 1939 found Kenya
much stronger and better prepared than in 1914. An efficient
and well-stocked railway and transport system was in being
and the Government machine had developed sufficiently to maintain
the economy and to administer what was to prove Britain's most
important strategic base in Africa. However, for the immediate
defence of Kenya at the outbreak of war there was only a Brigade
of 1,500 front-line African troops – well-trained it is true, but ill-
equipped for modern warfare. This Brigade of King's African
Rifles, formed initially for internal security, was subsequently enlarged and merged with the two settler military units – the Kenya
Defence Force and the Kenya Regiment – and fought successfully
as an infantry division in three separate campaigns: the defeat of the
Italians in Somalia and Abyssinia; the occupation of Madagascar,
and the reconquest of Burma. It was the first time that troops from
Kenya were to fight outside Africa on the side of Britain.

Ill-equipped as they were by modern standards, the Kenya forces
were not caught unawares by the outbreak of the Second World War.
In 1935, the Italians had invaded Abyssinia to add to their East
African empire and from then onwards they had been, with their
stong military forces strung out along the Northern Frontier, a
potential enemy for both Britain and Kenya. It was thought on the
outbreak of war that Italy, in order to preserve her East African
empire, would be obliged to threaten the Suez Canal, British Somaliland and Kenya by a main thrust along the East African Coast to
Mombasa. Military preparations were made on this assumption
and that in the early stages the small Kenya force could concentrate
on the defence of Mombasa and exploit the natural barriers of the
Northern Frontier District to contain any invasion of the Highlands.
As it turned out, Kenya was never invaded, although the Italians
with their superior land and air forces could have overrun the
country if they had wished.

Instead of being invaded, Kenya became the base from which the British eventually drove out the Italians from Somaliland and Abyssinia. Troops from Tanganyika, Uganda, West Africa, Nyasaland, Rhodesia and South Africa were all centred on Kenya and from the outbreak of war in September 1939 to the end of 1940 – the time taken by Italy to enter the war on Germany's side and conquer Somaliland – the British consolidated their position. A fully equipped invasion force – mainly of African troops – was formed, and on 23 January 1941, Kenya soldiers of the East African Brigade led the force across the frontier into Italian-held territory.[1] At the end of the campaign, in February 1942, when the last stronghold at Gondar had been captured and Italy's East African empire lay in ruins, the African soldier had proved – as in Tanganyika during the First World War – that with good leadership he was able to fight over country under the most adverse conditions.[2] He had also proved that he was more than a match for the modern, well-equipped Italian army. The same was true in the campaigns against the French in Madagascar and against the Japanese in Burma. Yet an unfortunate event at the end of the Abyssinian campaign clouded the image of the African soldier in the eyes of his British leaders. One of the East African Brigades, comprising a battalion from Kenya and two battalions from Uganda, had been concentrated in northern Abyssinia to await embarkation for service overseas to India. The African troops assumed that after their rigorous campaign they were bound for Kenya and Uganda on leave. They claimed that they had only taken military service for the defence of their homes in Africa; that they should be allowed to volunteer again if they were required to serve abroad; and that pay for such services should be at higher rates. It was near-mutiny and the British military authorities, anxious to avoid a major incident in occupied territory, and with insufficient troops to enforce the embarkation, withdrew the reluctant Brigade from overseas service and despatched it to Kenya by road.[3] The incident showed that the African soldier was also an individual and not afraid to stand up for his rights. It did not, however, prevent thousands more African soldiers from Kenya volunteering to fight for the British in the years that followed.

[1] The Brigade reached Addis Ababa on 6 April after what has been described as the longest and swiftest advance in military history: 1,687 miles at average rate of 76.6 miles a day for each day of movement. (Lt.-Col. H. Moyse-Bartlett, *The King's African Rifles*, p. 521.)
[2] Moyse-Bartlett, op. cit., p. 573.　　　[3] Moyse-Bartlett, op. cit., p. 568.

After the collapse of Italian resistance in the Abyssinian campaign, in which an army of 200,000 men with the whole of its equipment had been practically destroyed and nearly a million square miles of land occupied, Kenya and her neighbours were given another front to face. At the beginning of 1942 Japan was the dominant power in South-East Asia. British, Dutch and American forces had been overwhelmed in lightning campaigns and there was little to stop Japan from extending her influence across the Indian Ocean to the eastern seaboard of Africa. For Britain it was vital that any threat to this strategically important part of the world should be contained. The Mediterranean was virtually closed, and military convoys supporting the British armies in the Middle East had to be routed round the Cape of Good Hope and up the East African Coast. Mombasa, with its deep, sheltered harbour, was, therefore, developed as a base for the naval forces controlling this traffic and for the sea defence of India and Ceylon. It was from Mombasa that a large British fleet sailed in March 1942 to contain a strong Japanese naval excursion into the Indian Ocean. The port also provided a base for the invasion of Madagascar, and many of the troops employed in this successful campaign to take the island over from the Vichy French were soldiers from East African infantry battalions. Further afield, in India and Burma, troops from Kenya, Uganda and Tanganyika were helping the British in the land war against the Japanese. At the end of this war it was estimated that more than 40,000 African soldiers served with the East African infantry division and supporting units.

The war changed Kenya from a little-known, recalcitrant colony of Britain to a country that could stand on its own feet and was of some strategic and economic importance. As the military forces required by Britain built up, and the thousands of prisoners of war from Abyssinia and the evacuees from the Middle East arrived to take up residence in the country, there was a pressing need for more food production. Almost anything the land could produce was needed for the war effort: wheat, maize and animal products for internal consumption; cotton, copra, sisal, coffee, timber and pyrethrum for export. Agricultural production was given a welcome boost as demand for food rose far above pre-war levels. Money was plentiful and with consumer goods scarce the Kenya Budget was balanced with something to spare. The substantial financial aid given to Britain by the three East African territories, Northern

Rhodesia and Nyasaland was a measure of the general prosperity during the war. More than £7 million was lent free of interest and more than £11 million at low rates. Monetary gifts brought to the notice of the Secretary of State for the Colonies totalled £1,700,000 and it is certain that much more was contributed to the Red Cross and similar bodies.[1] In return, the territories shared £21 million of the £120 million provided by the British Government under the Colonial Development and Welfare Act of 1945.

The political scene in Kenya was quiescent throughout most of the war. Sir Henry Moore, Chief Secretary under two Kenya Governors, had succeeded Brooke-Popham in 1940. Looked upon as a man of 'great delicacy of feeling', he nevertheless inspired during his period of office a strong administration which stood the country in good stead throughout the war and into the post-war period.[2] Moore was helped by the Governors' Conference, whose permanent secretariat and Economic Council co-ordinated the East African war effort, and by the European and Asian communities who gave whole-hearted support to the Government through the various boards and committees set up to prosecute the war. Politically, the African community was less forthcoming. The Kikuyu Central Association, which had taken up an extreme position in African politics after the breakaway of Harry Thuku to form the Kikuyu Provincial Association, was banned by the Government a few months after the outbreak of war. It was accused of being a subversive organisation and its leaders of being 'in contact with the King's enemies or potential enemies'. Little documentary evidence was discovered by the Government to substantiate the charge, yet twenty of the Association's leaders were arrested. The General Secretary, Jomo Kenyatta, who was still in England, escaped arrest.

At the time of the ban, the K.C.A. claimed a membership of 7,000 and support from the Ukamba Members' Association and the Teita Hills Association; but its proscription as an illegal society created little interest among the Kikuyu, many of whom were in the army or employed in war work. The mantle of African political leader once again fell on Harry Thuku whose Kikuyu Provincial Association with its moderate approach to politics and loyalty to the Government was no risk to security. However, the K.C.A. was kept

[1] The British Territories in East and Central Africa 1945–1950, *Cmnd. 7987*, p. 36.
[2] Mitchell, op. cit., p. 189.

going secretly by a few of its members until the release of their leaders from detention towards the end of 1943. This coincided with the campaign, both inside and outside the Kenya Legislative Council, for the appointment of an African representative and the Rev. (later Archbishop) L. J. Beecher, who had been nominated earlier to the Council to represent African interests, said he looked forward to the day when Africans would sit alongside the nominated Europeans and would even replace them.[1] In the mood of co-operation engendered by the war there was little opposition to the appointment in October 1944 of the first African member of the Kenya Legislative Council. Competition for the post from a number of prominent Africans, including supporters of the banned K.C.A., was strong; in the event, Eliud Mathu, the Oxford-trained son of a Kikuyu medicine man, was nominated. Thuku's K.P.A. gave active support to the new member; but Mathu, feeling the need for the backing of a national political organisation, founded the Kenya African Study Union as 'a forum of all shades of articulate African opinion unhampered by the bounds of tribalism and with the following aims: to unite the African people towards an African nation; and to foster the social, economic and political interests of the Africans'.[2] The organisation changed its name later to the Kenya African Union with Thuku as President.

[1] Bennett, op. cit., p. 96.　　　　　　　　　　[2] *Cmnd. 1030.*

1 Fort Jesus, the seventeenth-century stronghold on Mombasa Island

2 Arab dhows, the type of ships that have been sailing along the monsoon trade routes to eastern Africa since the dawn of history

3 Kikuyu herd boys on the Limuru escarpment
overlooking the Great Rift Valley

4 An African farmer and his family picking pyrethrum
on his new farm in the former 'White' Highlands
of Kenya

5    The heart of Kenya's soda industry at Lake Magadi
     on the floor of the Great Rift Valley

6    Old Mombasa, *Mvita*, the Island of War

7   Modern Nairobi, Kenya's capital city

8  Harry Thuku, the angry young man of Kenya politics in the 1920's, pictured in retirement

9  Sir Philip Mitchell, Governor of Kenya from 1944 to 1952

10  Jomo Kenyatta in middle age, speaking during his campaign to end British rule in Kenya

11  Sir Evelyn Baring (later Lord Howick), Governor of Kenya from 1952 to 1959

12   Mr D. N. Pritt Q.C., who led the defence in the
Kenyatta trial, leaving the Supreme Court in Nairobi
in January 1952

13 Kikuyu tribesmen, suspected of Mau Mau activities, await screening in a fortified police post at Nyeri after a night round-up and breakfast on cooked *posho* or maize meal

14 Mau Mau detainees at the Thomson's Falls detention camp with temporary gallows in the background

15  A young Kikuyu, ragged follower of Mau Mau, arrested
by security forces in a forest action

16  Forest fighters of the Kenya Land Freedom Army after
their surrender under the 1963 amnesty

17    A Lincoln bomber of Britain's Royal Air Force on a
bombing run over the Aberdare forests

18    Bombs bursting on a Mau Mau forest hide-out

19  A political meeting outside a settlers' club at Thomson's Falls in January 1953 called to discuss tougher measures against Mau Mau and transfer of political responsibility from London to Nairobi

20  White settlers march on the Governor of Kenya's residence, Government House, Nairobi, in January 1953 after the murder of the Ruck family by Mau Mau

21 and 22  The end of settlerdom in Kenya: the statue of
Lord Delamere, 'father' of white settlement, being
removed from its position in the centre of Nairobi,
November 1962

23   Britain's Conservative Prime Minister, Mr Harold
Macmillan, and his Colonial Secretary, Mr Iain Macleod,
at a Lancaster House conference in December 1960

24   Mr Tom Mboya and Mr Michael (later Sir Michael)
Blundell, leaders of opposing parties, pictured in Marc[h]
1961 after the First Lancaster House Conference wher[e]
their differences were resolved

25  Kisoi Munyao, African leader of a multi-racial climbing
party, plants Kenya's new national flag on Nelion, the
highest peak of Mount Kenya, on Independence Day

26 Kenya's new leaders in happy mood under the tower of
Parliament House, Nairobi, after the announcement of
the one-party state: in front, Tom Mboya, Musinde
Muliro, Oginga Odinga, Jomo Kenyatta and Ronald
Ngala

27    Kenya soldiers with 'loyalist' irregulars during the Emergency

28    Mutinous soldiers of the Kenya African Rifles guarded by one of the contingent of British troops called in by Premier Kenyatta in January 1964 to put down the Kenya army mutiny

29 After talks on East African federation in Kampala, May 1964: Dr Milton Obote (Uganda), Jomo Kenyatta (Kenya) and Dr Julius Nyerere (Tanzania)

*Chapter 8*

# Multi-racial Society

IN SEPTEMBER 1944, Sir Philip Mitchell was nominated to succeed Moore as Governor. Mitchell had wide experience of East Africa as an administrator and he came from the governorship of Fiji where the multi-racial concept in politics was a reality; yet his term of office in Kenya – the longest of any previous Governor – ended in political chaos and violence. A brilliant man who had the capacity of getting his own way by persuasion, Mitchell introduced sweeping changes in the political life of the country, many of them liberal and unpopular with the settlers. The long despatches he wrote to his overlords in London outlined clearly the problems facing post-war Kenya; but the cleverness of his writings concealed the strong undercurrents that led to the stormy days of the 1950s. He did not, however, underrate the magnitude of his task when he noted in his diary on the day he was appointed: 'I am certainly very glad to go back to East Africa; and if I cannot retire, then I know of no job I would like better than Kenya, for it epitomises all East African problems and is the most difficult task in the continent; but has also many great attractions.'[1]

Before he left Fiji, Mitchell had already worked on the draft of a letter putting forward his ideas on Kenya politics to the then Secretary of State for the Colonies, Mr Oliver Stanley. He thought the Legislative Council was too much of a single chamber and that there would be great advantages if Bills had to come back to the Governor-in-Council; secondly, he thought the Legislative Council should have a Speaker instead of a President in the person of the Governor. This would make the Governor more effective as an impartial arbiter, would keep him out of controversy in the early stages and give a greater independence to the Legislative Council. Mitchell also thought that the unofficial members on the Governor's Executive Council should support the Government on major issues or resign; and that they should take charge of groups of subjects. In other

[1] Mitchell, op. cit., p. 313.

words, they would become members of the Government with ministerial responsibilities.

During the period in wartime Kenya when he was Deputy Chairman of the East African Governors' Conference and administrator of the joint secretariat, Mitchell had pressed for the establishment of a central authority for East Africa with full federal powers. In his discussion with the Secretary of State in London before taking up his appointment, he found Stanley held the view that although it would be useless to reopen the question of any form of political union in East Africa, or the creation of a central authority, it was necessary to devise some means of administering the services common to all three territories in East Africa. Accordingly, Mitchell saw Kenya's relations with Uganda and Tanganyika as the first problem to be tackled. His experience with the East African Governors' Conference and the joint war machinery he established had convinced him that nothing short of a central legislature and executive with powers deriving from an Order-in-Council would be of any use except to create controversy. The range of function to be assigned to such an authority had to be severely restricted because of lack of general agreement, but must include railways and harbours, customs and excise administration and if possible tariffs, defence, civil aviation and long-range research. It would be necessary for income tax to be administered by a single department and that would mean common rates and allowances. The Posts and Telegraphs Department was already a common service, but it was organised on the traditional department lines and Mitchell thought it should become 'self-accounting' and keep commercial accounts, otherwise there would certainly be controversy about who was to take surplus revenue or pay deficits and in what proportions. There were also a number of smaller services such as meteorology and statistics which would fit into the authority he had in mind. The rub was, he thought, the legislature; for there was no way to avoid raising the issue of representation which would certainly be controversial, inter-territorially and racially, but which was essential to a workable scheme. 'Anyone who had had experience of the attempt to run common services by means of identical legislation, including the voting of supply, would not need telling that it simply would not work.'[1] After his long service in Tanganyika and Uganda, Mitchell knew that neither country would willingly be associated with Kenya

[1] Mitchell, op. cit., p. 215.

in any joint authority; for Kenya European political activities were profoundly mistrusted.

Mitchell included his ideas in a draft scheme presented as a White Paper and published on 12 December 1945. Despite the expected controversy throughout East Africa, a compromise was reached and the East Africa High Commission with its constituent Central Assembly was set up two years later. The Commission consisted of the Governors of Kenya, Uganda and Tanganyika – the Governor of Kenya acting as permanent Chairman. The Common Services administered inter-territorially by the Commission were grouped under four principal executive officers: the Administrator, the Commissioner for Transport, the Finance Member and the Postmaster-General. The Central Assembly had twenty-three members of whom seven were *ex-officio* members, i.e. officers in the High Commission service; three were officials nominated by each territory; and thirteen unofficial members – one elected by the unofficial members of the Legislative Council of each territory; one European, one Indian and one African member nominated by the Governor of each territory (except Kenya where the European and Indian members were elected by the unofficial members of their communities in the Legislative Council); and one Arab member appointed by the High Commission.

In 1950, an official report noted:

'The High Commission and Central Assembly have completed, in the first two years of their existence, a great deal of the indispensable spadework on the integration and administration of the numerous inter-territorial services entrusted to them. In the field of research, they are responsible for the administration of important programmes, which may contribute greatly in the future to the advance of the whole region, in agriculture, veterinary science, medicine, fisheries and industry. They are also responsible for the campaigns against the tsetse, the mosquito and the locust, the three major pests of Africa. There is, in addition to the unified transport system covering ports, railways and inland waterways, on which the development of East Africa to a great extent depends, the amalgamated postal and telegraph services, the unified customs department and other important services. By the efficient despatch of its business, and the prevailing racial harmony, the East African Assembly has given a notable instance of success of a genuinely East African approach to common problems. The conduct of affairs in the Assembly and its committees is a good augury for the future.'[1]

The continued success of the East Africa High Commission was of course dependent on racial and political harmony in the constituent territories – particularly Kenya. Following the creation of the Central Assembly and the translation there of a number of Kenya Government members, Mitchell had decided to introduce an unofficial multi-racial majority into the Legislative Council in the hope that it 'might stimulate the development of party as opposed to racial groupings'. The official side was reduced to make way for an African representative and this brought the total number of African members up to four. Mitchell had, in fact, introduced the principle of racial parity to the Kenya Legislative Council as he had done in the Central Assembly. The number of European unofficials was equal to that of the other two races: eleven elected Europeans, five elected Asians, one nominated and one elected Arab, and four Africans. Mitchell, however, retained sufficient control over the Council by giving himself powers to force through essential legislation and the seven *ex-officio* and nine official members appointed by him were able to ensure for the Government a balancing role in the Council's affairs. He had, in 1945, organised his administration to take account of the need to modernise the Kenya Government in the post-war period. His principal executive, the Chief Secretary, was relieved of the burden of routine administration of all departments and was appointed Member for Development and Chairman of the Development and Reconstruction Authority, while remaining head of the Civil Service. The Financial Secretary became Member for Finance; and in 1947 a Secretary to the Treasury was appointed to take over as permanent head. The Attorney-General was made Member for Law and Order; the Chief Native Commissioner put in charge of African affairs; members appointed for Agriculture, Animal Husbandry and Natural Resources; Health and Local Government and, in 1948, for Commerce and Industry. The remaining Government departments were grouped under the Deputy Chief Secretary who was also Member for Education. All Government members sat on the Governor's Executive Council – the Kenya Cabinet. With the exception of Major Cavendish-Bentinck, the

[1] *Cmnd.* 7987, p. 29.

Member for Agriculture, and Mr E. A. Vasey, the Member for Health and Local Government, they were Colonial Service officials. When Cavendish-Bentinck and Vasey accepted their posts they crossed the floor of the Council and sat with the officials on the Government side, giving up their seats as European elected members; but they were still identified with settler politics and their appointments earned the hostility of the Asian and African communities. Such opposition was largely ineffective, for Mitchell was firmly in the saddle and determined that his concept of a multi-racial political society in Kenya should be made to work.

The Kenya community was now divided into four distinct, and racial, political groupings: the Electors' Union, which had succeeded the Convention of Associations in the last years of the war and was now the main platform for European opinion; the Indian National Congress which after the partition of India was now predominantly Hindu; the Central Muslim Association; and the Kenya African Union. The transformation of the latter body from a study group in support of the sole African member of the Legislative Council to a strong political association with definite aims for independence coincided with the return in 1946 of Jomo Kenyatta after a sojourn of more than fifteen years in Europe. A year later he was elected President of the K.A.U. in succession to Harry Thuku who virtually retired from African politics and became in the words of Mitchell 'a highly respected farmer in Kiambu'.

Kenyatta was the dynamic leader for whom the Kikuyu were waiting. They were still the most politically conscious and by far the biggest in number of all the tribes in Kenya. In 1958 they comprised 30 per cent of the total African population of five and a quarter million with the next largest tribe the Luo under half at 14 per cent. Many Kikuyu had served with the army during the war and on their return had been trained for civilian occupations; but opportunities for these ex-soldiers were few in post-war Kenya and so there built up against the Government a resentment which, as the years went by and the problems of unemployment and overcrowding in the Kikuyu reserve became acute, grew into open rebellion. Kenyatta on his return to Kenya found adequate grounds for his own resentment. He had approached Mitchell and said he wanted to take an active part in local affairs. Mitchell, while acknowledging Kenyatta's 'undoubted talents and considerable influence', failed to take the hint and with some condescension suggested that Kenyatta should make a start in local government and seek election to the Local Native Council of his area. Such a suggestion was of little help to a man who had been during his time in Europe one of the promoters of African nationalism. Although he accepted a seat on the African Land Settlement and Utilisation Board, Kenyatta went his own way and began the foundations of a career that was to lead him to the very top of Kenya politics. His position as President of the Kenya African Union gave him the opportunity to travel round the country and establish his influence with the other tribes. His greatest influence, of course, was with the predominantly Kikuyu organisations – the Independent Schools, the Githunguri Teachers' Training College, tribal age-groups, ex-soldiers' associations and the trade unions. These organisations were also a source of much-needed funds for Kenyatta to launch his campaign for African domination in Kenya affairs. At various private meetings he was reported to have said that he disliked Europeans and Asians, and that in course of time they would all be removed from Africa. Aware that his movements and speeches were being watched he was more cautious in public, though making it clear that the setting-up of an all-African state in Kenya was his ultimate aim. 'He often made constructive speeches, but was also an adept at cloaking his inner intentions in such a way that the meaning, while abundantly clear to the rest of his audience, was sufficiently "safe" and vague to escape action by the authorities.'[1]

Tom Mbotela, a non-Kikuyu of mixed tribal parentage, was Kenyatta's only rival within the K.A.U. Despite his reputation as a moderate in local government affairs – he had been active in the Nairobi African Advisory Council – Mbotela was just as firmly on the side of African advance. At a large public meeting, a few months after his appointment as K.A.U. Vice-President, he gave his views on what the aims of the Union should be: to unite the Africans in Kenya; to prepare to defend all Africans in Kenya; to fight for the African in education, labour and housing matters; to fight for equal rights with the European; to fight for freedom of speech; to fight for universal franchise. Where Mbotela differed from the extremist members of the K.A.U. was that he considered these aims should be achieved through non-violence and full co-operation with the Government. He persisted in his beliefs until his assassination in 1952 by Kikuyu gunmen.

[1] *Cmnd. 1030*, p. 26.

In 1950, the East African Indian National Congress approached
the K.A.U. with a view to forming an Afro-Asian front in Kenya
politics. Kenyatta received substantial financial aid from Indian
sources for his Teachers' Training College,[1] but he refrained from
any public association. His beliefs were based on undiluted African
nationalism and already the pace was being forced by the activities
of the district committees of the K.A.U. and other Kikuyu organisations. Mau Mau – the 'People of the Three Letters' and alleged to
be the K.C.A. in another guise – was given official recognition in
August 1950 when after prosecutions for illegal oath-taking in
Kiambu and Naivasha it was proscribed by the Government as being
an unlawful society. The traditional Kikuyu method of binding
people to a cause by oath-taking was now being used as a powerful
weapon to raise funds for political purposes and prosecutions in the
courts did little to stop the movement which made swift progress in
Kikuyuland and the surrounding settled areas. Much of the illegal
work was being done by young Kikuyu agitators, many of them ex-
soldiers and members of the 'Forty Group' – a 2,000-strong tribal
age-group circumcised in 1940. There is also evidence that the col-
lections they raised by intimidation were channelled back to the
Githunguri Teachers' College.[2]

Kenyatta was never apparently short of money for his campaign.
On the other hand, the Central Committee of the K.A.U. received
little financial support from district branches and was always short
of funds. This placed a limitation on its work and Kenyatta was
able to contain the influence of the moderates while extending his
own influence through superior financial backing. On his recommendation, the K.A.U. was affiliated to the Congress of Peoples
Against Imperialism and made a valuable contact in Mr Fenner
Brockway, M.P., the Labour supporter of African nationalism. Contacts were also made with embryo nationalist organisations in Tanganyika, Uganda and West Africa to affiliate the Union with a
wider pan-African movement; and there were suggestions that all
recognised African national movements should combine in a Congress Party, appointing Jomo Kenyatta as its first President, and with
the objective of achieving a United Africa recognised by the United
Nations Organisation. As 1950 neared its close, the stage was set
for Kenyatta to achieve his ambition of an all-African Kenya and to
be in the van of the movement towards independence already

[1] *Cmnd. 1030*, p. 34.  [2] *Cmnd. 1030*, p. 65.

making itself felt throughout the African continent. He undoubtedly gained encouragement from the announcement in that year by the British Government that 'the central purpose of British colonial policy is to guide the people of the colonial territories to responsible self-government'.

The year 1950 marked the end of Kenya's post-war period. The official report on the five years following the end of the war describes them thus: '. . . a time of material prosperity maintained, with the prices of East and Central African products remaining high or climbing higher; of plans for economic development that should lay the foundations of a permanently higher level of production and trade; of continued efforts to expand the social services for all communities, and to associate all communities in the administration of them; of the developments of local government; and of the political advances, impressive enough in themselves, but far more so when one reflects how brief is the history of British administration in eastern Africa . . .'[1] The rate of progress in Kenya during the post-war period was certainly impressive. Kenya was the first of the East and Central African territories to receive an unofficial majority in the Legislative Council, and the first to admit African unofficial members. In the field of local government, procedure and practice were brought into line with that of the United Kingdom; Local Native Councils were given more powers and renamed African District Councils; the White Highlands were split up into seven District Councils; and in the urban areas the expanding towns were given a large measure of autonomy. Nairobi was granted city status in March 1950 to mark the fiftieth year of municipal government – the first municipality to receive the 'honour' in an African colonial territory. When the monarch's brother, the Duke of Gloucester, handed over the letters patent to the Mayor, he received a silver pepper muffineer containing thirty East African peppercorns 'in discharge of the nominal rents payable for crown land of which the municipal council has been the tenant during the past 30 years'.[2]

The British authorities saw in the development of local government a key to political, social and economic development in Kenya. They considered that it was in this field that Africans could best learn to participate in self-government and that from local government bodies the leaders of the future would be largely drawn.

[1] Cmnd. 7987 (1950).                          [2] Cmnd. 7987.

Mitchell himself stated that Nairobi enjoyed a greater degree of practical autonomy than the central Government; but as it turned out few African councillors became national leaders in Kenya. Nevertheless, it is true that local government councils did much to improve social services and community development in the urban and rural areas. These improvements had, however, to be financed through contribution in the form of rates from the African community. In 1949, the revenue from rates amounted to £237,500 as against £65,000 in 1939 and represented 35 per cent of the total revenue of African local government bodies. Betterment funds, derived principally from a cess levied on the sale of maize, were also a source of revenue. In Nyanza province, the major area for African-grown maize, betterment funds were estimated to have produced in 1950 a total of £155,500.

Exports to finance the growing prosperity of post-war Kenya went up to £11 million by 1948; but imports also went up—to £27 million. Because of its geographical position, Kenya was the centre for East African trade and the bulk of imports came through Mombasa; so the apparently unfavourable balance of trade was offset by the returns from Uganda and Tanganyika. Another factor was the considerable investment of capital from outside sources to finance the £19 million Kenya Development and Reconstruction Authority and its Ten Year Plan of 1947. The plan was recast in 1950 to provide a total expenditure of £28,500,000 as a result of the population census two years earlier. This census was the most reliable count of all races yet carried out. It disclosed that the African population at 5,218,232 was much greater than previous estimates had suggested and meant a million more people to be fed, housed, educated and kept healthy. The European and Asian communities had also grown rapidly since the war through immigration. At the time of the census there were 29,660 Europeans and 98,000 Asians.

Throughout the post-war period there was a general drift towards the expanding towns. Housing was inadequate to deal with a bigger urban population and in Nairobi, where the African population went up by a third, 5,000 people were without satisfactory accommodation. The Housing Fund of £600,000 for municipal housing schemes, and drawn from colonial development and welfare schemes, was virtually exhausted. Investigations into a ten-day strike of railway and dock workers at Mombasa revealed that the workers' grievances over living conditions were well-founded and that regulations for their maintenance were not being observed. It was not surprising that developments during the post-war period included a steady increase in crime. The police force was expanded and in 1949 took over the policing of the African areas, previously the responsibility of local authorities. It was not before time. Three years later the Kenya police were faced with a complete breakdown in law and order, and the armed rebellion known as Mau Mau.

*Chapter 9*

# People of the Three Letters

---

T HERE WERE LITTLE outward signs of Mau Mau in the year preceding the 1952 declaration of a State of Emergency. Mitchell, who was coming to the end of his term of office – it had been extended two years for him to complete the political changes he had set in train after the war – could record in an account of his fishing trips to Kikuyuland: 'On these occasions one walked about all day among the village people, accompanied only by a small boy carrying spare gear and sandwiches, and never met anything but smiling faces and happy, cheerful people, delighted to see one and pass the time of day. Anything less like a people on the verge of revolt would not be possible to imagine...'[1] It seemed to Mitchell in 1951 that Kenya, a 'happy, cheerfully loyal country', was settling down well after the disturbing years of the post-war period, though he concedes that his approach to East African problems was 'first and above all, the promotion of good feeling between the races and dissipation of hate and fear'. His main consideration was the expansion of parity between races in the political life of the country, and he found a supporter in the Labour Secretary of State for the Colonies, Mr James Griffiths, who visited Kenya in May 1951. As a result of this visit, it was proposed that within twelve months of the election of the next Legislative Council in May 1952 there should be a constitutional conference and as interim measures that an African would join the Governor's Executive Council and the number of African seats increased in the Legislative Council from four to six; an additional seat given to the Indians and to the Arabs; and three more seats given to the Europeans to preserve the principle of parity. The K.A.U. did not, however, accept this interpretation of racial parity. Griffiths, who privately described Kenya as 'God's own country with the devil's own problems', had met Kenyatta as well as the elected members of the various groups during his visit. He had accepted from Kenyatta a memorandum presented in the name of the K.A.U.

[1] Mitchell, op. cit., p. 261.

It was a reasoned document stating in full African demands and pointing out the 'absurdity' of over five million Africans in Kenya being represented by only four African nominated members.[1] There were no indications in this document of any rebellious sentiments, though at a meeting the following September, the Central Committee of the K.A.U. approved the adoption of a Union flag which would become in time the 'Dominion Flag' when Africans had obtained self-government.[2]

By the end of 1951, Kenyatta had strengthened his hold on the K.A.U. He had caused Tom Mbotela to be removed from the office of Vice-President and with eight out of the nine members of the Central Committee from the Kikuyu tribe he dominated this powerful body. Nonetheless, Kenyatta was in a difficult position publicly, as the accepted leader of a tribe in which an anti-government and anti-European movement was gaining strength. He could not openly defy the Government, otherwise he would have suffered the fate of Harry Thuku in the 1920s. Yet he had to retain leadership of his people who were being taught – through the activities of the underground K.C.A., the Kikuyu Independent Schools' Association and the 'Forty Group' – that the Kikuyu should fight for their lost lands, regain complete freedom and force the British to abandon their interests in Kenya. Kenyatta no doubt knew that he was walking a political tightrope and he did this with particular skill during a year when secret and illegal oath-taking was widespread and Mau Mau was forming itself into a 'subversive movement based on the lethal mixture of pseudo-religion, nationalism and the evil forms of black magic'.[3] He had come under pressure from the Committee of the Kenya Citizens' Association to denounce Mau Mau publicly.[4]

[1] Appendix 2.
[2] Kenyatta's description of the flag to the mass K.A.U. meeting at Nyeri, 26 July 1952: 'It has three colours as you see – black at the top, red in the middle, green at the bottom. Black is to show that this is for black people. Red is to show that the blood of an African is the same colour as the blood of a European, and green is to show that when we were given this country by God it was green, fertile and good, but now you see the green is below the red and is suppressed. You also see on the flag a shield, a spear and an arrow. This means that we should remember our forefathers who used these weapons to guard our land for us.' *Cmnd. 1030*, p. 307.
[3] *Cmnd. 1279*, p. 103.
[4] The Kenya Citizens' Association, formed in October 1950, was sponsored by Peter Mbiu Koinange, the friend and supporter of Kenyatta. Its aim was to be a non-racial association for the 'fostering of human relationships' and for the free discussion of the problems involved. The inaugural meeting at

This he did, reluctantly, at a well-attended K.A.U. meeting at the Kaleoleni Hall in Nairobi; and he did so in such guarded terms that translations of his speech provided – as with all his public speeches reported at that time to the Director of Intelligence and Security – a number of double meanings. He simply said that he did not know this thing called Mau Mau and that he did not even know what language it was – the latter remark being greeted at the meeting with some mirth.[1]

The breeding ground for Mau Mau was in the European settled areas among the landless Kikuyu farm labour. Commenting in March 1951 on the arrest of six ringleaders of a typical oath-taking ceremony on a European farm, the Director of Intelligence and Security wrote: 'All six were Kikuyu and all were employed as farm labourers in the vicinity. Documents seized by the police at the time of the arrest reveal that the oath campaign is to continue until all Kikuyu are members. The name of Jomo Kenyatta is frequently mentioned as a superhuman who will guide the African towards freedom and remove the European from the Colony.'[2] Reports from Nyeri, on the boundary between Kikuyuland and the White Highlands, spoke of universal civil disobedience, a march of K.A.U. members on Government House, and the assassination of leading Government supporters among the Kikuyu chiefs. Yet in Nairobi, where those responsible for law and order appeared to be out of

the multi-racial United Kenya Club was attended by 17 Europeans, 8 Indians and 11 Africans – including Jomo Kenyatta.

[1] The words Mau Mau were first heard of in March 1948 but did not come into current use until early 1950. It is said that Mau Mau really means *Uma Uma* (Out Out) and is a code word based on the old pre-circumcision language of the Kikuyu young men. D. H. Rawcliffe says in *Struggle for Kenya*, his study on the Mau Mau movement, that the name of the cult probably came from the onomatopoeic imitation of the 'roaring like lions' by the priests of the *Watu wa Mungu* during their ceremonies. This Kikuyu religious sect, which was popular in the 1920s, has declined until there are only a few adherents left. However, their wild roaring like lions as a piece of symbolism based on the fifth chapter of Isaiah has survived: 'Their roaring shall be like a lion, they shall roar like young lions; yea, they shall roar, and lay hold of the prey, and shall carry it away safe, and none shall deliver it.' Another, more recent, explanation of the words Mau Mau is contained in *Mau Mau from Within* by Donald Barnett and Karari Njama. During the interrogation of witnesses at the Naivasha Oath Trials in 1950 one of them said he was given the 'Muma' oath. The European police officer taking the evidence misinterpreted the word and gave the pronunciation and spelling as 'Maumau'. Kenyatta was, therefore, probably correct in saying there was no such word in the Kikuyu language.

[2] *Cmnd. 1279*, p. 105.

touch with the district administration and the police, the reports
were discounted because of the 'natural cowardice of the Kikuyu,
the fact that threats of action had often been made in the past, and
known disagreement between Kikuyu K.A.U. leaders'.

Mitchell's government machine, while efficient in many respects
– particularly in its political and legislative work – was sorely lacking in the administration of internal security. There was no central
organisation to assess the general import of intelligence reports and
there was little excuse for this. In August 1950, following the
Naivasha Oath Trials, the Internal Security Working Committee
was set up under the chairmanship of the Secretary for Law and
Order. Its functions were to assess the internal risk in Kenya and to
review existing schemes to meet this risk. The Committee submitted
its first and last report to Mitchell in November 1951. It was a comprehensive review, not only of security but also of the factors which
influenced the political scene at the time and covered African
nationalism, communism, land hunger, detribalism, politicians and
agitators, European sympathisers, the Press, comparison with other
countries, and Indian influence. On Mau Mau it had this to say:

'This is a Kikuyu secret society which is probably another
manifestation of the suppressed Kikuyu Central Association. Its
objects are anti-European and its intention is to dispossess Europeans of the White Highlands. Its members take an oath not to
give information to the police, and may also swear not to obey
certain orders of the Government. It is suspected that some members employed on European farms indulge in a "go-slow" policy,
and that they may also have committed minor acts of sabotage
on farms. Successful prosecutions against the society are believed
to have checked its growth; or at least to have curbed the forceful
recruitment of adherents. The potency of the organisation
depends on the extent to which it possesses the power, latent in all
secret societies, of being more feared than the forces of law and
order. It is possible that as soon as the Sh. 60 entrance fees are
no longer forthcoming little more will be heard of Mau Mau;
but in the meantime, this society, like the religious sects, remains a
possible instrument for mischief in the hands of agitators . . .'

The report summarised its findings thus:

'The main underlying factors which condition the climate of
anti-European feeling amongst the Africans are the disparity of

wealth, land-hunger, the urge to run their own affairs, a com-
bination of the often rather nebulous elements that go to produce
feelings of racial discrimination, and among the better-educated
and personally ambitious the fact that progress towards self-
government in Kenya is apparently slower than in other territories where Europeans are not a permanent element in the
community.'

The Government no doubt took comfort from the Committee's
view that as soon as entrance fees were no longer forthcoming little
more would be heard of Mau Mau — a statement of wishful thinking
in an otherwise accurate assessment of the movement and the surrounding political conditions. It seems certain, however, that if
the Government had taken action on the report the violence of the
eventual outbreak might have been lessened. On the other hand, the
movement towards independence from British rule would have
slowed down and might have been halted altogether.

In a letter attached to the report which was circulated under
secret cover, Mitchell noted:

'... it is as well to bear in mind that although a sentiment such
as nationalism may acquire great strength and momentum, quite
apart from the existence of poverty or other causes of social discontent, the major problem in Kenya and East Africa generally
is social and agrarian and not nationalistic. Moreover, we are at
present at a stage when improvement in social conditions and
such land reform as is practicable could bring about a marked
betterment in the attitude to Government, and it is for that reason
that we can regard such improvement and reform as a major
security measure. In particular, improvements in wages, housing
and education are within our power and of great importance,
while the greatest importance attaches to everything that can
be done to create better conditions on the land.'

Mitchell was at the end of his term of office and it is understandable that he had no wish to give the impression that the country was
on the verge of revolt. He had chosen to retire to his farm in Kenya,
which confirmed his faith in the country's 'peaceful progress'; but
personal pride in forty years of successful service to East Africa
would in itself have made him present to his Colonial Office masters
in London a rosier picture of the situation in Kenya than was wise.
His final views were contained in a mammoth despatch to the

Colonial Secretary and entitled 'Land and Population in East
Africa'. Published in early 1952, it was a comprehensive and searching document on one of the great problems of the day – the use (or
misuse) of land in a country of limited natural resources and expanding population. The despatch did not, however, face the reali-
ties of the situation in Kenya or suggest any solution to growing
discontent other than the appointment of a Royal Commission to
examine further the problems outlined. Mau Mau was neither a
manifestation of poverty and other causes of social discontent; nor
was it some evil reaction to the pressures of a white civilisation on
an ignorant, primitive people. It was a movement which used every
weapon it could to enslave the mass of the Kikuyu people to the
ideals of African nationalism and to the campaign to free Kenya
from alien rule. As will be seen, the methods used by Mau Mau
were undoubtedly primitive and evil; but terrorism as a political
weapon knows no bounds in Africa or in any other continent.

As Kenya entered the fateful year of 1952 Mau Mau intensified
its efforts. The movement was still underground, although where
persuasion failed intimidation by force was being used to gain support. Not all Kikuyu were willing to take the Mau Mau oath and
the first signs of resistance were the increasing number of arson
cases. In each case, the victim was a known supporter of Government policy and on 23 February the District Commissioner for
Nyeri – where arson was rife – appealed to the authorities in Nairobi
for the Collective Punishment Ordinance to be implemented in the
locations concerned. He wrote: 'In view of the fact that we have
been unable to arrest the actual culprits, it now becomes essential to
ensure that Government servants and supporters should not suffer
severe financial loss as a result of their loyalty to the Government. It
is equally vital that we should prove to the general public that we
are not prepared to tolerate such outrages and that if the rank and
file are unwilling to assist the administration and the police, then the
community must suffer.' There was some resistance to the suggestion
and it was only after strong personal representation by the District
Commissioner (he had become acting Provincial Commissioner)
who saw in the outbreaks of arson a preliminary to 'further lawlessness spreading to other areas' that Mitchell on 8 April signed an
order imposing a fine of £2,500. The apparently organised campaign of arson was not confined to the Nyeri district. In the neigh-

bouring settled areas of Timau, Nanyuki and Naro Moru there were a number of unexplained fires in which grain stores and thousands of acres of grazing on European farms were destroyed.

Mitchell's reluctance to acknowledge the deteriorating situation and his delay in signing the order to implement the first Government action against Mau Mau were no doubt conditioned by the arrival in February of Princess Elizabeth and the Duke of Edinburgh on a Royal Visit to Kenya. This was 'a final and unforgettable climax' to Mitchell's forty years of service in East Africa and on behalf of the people of Kenya he had presented to the Princess a hunting lodge on the slopes of Mount Kenya – in the forest adjoining the area where Mau Mau was beginning to show its teeth. In Mitchell's view there had always been discontent among the Kikuyu and the country was still 'cheerful and loyal' despite urgent representations from his officers in the field that the Royal Visit – which coincided with the outbreaks of arson – should not take place. As it turned out, the Princess was in the country for less than a week; for she was called home on the death of her father. If the Kenya Government had known that Treetops in the Aberdare forests, where Princess Elizabeth succeeded to the British throne while she was watching wild-life, was to become in under a year the hunting ground of well-armed and ferocious Mau Mau gangs, they might have hesitated to take such an appalling risk. Later, in July, the Kenya Commissioner of Police was to write to the Member for Law and Order that the events of the previous seven months had indicated that a plan by the Kikuyu to revolt against the settlers and the Government had been put into effect. Arson had been replaced by assassination as a weapon of intimidation. On 15 May the bodies of two Kikuyu informers were taken out of the Kirichwa River near Nairobi and from confessions made later it was found that an organised campaign of Mau Mau executions increased in intensity about this time. In the Kiambu district, the centre of Kikuyu resistance to Mau Mau oath-taking, 500 bodies were eventually found.

The Kenya Government was forced to recognise the situation and on 12 June when he addressed the opening of the new and enlarged Legislative Council Mitchell stated: 'The Government views with concern the recent threat to law and order occasioned by the activities of proscribed societies. Urgent and continuous attention will be given to the task of maintaining the fullest confidence in the peaceful administration of the Colony. Measures to this end must include more extensive policing of the African Land Units . . . to preserve law and order.'[1] Nine days later, Mitchell gave up his post on retirement and the Chief Secretary, Mr (later Sir) Henry Potter, took over as Acting Governor until the arrival of a successor.

Intensive police activity throughout the month of June revealed that Mau Mau was gaining ground rapidly: the Mau Mau oath had now become a killing oath aimed directly at Europeans.[2] Alarmed at these developments, and the threats to European lives and property, the European members of Legislative Council introduced a resolution urging the Government to take more positive action. The subsequent debate – led by Michael (later Sir Michael) Blundell, the settlers' new leader, was the first occasion on which the issue of Kikuyu subversion and Mau Mau was brought openly into public discussion. Blundell alleged that the country was being faced with 'a subversive organisation which was like a disease spreading through the Colony and the leaders have a target and that target is the overthrowing of the Government and my information leads me to believe that the target may well be within nine months'. The debate, however, failed to change the Government's opinion that public security was not in danger and that there was full confidence in the actions taken by the Government to maintain law and order.

On 26 July a mass meeting was held in Nyeri by the Kenya African Union. The Government had agreed to the meeting reluctantly – all public meetings had been banned except under licence – and only if Jomo Kenyatta gave an undertaking that he would use the meeting to denounce Mau Mau. As it turned out, the meeting, which was attended by 25,000 Kikuyu and spurred on by lorryloads of agitators from Nairobi, was a near riot. It gave little comfort to the Government; for Kenyatta was again ambivalent and instead of delivering an outright denunciation repeated that he did not know the 'thing called Mau Mau'. Instead, he used the occasion to make an appeal for African unity and freedom: recovery of lost lands and equal rights with Europeans. Above all, he asked

---

[1] D. H. Rawcliffe, *The Struggle for Kenya*, p. 53.

[2] The oath had several variations but the official version was: (a) If I am sent with four others to kill the European enemies of this organisation and I refuse, may this oath kill me; (b) When the reed-buck horn is blown, if I leave the European farm before killing the owner, may this oath kill me; (c) If Jomo Kenyatta is arrested by our enemy, I will die if I do not follow him wherever he is, and free him. *Cmnd. 1030*, p. 136.

for 'good behaviour' from his audience so that mass K.A.U. meetings would be allowed to continue. The remarkable thing about the
Nyeri meeting was that while Kenyatta was said to have been visibly
shaken by the unruly behaviour of a large section of the crowd he
was able to dominate it by his personal magnetism and prove that
he was the 'leader of Mumbi'.[1] The Nyeri meeting was widely
reported and enlarged the reputation of Kenyatta and the K.A.U.;
but it left the Nyeri district in a 'mental turmoil'.[2]

Although there was now evidence that a large majority of Kikuyu
were bound to Mau Mau and its aims to overthrow the Government
by illegal means, the Government was still hesitant to exert its full
authority. The Acting Governor believed, despite adverse reports on
the situation coming in from district administrations, that there was
no cause for alarm. At a meeting with a deputation from the European elected members who pressed for the 'utmost urgency in taking
action', Potter went so far as to 'categorically deny that a State of
Emergency existed'. The Government was certainly in a difficult
position, as recognition of a State of Emergency would have been an
admission that the 'ordinary processes for the maintenance of security' had broken down: under the existing laws, there were no means
of dealing with a threatened revolt until the law had actually been
broken. Oath-taking ceremonies – and they were becoming more
effective through the activities of motorised oathing teams from
Nairobi – were difficult to detect and the execution system dealt
effectively with refusals and informers. Many of the recognised
political leaders of the Kikuyu were publicly airing their policies in
anti-Government and anti-European terms, but 'nothing of a sufficiently criminal nature was uttered'. Most of the evidence associating
these leaders with Mau Mau activities was by hearsay, much of it
based on fear and prejudice, and the Government's argument was
that under the existing laws of the country none of this evidence
would stand up in the courts. Only by the assumption of emergency
powers and the right to detain without trial could the Government
assert its authority. As these powers would have to be approved by
the British Government and stand up to the test of public opinion in
Britain – a vociferous section of which was anti-colonial – it was

---

[1] Mumbi was the wife of Gikuyu, the mythical founding ancestor of the
Kikuyu tribe. *Gikuyu na Mumbi* was also used as an undercover name for
Mau Mau.
[2] *Cmnd. 1030,* p. 138.

understandable that the Acting Governor hesitated before taking a decision, especially as Mitchell had convinced the authorities in London, however wrongly, that 'the suggestion that there was serious unrest in Kenya was a fabrication of mischievous agitators and unscrupulous journalists'. Nevertheless, the Colonial Office was given the first indication of trouble on 17 August in a letter from Potter to one of the Under-Secretaries:

'You will have seen from our recent political intelligence summaries that there has been a progressive deterioration in the state of law and order in the areas of the Colony where the Kikuyu tribe preponderate ... The main overt Kikuyu political organisation is the Kenya African Union which, while purporting to represent all Africans, does not do so, but is in fact Kikuyu-controlled, under the leadership of Jomo Kenyatta ... The covert organisation is the proscribed Mau Mau secret society, the terms of whose illegal oath include the killing of Europeans, "when the war horn blows", and the rescue of Kenyatta should he ever be arrested, and there need be little doubt, though there is no proof, that he controls this revolutionary organisation in so far as it is susceptible to control ... In brief, public opinion of all races is greatly disturbed and the Kikuyu are sullen, mutinous and organising for mischief. It is because I fear that we are in for a difficult and very troublesome time that I have thought it well to give you informally this brief personal appreciation. When I have further consulted my advisers I shall refer formally to the Colonial Office some proposals for drastic legislation of a kind which has become necessary to support our attempt to deal with the situation I have described.'[1]

The legislation Potter had in mind allowed a confession to a senior police officer to be accepted as evidence; gave additional protection to witnesses; power to restrict the place of residence of persons associating with unlawful societies; power to control traffic at night; to control printing presses; and to increase the maximum penalties for certain offences. In the event, the new legislation was too late to be implemented. The Government's hesitancy in dealing with the 'twilight period of revolt' had the effect of convincing a number of Kikuyu that while their leaders could be outspoken with impunity about the shortcomings of the Government in dealing with

[1] *Cmnd. 1030*, p. 151.

their grievances on land and democratic rights, their cause, no matter
the methods, was a true and just one, and that their leaders were
'powerful and honoured men'.[1] Events in West Africa where
Kwame Nkrumah had risen to power on a platform of extreme
African nationalism also had their effect on the Kenya situation.
This was recognised by the settlers who urged the Government to
make a statement that 'African nationalism on the lines of West
Africa was not H.M. Government's policy for Kenya and that once
this had been made perfectly clear, any statements which suggested
that such a thing were possible should be considered as seditious.'[2]
The Government went as far as it could to meet the demands of the
settlers and in an endeavour to ease the growing tension issued a
Press communiqué on 23 August. After drawing attention to the
repeated statements by certain African leaders claiming self-government and the eviction of the other races in the Colony, it reiterated
the declared policy of H.M. Government, announced in the House
of Commons on 13 December 1950, that the rights of all races would
be respected. It ended with a warning that the Government would
not tolerate the continuance of the state of unrest resulting from the
attempts of 'irresponsible African' politicians to attack and under-
mine that policy, and would use every means at its disposal to enforce a respect for the law. The communiqué was translated into the
vernacular and distributed widely; but it failed to halt the growing
feeling of tension.

Other attempts were also made to contain Mau Mau. A team of
Kikuyu moderates led by Senior Chief Waruhiu organised a movement by African Church leaders in an attempt to counteract the
subversive activities of Mau Mau. Counter oath-taking ceremonies
to 'cleanse' Kikuyu forced to support Mau Mau were held and
although successful the scope was, however, too narrow and they
acted as a 'palliative rather than a purge'. Yet another mass meeting
was held, this time at Kiambu, for Kenyatta to denounce Mau Mau.
He began his speech with the following words: 'Many people were
asked what this meeting is about and who the organisers are. This
meeting is of the Kikuyu elders and leaders who have decided to
address a public meeting and see what the disease in Kikuyuland is,
and how this disease can be cured. We are being harmed by a thing
which some people seem to call Mau Mau.' Unlike the crowd at

[1] Donald Barnett and Karari Njama, *Mau Mau from Within*, p. 121.
[2] *Cmnd. 1030*, p. 144.

Nyeri, the 25,000 Kikuyu at the Kiambu meeting were in a 'reasonable and pleasant mood' and the meeting was hailed as a resounding victory for African moderate opinion. Nevertheless, it failed to halt the inexorable march to a complete breakdown in law and order.

The first intimation to the outside world of the serious nature of the situation in Kenya was contained in the London *Sunday Dispatch* of 24 August 1952. Under the banner headline 'Night of the Long Knives in Kenya', the article told of a Mau Mau plot to murder all Europeans in their beds in a general uprising. Although sensationalised, the article was not based entirely on speculation. Most Europeans in the colony were in the happy position of employing one or more African servants – the bulk of whom were Kikuyu – and it was possible that if the Government had not provoked Mau Mau into showing its hand earlier than was possibly intended, such a plan could have had some success.[1]

In Kenya at the end of September, the Government was confident that it could contain Mau Mau. Its first major test was the mass Mau Mau oath-taking ceremony at a European farm at Timau which had been followed by arson and indiscriminate attacks on farm livestock by groups of indoctrinated Africans: few of the animals were killed outright and many were left to die a slow and painful death. The attack, seen as insensate cruelty to animals, created widespread indignation among Europeans in Kenya and Britain and police action was vigorous, and by 6 October thirty-nine Kikuyu and one Meru tribesmen had been arrested and sentenced to imprisonment. The Government had proved that it could deal effectively with any outward manifestation of Mau Mau; but it was not long before humans began to take the place of animals in outbreaks of Mau Mau ferocity. On 7 October, Senior Chief Waruhiu, the widely respected Christian leader of the Kikuyu moderates, was shot down in broad daylight by gunmen as he was driving home to his farm on the outskirts of Nairobi. The murder was followed by isolated attacks on European settlers and on 20 October the Govern-

---

[1] ' "What do you think", I enquired, "of *Utuku was Hiu Ndaihu* (The Night of the Long Swords)? As the rumour goes, if all the Kenya tribes are taking the oath as we are doing . . . it may be possible to kill all Europeans . . ." ' Barnett and Njama, op. cit., p. 133. 'European farmers are very reasonable but all indications are that there will be a planned assassination of Europeans. Reprisals will then be absolutely inevitable.' Passage in letter from Sir Evelyn Baring to the Secretary of State. *Cmnd. 1030*, p. 158.

ment issued a proclamation declaring that a State of Emergency existed in Kenya.

The proclamation was signed by the new Governor, Sir Evelyn Baring, who had been sworn in the day before the Waruhiu murder. A member of the distinguished banking family and with experience of Africa as a popular wartime Governor of Southern Rhodesia, Baring had a standing with his Colonial Office masters in London that few Kenya Governors possessed. He very soon appreciated after only a few days in Kenya that unless the Mau Mau movement could be stopped there would be 'administrative breakdown, followed by bloodshed amounting to civil war'. Baring was given the opportunity to outline his views on the Kenya situation and the policies he intended to pursue in a broadcast speech on the proclamation of the State of Emergency. He said:

'This grave step was taken most unwillingly and with great reluctance by the Government of Kenya. But there was no alternative in face of the mounting lawlessness, violence and disorder in a part of the Colony. This state of affairs has developed as a result of the activities of the Mau Mau movement. There is every sign that these activities have followed a regular course in accordance with a considered plan. There is a pattern in the acts of violence; and there can be no such pattern unless someone has made a plan. In order to restore law and order and to allow peaceable and loyal people of all races to go about their business in safety, the Government have made emergency regulations to enable them to take into custody certain persons who, in their opinion, constitute a danger to public order.

'Many have suffered from the attempts of the members of the Mau Mau society to gain their aims by widespread and carefully planned violence and intimidation; and most of the sufferers are peaceful and law-abiding Africans. Many African chiefs, headmen, missionaries, Government servants and teachers have shown the greatest courage and devotion to duty by continuing their work for their people in the face of constant threats and frequent attacks. Unfortunately, at first gradually and now swiftly, the Mau Mau crimes have increased in number, in daring and in savagery. Recently, persecution of Kikuyu Christians has increased in severity, churches have been desecrated, missions have been attacked, and teachers and children in mission schools have been assaulted and threatened. At one time most of these crimes were committed by stealth, now one of the best-loved and most revered African chiefs in Kenya has been assassinated on the high road in broad daylight by a band of armed men. In short, within a restricted but important area this movement, which shows every sign of careful planning by clever and cruel men, has either by direct or indirect means produced a serious state of disorder.

'Such is the position today in a part of Kenya; and Kenya is a country with many and peculiarly complex problems. It is understandable that many people in this country nurse grievances, but it is wrong that they should attempt to remedy these grievances by force and by secret plotting against society and the State. Problems of the nature and complexity of Kenya cannot be resolved suddenly and by violence. The Government have, therefore, with the full knowledge and concurrence of the Secretary of State for the Colonies, taken drastic action in order to stop the spread of violence. This has been taken not against men who hold any particular political views, but against those who have had recourse to violent measures. This is in the interests of all. It is in the interests of Africans in those wide areas of the Colony which have remained peaceful and of loyal Kikuyu who have been the main sufferers. It is in the interests of Asians who have been the object of attacks by criminal gangs especially in Nairobi, but who have shown commendable steadiness under the strain. It is in the interests of Europeans whose persons and property have more recently been subject to outrage and who have very properly shown great restraint.

'Kenya has before it a bright future with a good prospect of a rising standard of living for people of all races, provided that there is peace and order. In peaceful conditions, plans were being made for economic development and particularly for help to the poorer inhabitants of this country. There were, for example, good hopes of accelerating the pace of the construction of houses for Africans, of expanding African education and of improving the position of Africans in the Civil Service. All these things will be impossible of realisation if conditions of disorder continue. Disorder leads to lack of confidence and where there is no confidence there is economic stagnation. In a state of economic stagnation the standard of life falls and social services, such as education and health, suffer – but once peace and quiet have been restored,

Kenya should enjoy an expanding economy; and before the present disorders there were most encouraging signs of this. The Government have every intention of continuing work on their plans, and indeed of speeding them up.'[1]

The day of Baring's broadcast there were widespread arrests by Government forces in Operation 'Jock Scott'. K.A.U. leaders, including Jomo Kenyatta, were taken out of their beds in dawn raids and by nightfall ninety-nine had been detained.[2] There was no resistance and the Government believed that it had cut off the head of Mau; that it had 'won the race' in showing that the forces of law and order were to be more feared than the power of Mau Mau. The race, however, was not yet over. Mau Mau was a hydra, a many-headed movement run on traditional Kikuyu lines of small, autonomous groups and cells. It had yet to be proved, in a long-drawn-out legal battle, that Kenyatta and his fellow leaders were the managers of Mau Mau: £55,585,424 and 13,547 lives were to be expended before the State of Emergency was ended seven years later. The decisive chapter in the history of Kenya, 'God's own country with the devil's own problems', was only just beginning.

[1] *Cmnd. 1030*, p. 160.
[2] On the declaration of a State of Emergency, the Governor signed orders immediately authorising the detention of 183 Africans. Eight, including Jesse Kariuki in jail for sedition, were already under arrest for other offences. *Cmnd. 1030*, p. 159.

# Part Three

# STATE OF EMERGENCY

## Chapter 10

# Mau Mau on Trial

A T THE TIME of the declaration of a State of Emergency there was as yet no evidence of a coherent plan of revolt by Mau Mau. The movement had a loose system of control leading from local cell councils through district and provincial committees to the Nairobi-based Central Committee – allegedly the militant wing of the Kenya African Union. When the Central Committee was virtually wiped out by Operation 'Jock Scott', leadership passed to the lower-level committees and councils who grouped together where possible to keep the movement in being. From then on, the revolt took shape as local conditions, and the whims of local leaders, decided. The struggle was confined to the Central province (including Nairobi and the Kikuyu, Embu and Meru reserves) and the four settler districts of Nanyuki, Laikipia, Naivasha, and Nakuru in the adjoining Rift Valley province: in all, an area of about 14,000 square miles in the very heart of the country. With an estimated two-thirds of the Kikuyu and the related Embu and Meru people having taken the Mau Mau Oath of Unity the Government faced a potential enemy of about three-quarters of a million.

The first targets for the Government were the forces gathering in the Aberdare and Mount Kenya forests. These steeply-sloping forests, rising high above the surrounding countryside, were the traditional refuge of the Kikuyu in troubled times and had a permanent population of some three hundred or so criminals on the run. In the latter half of 1952, a steady stream of young Kikuyu under the influence of Mau Mau propaganda joined this band of outlaws which included a number of oath-takers and K.A.U. strong-arm men wanted by the police. Although they had no plan of action, the militant men of Mau Mau recognised the force of the gun as the principal weapon in any fight for freedom and, as a result of systematic thefts from military camps and settler homes, they could claim at the outset of the Emergency to have over 500 firearms and a

quarter of a million rounds of ammunition for the nucleus of the
'Kenya Land and Freedom Armies'.

The Kenya Government's assumption of wide powers under the
Emergency regulations enabled an all-out war to be waged against
Mau Mau but almost a year passed before there was any effective
action by the forces of law and order. The dramatic suddenness of
Kenyatta's arrest; Baring's broadcast to the people; the arrival of
British troops by air to reinforce the six battalions of the King's
African Rifles; and the call to arms of the Kenya Regiment and the
Kenya Police Reserve (both European bodies) had been well-
received by the settlers and supporters of the Government: then
disillusionment set in as the initiative appeared to pass to Mau Mau.
As the 1st Battalion of the Lancashire Fusiliers paraded in Nairobi
and neighbouring districts, and the armed cruiser H.M.S. *Kenya*
showed the flag in Mombasa, Mau Mau struck the first blows of
the Emergency: Senior Chief Nderi, who had denounced Mau Mau
at the Nyeri K.A.U. meeting, was ambushed and slashed to death
while making his way with tribal retainers to break up a mass oath-
taking ceremony in his location; and Eric Bowyer, Mau Mau's first
settler victim, was brutally murdered together with his two African
servants. More attacks followed and the list of Mau Mau victims
grew. Tom Mbotela, the moderate K.A.U. leader and a main prosecution witness for the Kenyatta trial, was assassinated, at the third
attempt, by gunmen in the heart of Nairobi. Nobody appeared to be
safe from the slashing knives and guns of Mau Mau: the pro-
Government supporter in Kikuyuland or the European farmer on
his lonely farm. It seemed that the Government, even with its growing weight in men and arms, was powerless to contain the Mau Mau
threat.

On the other hand, the Government was still recovering from the
'head in the sand' policies of Mitchell. Baring was surrounded by
the same advisers who firmly believed that the arrests under 'Jock
Scott' had broken Mau Mau and that the spread of lawlessness
could be contained by police action, with the military in support.
As it turned out, the restrictive measures imposed on the Kikuyu
precipitated the revolt the Government sought to prevent. The
forces of Mau Mau built up in the forests as more and more of the
militant and criminal elements in Kikuyu society sought refuge
from the police. In Nairobi, the centre of government, there was
evidence later that the underground movement was very much in

control of the Kikuyu population and that the Central Committee had re-formed to build up a passive wing and organise a system of supply for the forces in the forests. Throughout that first year of the Emergency, the main concern of the Government seemed to be with the head of Mau Mau rather than with the tail which constituted the real menace.

Kenyatta and the other leaders were brought to trial at the remote schoolhouse of Kapenguria in the farthest corner of north-west Kenya: 280 miles from Nairobi.[1] The case was the Crown against Kenyatta and others for managing an unlawful society (i.e. Mau Mau). It opened on 25 November 1952 and lasted five months: another fifteen months passed before the last appeal was heard and the sentences confirmed. The Crown's argument was that this was a criminal case, but with Kenyatta's stature as an African leader and the world-wide interest in Mau Mau, the whole atmosphere was that of a State trial. Helped by experienced lawyers from Britain, India, Goa, Jamaica and Nigeria, Kenyatta turned the trial to his advantage and used it as a platform to justify his position as the leader of Kenya Africans and the movement towards independence from alien rule. The Government was to regret the decision to bring Kenyatta and his five colleagues to trial: under the Emergency regulations they could have been detained in 'a remote place indefinitely' without trial. It seems obvious that the intention was to use the trial as a propaganda weapon to discredit the Kikuyu leaders and reduce them to the level of criminals. In the event, the proceedings at Kapenguria and the subsequent lengthy process of appeals to the Supreme Court and the Privy Council in London enhanced Kenyatta's prestige and gave him world-wide publicity. His case rested on a denial of complicity in Mau Mau and an assertion that the Government instead of fighting Mau Mau had arrested the very people who could have helped to stamp it out. In retrospect the evidence produced by the prosecution to support the Crown case appears flimsy;[2] but in the emotional atmosphere of the time it was

[1] The nearest town of any significance was the settler centre of Kitale, 24 miles away. To hold the trial in such a place caused great inconvenience to both the prosecution and the defence; but the decision was taken by the Government for security reasons, Kapenguria being declared a special area from which all unauthorised persons were excluded.

[2] Later, in 1959, a leading prosecution witness, Rawson Macharia, denounced his own evidence as false, suborned he said with bribes to testify against Kenyatta. Macharia was eventually convicted in court for perjury and pronounced by the judge to be a pathological liar. An uneasy suspicion

strong enough to convict Kenyatta and the five others to the maximum sentence of seven years' hard labour[1] and for the Governor
subsequently to decree that they should be restricted to residence in
the Northern province for life. In pronouncing sentence, the Magistrate, Mr R. S. Thacker, Q.C., a retired Judge of the Kenya Supreme
Court, had this to say:

> 'You have let loose upon this land a flood of misery and un-
> happiness affecting the daily lives of all races in it, including your
> own people. You have put the clock back many years and by your
> deeds much of the respect for your tribe has been lost, at least for
> the time being. You have much to answer for and for that you will
> be punished. The maximum sentences which this Court is em-
> powered to pass are the sentences which I do pass and I can only
> comment that in my opinion they are inadequate for what you
> have done.'[2]

In contrast to the Magistrate's pronouncement, Kenyatta's personal statement from the dock was reasonable:

> 'Without taking up much of your time, I will tell Your Honour
> that we as political bodies or political leaders stand constitutionally
> by our demands which no doubt are known to you and to the
> Government of this country, and in saying this I am asking for no
> mercy at all on behalf of my colleagues. We are asking that justice
> may be done and that the injustices that exist may be righted. No
> doubt we have grievances, and everybody in this country, high or
> low, knows perfectly well that there are such grievances, and it is
> those grievances which affect the African people that we have
> been fighting for. We will not ask to be excused for asking for
> those grievances to be righted. . . . We stand for the rights of the
> African people, that Africans may find a place among the
> nations.'[3]

The Kenyatta affair followed its tortuous course till July 1954
when the Privy Council refused the final appeal. Through extensive

was left among many people that the original case against Kenyatta had
been weakened. The Kenya Government refused demands to reopen the case.

[1] The number seven has mystical significance of great potency among the
Kikuyu and was used extensively in Mau Mau oath-taking procedure. Kenyatta's seven-year sentence must also have had mystical significance to his
supporters.
[2] Montagu Slater, *The Trial of Jomo Kenyatta*, p. 242.
[3] Slater, op. cit., p. 240.

Press coverage, it had been kept continually before the public eye and when the time came for the final court of British justice to make its decision, Kenyatta, the 'great and loved one' to his people, was a martyred leader. He disappeared into the oblivion of the desert and the hot, dusty jail at Lokitaung; but he continued to dominate the thoughts of his many followers and to provide inspiration for the Land and Freedom Armies in the forests who were at a crucial stage in their fight against by now overwhelming odds.

Throughout 1953, the initiative was still firmly in the hands of Mau Mau. The forces in the forests under the leadership of Dedan Kimathi and Stanley Mathenge had become better organised. These two men, Mau Mau's most powerful and successful oath-takers, had entered the forest in 1952 with prices on their heads. Their first objective was to enforce complete unity among the Kikuyu before turning on the settlers and the security forces. Hence, the pro-Government supporters, or loyalists, among the Kikuyu who had formed themselves into a Home Guard were a major target.[1]

Most of the tip-and-run battles fought in early 1953 were in the Central province, but isolated attacks by independent groups kept up the tension in the neighbouring Rift Valley province where the patience of the settlers at the apparent dilatory methods of the Government in dealing with the unseen enemy was almost exhausted. The score in the first two weeks of the New Year was two Europeans, thirty-five Africans killed, including a Kikuyu chief murdered as he lay wounded in hospital after an encounter with a Mau Mau gang; and at a series of excited meetings at Thomson's Falls and Nakuru armed settlers threatened independent and un-constitutional action. There were demands for self-government and approaches to be made for help from Dr Malan, the South African Prime Minister. At a meeting in Nakuru, the 'capital' of the White Highlands, there was even a demand for the immediate shooting of 50,000 Kikuyu until they were literally killed into submission.[2] The mood of the settlers was made almost insensate by the savage murder on Saturday 24 January of Mr and Mrs Roger Ruck and their young son Michael on their farm by the edge of the West Aberdares

[1] The Kikuyu (Home) Guard was the resistance movement to Mau Mau and by January 1953 had a strength of 10,000 – almost equal to the force of Mau Mau 'warriors' gathering in the forests.
[2] Sir Michael Blundell, *So Rough a Wind*, p. 137.

forest. It seemed a senseless killing, for the Rucks were noted for
their liberal and kindly attitude towards Africans. The local and
world Press erupted in protestations of horror at the killings, and the
following Tuesday an angry crowd of 1,500 Europeans marched on
Government House in Nairobi to demand action from the Governor.
Baring refused to appear and it was only by persuasion from the
European members of Legislative Council who happened to be
meeting there that the crowd was prevented from invading his
residence. It was a nasty moment and although the demonstrators
were mainly European businessmen and office workers, their mood
reflected the highly emotional state of the settler community at the
time.

Baring was in a difficult position. He had shown the ability to take
decisive action by declaring a State of Emergency only two weeks
after his arrival in the country; but he had inherited a government
machine entirely unprepared for the situation he had taken over.
He was also faced with the need to preserve confidence in Kenya
abroad, and thereby the main source of economic help, while at the
same time dealing firmly with the breakdown in law and order
among a powerful section of the people. Nevertheless, Baring had
no cause to be completely dissatisfied with the achievements during
his first few months of office. He had decentralised much of the
Government's authority by giving more power of decision to his
officers in the field. A system of Emergency committees composed of
administration, police, military and civilian representatives had
been set up in the provinces and districts: the Kikuyu (Home) Guard
under his personal encouragement was expanding rapidly; a chain
of fortified police and guard posts and a wide barrier ditch to protect the surrounding population were being built along the borders
of Kikuyuland and the forests; a network of intelligence had been
established to break the silence barrier created by the Mau Mau
oath; a distinguished British general had been appoined Director of
Military Operations to co-ordinate the work of the security forces;[1]
and the legal system was being overhauled to hasten the work of the
courts and deal more effectively with the increasing number of cases
as the police strengthened their hold on Mau Mau. Notwithstanding
all this, the initiative was still with Mau Mau at the time of the
Government House demonstration and the men from the forest

[1] Major-General Sir Robert Hinde, K.B.E., C.B., D.S.O.

showed how dangerous they could be in two well-planned operations carried out on the same night – 26 March.

The first operation was conducted with military precision when a force of eighty-five forest fighters raided the divisional police head-quarters at Naivasha and overran the report office and armoury. The operation succeeded beyond all hopes and the raiding force, which had found the headquarters virtually unguarded, was able to return to the forest fully equipped with automatic weapons, rifles and ammunition, releasing 173 prisoners from the detention camp near-by as a final gesture of contempt. The raid was humiliating and confirmed suspicions that the Kenya police, which had expanded so quickly since the beginning of the Emergency, needed strengthening within its own ranks. Plans were put in hand immediately to make the police more efficient and less vulnerable to Mau Mau attacks; but the loss of such a large quantity of arms and ammunition was to take its toll in the months to come.

The second operation not only removed any complacency that Mau Mau activity was restricted to hit-and-run raids by small forest gangs, but also shocked the world by its ruthlessness. A force of about a thousand Mau Mau under the command of Dedan Kimathi descended on the loyalist location of Lari in the uplands overlooking the Rift Valley near Kedong with orders to wipe out every man, woman and child. This they attempted to do, by ringing each home-stead and setting fire to the whole location and the plain beyond. Those who escaped the flames were butchered as they fled and very few survived the slashing knives and the hacking swords of the raiders. The military force guarding the area had been called away and all the able-bodied men were patrolling the forest some distance from the location, so there was no interference in the mass slaughter of the defenceless inhabitants.

The Lari Massacre, in which over 200 homes were destroyed and as many killed, eliminated much of the erstwhile support for Mau Mau among the Kikuyu people and the other tribes viewing with sympathy the struggle against the Government and the settlers. Such indiscriminate slaughter in one mad act was not only seen as an attempt to crush any opposition by loyalist Kikuyu to Mau Mau; but also as a frightening example of what African society would face if the militant nationalists came to power. The Government made much of the stunning effect of the massacre on local and world opinion to show that Mau Mau was Africans terrorising, killing and maiming Africans and not just a movement to free Kenya from alien rule. In reply, Mau Mau, realising that it had gone too far, blamed Government forces for the massacre and said that they had tried 'to cover Mau Mau aims by a horrible action to the eyes of the people'. Whatever use the Government made in publicising the Lari Massacre to the world, the fact remains that it was the turning point against Mau Mau; many more rallied to the Kikuyu Guard and from this time on Mau Mau would meet increasing resistance from the people they sought to liberate.

Since the beginning of the year, the Government had been under constant pressure from the settlers to remove all Kikuyu from the White Highlands and send them back to their reserve. The Government had resisted, except for an evacuation of all Kikuyu from the operational areas near the forests; but now as a result of the growing number of attacks on Europeans and Africans in the settled areas there were widespread dismissals of Kikuyu employees by the settlers – despite the great costs to themselves as the Kikuyu made up the great bulk of the farm labour force – and the trek back to Kikuyuland grew. There were other factors involved as well: the Government had passed the Kikuyu Registration Ordinance requiring every Kikuyu living outside the reserve to have an identity certificate with photograph; and Mau Mau spread the rumour that those who submitted to being photographed would be 'forced all their lives to work on European farms'. A decree went out therefore to all those who had taken the Oath of Unity to resist having their photographs taken. Rather than submit to the Government's measures, and incur the wrath of Mau Mau, thousands of Kikuyu from all over Kenya, and from as far as northern Tanganyika, made the long trek back to their homeland. The result was overcrowding in the reserve for most of the estimated returning 100,000 Kikuyu were landless and had to find what accommodation they could in the locations and villages. As the Government had feared, the return to Kikuyuland created a major problem for the administration at a difficult time. On the other hand, the Land and Freedom Armies received substantial reinforcements from the thousands of younger men among the returning Kikuyu who eventually found their way into the forests.

## Chapter 11

# War and Politics

IN JUNE 1953, there was a major change by the Government in the conduct of the war against Mau Mau. Baring was nominally Commander-in-Chief as well as Governor; but with the growing armies of Mau Mau constituting a major military threat, the British Government decided to appoint a senior General to take command of all the security forces in Kenya and at the same time to set up an independent military command in East Africa responsible direct to the War Office in London. General Sir George Erskine, a successful wartime commander, was appointed to the post. He soon decided to move away from the previous policy of defence and shortly after his arrival launched a major offensive in the forests to clear them once and for all. For this task, he had under his command an army of about 10,000 European and African front-line troops, a squadron of heavy bombers and two flights of light bombers, and at his disposal an armed police strength of 21,000 and Kikuyu Guard (also armed) of 25,000. Facing him in the forests were the so-called Kenya Land and Freedom Armies totalling an estimated 12,000 in small and loosely-controlled fighting groups, only some 12 per cent of whom were armed with precision weapons: the remainder had a variety of home-made guns and the vicious Kikuyu *simi* or sharp, double-edged sword. Supporting the forest groups was a closely-integrated system of supply – the passive wing of Mau Mau – involving about 30,000 men, women and sometimes children, in the reserve and in Nairobi.

Government forces had the advantage of superior numbers and equipment; but Mau Mau, even with its completely untrained army, had the advantage of fighting over its own ground – the Aberdare and Mount Kenya forests – and from a military point of view the most difficult country that could be imagined. The thick mountain forests with their steep gorges and swiftly-running rivers provided perfect cover and almost impenetrable defences for the Land and

Freedom Armies, and being full of game supported them for many
months when their sources of supply were cut off by the security
forces. The men in the forest guerilla groups were not, however, the
cream of the Kikuyu. While some of them possessed a few years'
schooling and experience in the army, the vast majority were
'illiterate peasants' and farmworkers interspersed with criminal
types.[1] Nonetheless, there existed within the various groups a military hierarchy based on traditional, tribal methods of selecting
leaders for their skill and reputation. Discipline was tight and enforced ruthlessly, with the death penalty by strangling for the most
minor offences. The men were brave and had tremendous powers of
endurance: only their lack of training in guerilla warfare and
sabotage, which would have made their hit-and-run affrays more
disruptive in terms of attacks on services rather than on people,
prevented them from becoming a more serious menace.

Erskine's offensive launched at the end of June was slow to build
up; but as more of his purely military forces were released from their
security role in support of the civil authorities in the Central
province and the settled areas, and his troops learnt to operate more
effectively in the forests, the military tide began to turn against
Mau Mau. By the end of the year, and fourteen months of the
Emergency, the Land and Freedom Armies had lost 3,064 killed and
over a thousand captured at a cost of negligible losses to the British
forces. The activities of the security forces in the Kikuyu reserve and
Nairobi had resulted in 64,000 Mau Mau supporters being brought
to trial. On the other hand, 970 African loyalists and twenty-one
Europeans had been killed or wounded.

At the beginning of 1954, the Government had contained Mau
Mau and removed the threat of a general uprising. Under Baring's
guidance, closer administration was being introduced in all the
affected areas. The settlers, too, had their farm defences better
organised and with many of them part-time police officers, they
were able to give positive support to the security forces and in some
cases to the military offensive in the forest. Yet Mau Mau was still
some way from being defeated and as the costs of the Emergency
continued to rise the movement had become a running sore on the

---

[1] Karari Njama, a 25-year-old teacher in the Kikuyu Independent Schools'
Association with only two years' formal schooling at Alliance High School
and with no form of teacher training, was considered to be the most educated man in the forests. Barnett and Njama, op. cit., p. 151.

economy.[1] The financial surplus of one and a half million pounds in
1952 had been whittled away and with extra costs due to the Emergency amounting to a million pounds a month, the Government was
forced to appeal to Britain for substantial aid.[2]

On the political front, the first year of the Emergency was
dominated by the settlers. Their leader Michael Blundell, a successful farmer and soldier, had established himself as one of the most
powerful men in the country. He was often at the centre of
controversy for his radical and highly personal views, but he had
great influence with the Kenya and British governments.[3] He
believed that unless unofficial opinion of all races could be integrated
into the Government 'grave racial chaos would develop'—a view
which was accepted with reservations by the European Elected
Members' Organisation, at that time the main body of settler
opinion. Nevertheless, Blundell's objective, shared by all his colleagues, was that there should be greater control of affairs away
from the Colonial Office. His argument was that much of the indecision and lack of effective action by the Government in the early
days of the Emergency had been due to the necessity of referring all
matters of policy to the Colonial Secretary first. This then became
the main political platform for the settlers: the differences arose
with regard to who was to share with them in this control, if anybody.

The British Government was reluctant to introduce any form of
constitutional advance in Kenya while there was a State of Emergency and, through the expressed views of the Colonial Secretary,
Mr Oliver Lyttelton, was adamant that any change could not be
built on a small European minority only, and would have to embrace
all races. After the Emergency, greater local responsibility might be

[1] It was worked out that each Mau Mau fighter killed cost the Government
£10,000.
[2] The Budget showed estimated expenditure 30/6/54–1/7/55 at £29
million, including £8 million for the Emergency, and a deficit of £2 million.
Britain contributed £6 million for the Emergency and £5 million for economic development. A further grant of £4 million was made in July plus an
interest-free loan of £1½ million for Emergency expenses.
[3] Blundell credits himself with having secured the appointment of Sir
Frederick Crawford as Deputy-Governor to relieve Baring of much of the
day-to-day business of government and to carry out the detailed planning
and co-ordination of Government departments for many aspects of the
Emergency. Blundell, op. cit., p. 142.

achieved by an extension of the membership system, but with the individuals concerned answerable to an electorate based on a selective franchise. Such caution was understandable. The Conservative Government of Churchill was in power with the slenderest of majorities and under constant attack from the Labour Opposition. Kenya had achieved notoriety through extensive Press and radio coverage of the Emergency, with world public opinion divided in its attitude to Mau Mau; some taking the pro-settler line that Mau Mau was a savage, atavistic cult; others that it was a morally-justified rebellion by an oppressed people. While not excusing the barbaric manifestations of Mau Mau and the campaign of terror against the Kikuyu people, the Labour Opposition in the House of Commons tended to support the latter view. The report of a Parliamentary Delegation published in January 1954 confirmed their suspicions that the course of justice in Kenya was not running at all smoothly, and they used this as a weapon with which to harass the Conservative Government.[1]

The Parliamentary Delegation had supported the conclusions of a recent Commission of Inquiry into the Kenya police and recorded its 'serious disquiet' at the evidence of bribery and corruption in the lower ranks. The swift expansion of the police forces, and serious nature of the problems involved, helped to explain, but did not excuse, the fact that brutality and malpractices by the police had occurred on a scale which constituted a threat to public confidence in the forces of law and order. Official records had shown that (up to the end of 1953) there had been 130 prosecutions for brutality among the police forces ending in seventy-three convictions. An even larger volume of complaints, many no doubt false but others possibly justified, were said to have been made to people in close touch with Africans. The Parliamentary Delegation noted that demands had been made for 'summary justice' in Kenya by members of the various communities and that increasing political pressure had been brought to bear on the Government with a view to securing the abandonment of at least some of the principles upon which British justice was founded. They desired to make clear 'beyond any possibility of doubt' that they were firmly opposed to any demand for martial law or for summary justice. It was important, they said, that in the administration of justice the highest standards should prevail in Kenya, for upon them public confidence and support of

[1] *Cmnd. 9081.*

the Government would ultimately depend. As Kenya became, increasingly, a pawn once more in British politics these views by a delegation from all political parties were to govern the thinking of the British Government in the years ahead.

African political opinion, which had not been altogether stifled by the detention of Kenyatta and his fellow leaders, was constantly critical of the various measures introduced by the Government to contain Mau Mau. This criticism came mainly from the nominated African members of Legislative Council, two of whom, Fanuel Odede and W. W. W. Awori, had taken over the leadership of the Kenya African Union on their appointment as President and Vice-President. The Government allowed the K.A.U. to continue its existence under these two 'moderate nationalists' until it became clear that they and their supporters had no intention of making the Union a pro-Government loyalist organisation. The Government considered it was the duty of all law-abiding citizens to aid in the suppression of Mau Mau and as the leaders of the K.A.U. made no move away from their deliberately neutral position, the organisation was proscribed on 8 June 1953: three months earlier Odede had been arrested and detained on the grounds that he was in touch with Mau Mau and had tried to spread its 'violent methods' against the Luo tribe.[1] The remaining three African members continued to press in Legislative Council for immediate reforms that would remove the political and social grievances they maintained were the root causes of Mau Mau; but their numbers were small and although they had nominal support from the Asian members, they were unable to deflect the Government from the policy of delaying any far-reaching reforms until the end of the Emergency.

The second year of the Emergency was a crucial year for Mau Mau. As the military forces established control in the forests and whittled down the strength of the Land and Freedom Armies, the Government concentrated on the task of eliminating the passive wing and weaning the Kikuyu people away from their tacit support of Mau Mau. Here, the results were more spectacular than the purely military operations. The first major target was Nairobi where

---

[1] Under the Emergency regulations the Government was not obliged to disclose the source of its information and it was suspected that the evidence laid against Odede was slight, and had come from fellow Luos, who were political rivals and disapproved of Odede's association with a mainly Kikuyu organisation. Rawcliffe, op. cit., p. 119.

the underground Central Committee administered a base from which the forest fighters were supplied with weapons, ammunition, recruits and money. The numbers of Kikuyu in Nairobi had swollen to 65,000 – one-third of the entire population – and were distributed throughout most of the city activities, in public services and commerce. Mau Mau openly flaunted its power and had embarked upon a campaign of crime and violence. So at the end of April 1954 the Government, hitherto fully occupied on the security front in the Central and Rift Valley provinces, decided upon a massive swoop on the city to remove it from the grip of terrorism. In a co-ordinated operation with the code-name 'Anvil', security forces sealed off the city and combed through it, making over 30,000 arrests. Those arrested, most of them Kikuyu, were taken to special camps and in a mass screening operation over 16,000 were detained as active Mau Mau supporters. Similar operations in other areas produced for the Government rich rewards through information about Mau Mau activities and strength which had been sorely lacking from the first days of the Emergency. Interrogators, with the help of loyalists and informers, successfully 'brainwashed' many thousands of Kikuyu and this form of psychological warfare was to be the Government's main weapon in turning not only the passive wing and other supporters away from Mau Mau but also the deeply-committed fighters in the forests. A start had already been made earlier in the year to induce the Land and Freedom Armies to come out of the forest and surrender. A former K.A.R. Corporal, Waruhiu Itote, the self-styled General China and Commander-in-Chief of the armies on Mount Kenya, had been captured in a clash with security forces. Skilful interrogation had persuaded him to turn informer and in return for his life he offered to help arrange the mass surrender of his army of 5,000 on Mount Kenya. However, a misunderstanding at the end of protracted negotiations when China's men were massing on the edge of the forest at Nyeri, caused the surrender talks to break down and the opportunity of eliminating half the militant wing of Mau Mau was lost. Nevertheless, a great deal of information was gleaned from China and many Mau Mau leaders outside the forests were arrested.

Throughout 1954, security forces kept up their pressure on Nairobi. There was a spectacular fall in the Mau Mau crime rate and evidence that the Central Committee organisation had been smashed. The Land and Freedom Armies were now without essential lines of supply, for in the reserve contacts with passive supporters had also been stopped. The loyalist groups there had been strengthened and the bulk of the Kikuyu were proving more co-operative as they began to see that the Government was slowly regaining control. One of the major influences on the situation in Kikuyuland was the forced collectivisation of thousands of scattered homesteads into villages. Although there was initial resistance to the scheme – there is no such thing as a village in Kikuyu tribal tradition – the advantages of living in well-planned settlements with a pro-tected, community life became obvious, and had far-reaching effects not least on the land consolidation programmes of later years.

The intensification of Government measures in 1954 was due largely to the setting up of the War Council. This body had come into being in March as a result of pressure from the settlers for more effective direction of the Emergency.[1] It had as members the Gover-nor, Deputy-Governor, Commander-in-Chief and Blundell as Minister without Portfolio. Lyttelton had changed his mind about making constitutional changes before the end of the Emergency and had introduced a plan for representative government through a Council of Ministers chosen from the main racial groups. The new multi-racial constitution provided for a council of fourteen Ministers with the Governor as Chairman; six Colonial Service members of Legislative Council; two European nominated members; three European elected members; one Indian elected member; one Muslim elected member; and one African nominated member. A system of parliamentary secretaryships was also introduced with one of the posts being offered to an African. Although the Lyttelton constitu-tion had the initial support of the European Elected Members' Organisation, it later caused a split among the settlers which was never to be healed: there were the liberal multi-racialists under Blundell who saw in the new constitution a national Government of all races; and the independently minded who considered it the thin end of the wedge and the end of the European supremacy. The European elected members had accepted the Lyttelton constitution reluctantly and only as a means of divorcing Kenya from Colonial

[1] One of the War Council's main tasks was to keep a close watch on the soaring costs of the security forces and military operations: for example, the British Air Ministry was charging the full rate for the obsolete bombs being used by Lincoln aircraft bombing Mau Mau encampments in the forests. After representations from the War Council, the costs of the bombing were substantially reduced. Blundell, op. cit., p. 169.

Office control. They had insisted on 'standstill agreements' on land, education and franchise to preserve their rights and in so doing undermined what, for Kenya, was a considerable advance towards the principle of partnership. The African members for their part, while promised that ways and means of initiating direct elections for Africans would be studied, refused to accept the Lyttelton constitution on the grounds that it treated them as third-class citizens.[1] However, one of their number, Mr B. A. Ohanga, a Luo, accepted the African Ministry for Community Development, but only after a month of hesitation and a personal plebiscite in his own district in Nyanza. He was supported in the Government by the nominated African Parliamentary Secretary, Mr Jimmy Jeremiah. Ohanga and Jeremiah were the first African Ministers in a Kenya Government and although they were popular with their European and Asian colleagues, their careers did not last for very long and they were both swept away in the direct African elections three years later.

Following the introduction of the Lyttelton constitution the country settled down to a period of political truce and continuing success against Mau Mau. The Government was in a much stronger position and in October the new Colonial Secretary, Mr Alan Lennox-Boyd (later Lord Boyd), visited Kenya to appraise the results of his predecessor's innovations. He reassured the settlers by stating that they had an essential part to play in Kenya and that they had the support of the British Government: moreover, he himself believed in further European immigration. This statement made Lennox-Boyd the settlers' friend: they were to remember it six years later in their campaign against the alleged 'sell-out' by the British Government of the Europeans. Lennox-Boyd gave another assurance, which was also to be proved false, when he supported the Governor's announcement that Jomo Kenyatta would never be allowed to return to Kikuyuland after the expiry of his seven-year sentence.

In January 1955, the final phase of the military operations against Mau Mau began. Most of the Land and Freedom Armies had been split up into small groups of ten and twenty, fighting for their existence under heavy pressure from security patrols and bombing. The

[1] The surrender talks of 1955 caused almost as much controversy among inquire into the method of introducing African elections for the Legislative Council.

military authorities hoped that by the sheer weight and density of
the Government forces involved – equivalent to a full infantry division – Mau Mau would be 'flushed from their lair' to be caught in
ambushes by the Kikuyu Guard along the forest edge. The results,
however, were disappointing: Mau Mau casualties amounted to only
161 dead, captured or surrendered. The forest fighters were too
skilful to be caught by set-piece military tactics and a second operation in which small army units were stationed in the forests for two
months with their own patrol areas was more successful and
accounted for 277 Mau Mau. Even then the results were disappointing in view of the massive effort and cost involved.

It was obvious that orthodox military methods were not going to
clear the forests quickly and another attempt was made to induce
large numbers of Mau Mau to surrender. There were indications
that the battle for freedom had lost its glamour for the many Kikuyu
who had taken to the forests now that they had been cut off from
their sources of supply and were being forced to live like hunted
animals. So a number of them who had been captured and brainwashed were allowed back into the forests to try and persuade their
ex-colleagues to surrender. The War Council, sceptical after the
failure of the China negotiations which were conducted when the
Government were not in a strong enough position and were viewed
by Mau Mau as a sign of weakness, agreed reluctantly to the proposals for new surrender talks, even though a genuine approach had
been made from some of the forest leaders to surrender all their
forces in the Aberdare and Mount Kenya forests. There was also the
factor that when the surrender operation was made public it would
create a political storm.[1] The situation, however, was radically
altered now that the Government had the initiative. An immediate
end to the strains of a State of Emergency was also not to be dis-
carded lightly: economic development was almost at a halt and the
heavy burden of the Emergency on manpower and financial resources was becoming intolerable.[2]

The Government's efforts to subvert leading elements of the Land
and Freedom Armies was helped by a split in the forest organisation.
Dedan Kimathi, once all-powerful through his dominance of the
Nyandarua (Aberdare) Defence Council, and its successor the

---

[1] The surrender talks of 1955 caused almost as much controversy among
the settlers as the Indian Question thirty years earlier.
[2] Blundell, op. cit., p. 189.

'Kenya parliament' to which all the leaders of the main fighting groups belonged, had finally broken with his rival, Stanley Mathenge, in a struggle for power. Mathenge, who was more of a soldier than a politician, and other dissident forest leaders, had seen that the tide was running too strongly against Mau Mau for them to resist, and had broken away to form a new Central Council – the Kenya Riigi.[1] It was this body which entered into protracted negotiations with the Government.

The new negotiations, conducted under maximum security precautions, went on for some weeks. At first, the talks were at a 'junior' level in the forest. Later in Nairobi they were conducted on the Government side by the Minister of African Affairs, Mr E. H. (later Sir Edward) Windley, a former Commissioner for the Central province; the Army Chief of Staff Major-General G. D. G. Heyman; and Mr Eliud Mathu in an advisory capacity. The Kenya Riigi party was led by 'General' Kahinga Wachanga, the self-styled 'Colonial Secretary of States'.[2] Although there were strong indications that a majority of the forest Mau Mau wished to surrender, they were so divided among themselves over the Kimathi and Mathenge rivalries that their spokesmen were unable to enforce any agreement. The Government had refused to barter on political concessions and restricted the bargain to an offer to the forest fighters of their lives in exchange for a stop to the fighting. Kimathi and his Kenya parliament had also waged a successful counter-campaign to prevent a mass surrender and so the talks failed; but nearly a thousand of the 'softer' fighters gave up, leaving the hard-core, including Kimathi and Mathenge, still in the forest. Mathenge eventually disappeared and was never accounted for: it is thought that he may have led the trek of some of the forest Mau Mau out of Kenya to Ethiopia and the Sudan.

In May 1955, there was a change in the British military command and Lt.-General (later Sir) Gerald Lathbury succeeded General Erskine as Commander-in-Chief. The strength of the Land and Freedom Armies had been reduced from 12,000 to 5,000 fighting at section leader level over a wide area and Lathbury decided that the days of the massive military operation were over. He introduced a new strategy whereby the forests would be turned over to 'special

[1] By the middle of 1955 the rate of losses by the forest Mau Mau had risen to over 300 a month.
[2] Barnett and Njama, op. cit., p. 467.

forces' composed of highly-skilled tracker teams who used surrendered and captured forest fighters to lead them. It was the most successful and, in terms of manpower and effort, the most economical way of eliminating the remnants of the Mau Mau militant wing from the forests: by the end of the year, twenty-four out of the fifty-one listed forest leaders had been captured and the total strength of Land and Freedom Armies reduced to about 2,000.

With the much-improved security position in Nairobi and the Central and Rift Valley provinces, the Mau Mau revolt could now be described officially as a 'nuisance'; but there was still a danger of resurgence while any of the forest leaders remained at large and of these the best-known and potentially the most powerful Kikuyu after Kenyatta was Dedan Kimathi, 'Prime Minister of the Kenya African Government'. The Government's security forces mounted a special operation to capture Kimathi and this they did after a manhunt lasting almost a year, and in which all the forest leaders of any note were eliminated and their followers reduced to a few hundred. In the last days of his freedom Kimathi roamed the forests like a crazed animal, deserted by his followers who had either been shot or captured. He ended his career as the leader of the Mau Mau revolt in Nyeri, the 'capital' of Kikuyuland, where he was tried and sentenced to death. Kimathi has been described as a demented, vicious criminal – a dangerous killer who terrorised his followers as much as the enemy and the man above all others responsible for the worst features of Mau Mau. Yet at one time, with an army of some 13,000 and the support of a majority of the Kikuyu, he was in a position to dominate the Kenya scene and to hasten the end of alien rule. That he and the other Mau Mau leaders failed in their objective of bringing down the Government and driving out the British does not alter the fact that Kenya was never the same country again. International politics and events in other parts of Africa were to have a more profound effect on the movement towards independence; but the Mau Mau revolt was an ever-present reminder of the costly nature of alien rule when it became unacceptable to a powerful section of the people.

Kimathi's capture in October 1956 marked the end of the operational phase of the Emergency. The costs were considerable: Mau Mau, 11,503 killed, 12,585 captured; Security Forces, 63 Europeans, 3 Asians, 101 Africans killed and 101 Europeans, 12 Asians, 1,469 Africans wounded; Civilians, 1,819 Africans, 32 Europeans, 26

Asians killed and 916 Africans, 26 Europeans, 36 Asians wounded; total number of Mau Mau and supporters in detention camps, 40,000 – it was as high as 77,000 at the end of 1954; Emergency expenses, £55,585,424.

*Chapter 12*

# The Wall is Breached

ALTHOUGH THE FIGHT against Mau Mau was virtually over at the end of 1956, the State of Emergency was to last another three years. The Government retained its sweeping powers under the Emergency regulations, but they were rarely used and had little effect on the upsurge of political activity following the improvement in the security situation. Africans were allowed again to form political associations, although only on a district or tribal basis as the Government had no wish during the difficult period of recovery to be faced by a single, national body dominated by the chauvinistic Kikuyu. The vacuum in the centre was filled by the Kenya Federation of Labour and its General Secretary, the young Luo, Tom Mboya. As a trade union, the Federation was, in theory, restricted to labour affairs and banned from indulging in political activities; but under Mboya's brilliant leadership it provided a platform for African public opinion both in Kenya and overseas. Mboya, who travelled extensively in America and England where he received wide publicity and at the same time substantial financial support for his movement, had the advantage of not being a Kikuyu or of being implicated in any way with Mau Mau; yet his demands for constitutional reforms were similar to those of the old Kenya African Union.[1] He rejected multi-racialism as a basis for political advance: Africa was for the Africans and compromises such as the Lyttelton constitution were only a bar to progress. To Mboya and the new generation of African leaders the target was one man one vote and African majority rule. It was, however, the Coutts Report with its leanings towards a selective franchise which provided the first step towards their goal.[2]

Mr W. F. Coutts, the Special Commissioner, had found that Africans throughout the country were more concerned with getting

[1] Appendix 2.
[2] Report of the Commissioner Appointed to Enquire into Methods for the Selection of African Representatives to the Legislative Council (1955).

145

direct representation than with the actual form of election. He
considered that the vote was a privilege, not a right, and that it
should be based on such qualifications as age, education and experience in positions of responsibility. So he recommended a multiple-
voting system with extra votes allowed for more than one of these
qualifications. The Government accepted the Report, but widened
the qualifications for the multiple vote to enfranchise at least 60 per
cent of the adult African population. Because of the delays in
countrywide registration, and the difficulties of establishing a new
electoral procedure, African elections were not held till May 1957.[1]
The European and Asian elections, the first opportunity the electorate had been given either to accept or reject the Lyttelton constitution, were held during the previous October. On the whole, the
Asians accepted the constitution while maintaining their position on
the Common Roll; but the settlers, split by now into three groups,
rejected any form of multi-racialism that would weaken the position
of Europeans and upset the parity system in the Legislative Council.
The United Country Party, the multi-racialists, were led by
Blundell; the Independents, the middle-of-the-road settlers, by
Group Captain L. R. Briggs; the Kenya Empire Party, the extremists, by Major B. P. Roberts. At the expense of his own popularity, Blundell had founded the U.C.P. as a means of forming a
*rapprochement* with the Africans and Asians. His place as leader of
the settlers was taken over by Briggs whose Independents won eight
seats in the elections to the multi-racialists' six seats. The Kenya
Empire Party failed to gain a seat and Briggs found himself, therefore, in a position of power among the Europeans. A good-natured,
rather naïve man for a politician, he personified the settler image:
ex-service, farmer and a firm believer in the rights of Europeans to
rule by 'merit and ability'. It was around Briggs, and not the forceful and sagacious Blundell, that the settler forces rallied during their
last years in Kenya. Even the extremists of the Federal Independence
Party (the successor to the Kenya Empire Party) found in Briggs a
refuge when their plans for partition and a separate white state were
rejected.

The British Government had made clear to all the conflicting
parties and racial groups before the elections that the only alternative to the Lyttelton constitution was a return to the purely-
colonial form of Government of previous years. For the settlers, who

[1] Seventy-eight per cent of a registered electorate of 126,000 voted.

disliked the constitution almost as much as the Africans but for
different reasons, there was little choice and Briggs was forced
against his own inclinations, and pronouncements during the elections, to join the new multi-racial Government as Minister without
Portfolio on the War Council, succeeding Blundell who had moved
to the Ministry of Agriculture on the appointment of Cavendish-
Bentinck as Speaker of the Legislative Council. Later, when the
African elections had taken place, the newly-elected African members were more forthright. They denounced the Lyttelton constitution as an Emergency measure, refused to take office in the
Government, and demanded a total of fifteen seats in the legislature.
All the former nominated African members had been defeated in
the elections, including Mathu. The new leader was Mboya who
had secured the Nairobi seat with the support of his own Nairobi
Peoples' Convention Party. He quickly made his mark in the
Legislative Council and took every advantage of his new position to
force the pace of African nationalism. The reported view of Coutts
that a majority of Africans were in favour of a multi-racial form of
Government and partnership with the other races was out of date:
only a self-governing African state would now meet the demands of
Kenya Africans. Mboya was no doubt encouraged in his attitude by
the fact that, in West Africa, Ghana had been granted independence
a few days before the first African elections in Kenya; that within a
short time of the elections his campaign for more representation in
the Legislative Council was already meeting with success. It had
become obvious that the eight African members could not, with the
large distances involved, look after the interests of some 5,000,000
people and it was agreed by the Government, and a majority of the
European Elected Members' Organisation, that there should be an
increase in representation. The agreement was seen as a major
break-through for the Africans as the Europeans did not insist
on an increase in their own seats to maintain parity in the
Legislative Council. 'The wall protecting us from the sea was
breached and the waters of African nationalism were pouring in
around us.'[1]

The determined attitude of Mboya and his colleagues not to
accept any position in the new Government, or to agree to any form
of collaboration with the other racial groups in pressing for self-
government, indicated that the multi-racial constitution was not

[1] Blundell, op. cit., p. 220.

working. Under Lyttelton's plan the British Government, through the Colonial Secretary, had the power to impose changes if the constitution should become unworkable. Accordingly, Lennox-Boyd revisited Kenya in October 1957 and after protracted negotiations with the various political groups, the European and Asian elected Ministers resigned from the Government to allow for a new constitution. Africans were given an extra Ministry and six more seats; twelve Common Roll seats, four for each of the main racial groups and elected by the Legislative Council voting as an electoral college, were created; and a Council of State set up 'to examine legislation that might be held to be discriminatory against any race in the country'. The Lennox-Boyd constitution was every bit as controversial as its predecessor and pleased only the Asians who saw in it the beginnings of their cherished Common Roll.

The Africans rejected Lennox-Boyd's plan outright as an 'imposed' constitution. They declared that they would be satisfied with nothing less than 'undiluted democracy' and such devices as specially elected members and a Council of State were no substitute for majority rule. Six new African members were elected in March 1958 to oppose the new constitution, but despite this, and the label of 'traitors to the African cause', eight candidates put their names forward for the four African specially elected seats.[1] Blundell gave up his influential Rift Valley seat and his closest multi-racial supporter, Mr Humphrey Slade, gave up his equally influential Aberdare seat to become European specially elected members. They were both replaced by Federal Independence Party extremists. Briggs did not rejoin the Government and thereafter devoted himself to the task of moulding his Independent Group into a last bastion of settlerdom. Musa Amalemba, a Baluyha from Nyanza, and one of the successful candidates for the African specially elected seats, became the Minister of Housing and the first 'elected' African Minister. No suitable candidate was found for the Ministry of Community Development vacated by the defeated B. A. Ohanga after the first African elections.

During the first year of the Lennox-Boyd constitution, the European special members under Blundell's leadership led the

---

[1] The allegation was the subject of a High Court case in which seven of the African elected members, including Mboya, were fined £75 for defamation of the candidates.

struggle to establish a multi-racial Kenya.[1] Blundell was also considered a traitor by a section of his community, but he still had considerable influence with the settlers and was not afraid to tell them in 1958 at a public meeting in Sotik that Kenya could not now avoid an African majority, and that European policies should be 'simply and clearly' designed to see that this 'great mass of people' was as educated and mature as could be contrived, and as unembittered as possible by removal of barriers and discrimination while the settlers still had the protection of British rule. In March 1959, Blundell resigned from the Government and formed the New Kenya Group composed of all the European, African and Asian specially elected and nominated members of Legislative Council plus ten of the fourteen European elected members. In its first policy statement, the Group put forward the view that Africans would ultimately rule Kenya and advocated the opening of the White Highlands to all races, qualified entry of all races into all schools and the introduction of a Common Roll. The policy, though signed by a majority of leading European politicians, was against all the settlers had fought for from the first days of white settlement and created among them a furious storm which lasted till the Day of Independence. On the other hand, it attempted to provide safeguards for minorities in the event of an African majority while admitting, in effect, that like the Federal Independence Party's policy of a protected settler state within an independent Kenya, multi-racialism could not withstand the swiftly-rising tide of African nationalism. '... The plain truth is that in 1959, after 60 years of British rule, with the heady wine of race and colour sweeping the world, the menace of communism, and the anxiety of the United States of America to demonstrate to Africa that Little Rock never happened, the European is not in a position to stand alone in glorious isolation.'[2]

The first year of the Lennox-Boyd constitution was also marked by disputes within the ranks of the African nationalists through the natural rivalries of ambitious young men and the entry into the Legislative Council of the first Kikuyu elected members. Mboya, however, was still head and shoulders above his nearest rivals for

[1] The United Country Party was disbanded in February 1957 when it was seen from the results of the elections that Europeans did not like political parties, and differences between Blundell and Briggs had been reconciled.

[2] Blundell, op. cit., p. 250.

power: his personality and brilliant oratory, coupled with skill in negotiation, made him respected on all sides. A Nairobi constituency and dominance in trade union affairs also gave him a large following; yet this was insufficient to achieve a united independence movement. Tribal and regional differences were strong and even Mboya with his non-tribal approach to politics found them a formidable barrier. Jomo Kenyatta at the end of his prison sentence and about to be banished for life to Lodwar in the remote Northern Frontier district was in the eyes of many people the only man who could unite the nationalist cause. Although discredited in the eyes of the British and Kenya Governments for his connection with Mau Mau, he had never lost his following among the Kikuyu people or the admiration of the other tribes. The so-called loyalists who had played the major role in crushing Mau Mau looked on him as a leader of the Kikuyu people and therefore of Kenya: it was the methods used and the hopeless cause of an army of 12,000 illiterate and poorly armed peasants attempting to overthrow a Government with all the forces of modern war at its disposal which had ultimately caused them to reject Mau Mau. They had never rejected Kenyatta and his aims for their emancipation; and so in 1958 he became the focal point of African politics. The Kenyatta cult, as it was called, grew quite rapidly and Baring, with a number of Emergency problems still unsettled, was forced in November, while opening a session of Legislative Council, to give a warning to 'those who would develop a cult of Jomo Kenyatta'.[1] This did not, however, deter the African politicians from using the cult in their struggle for power. Kenyatta was safely out of the political arena – a 'father figure' of African nationalism – and the politicians, regardless of their tribal affinities, vied with each other to vindicate him and thereby gain popular support. The anniversary of Kenyatta's arrest was marked by a day of fasting in Nairobi and at the Africa Peoples' Conference in Accra he was praised as a 'freedom fighter equal to Nkrumah'.

The African elected members were united of course in the main purpose of getting rid of the Lennox-Boyd constitution. In January 1959 they announced a boycott of Legislative Council proceedings

---

[1] Baring had cause for alarm: a new underground movement similar to Mau Mau and called K.K.M. (*Kiama Kia Muigi* – the party of the people) had appeared. By the end of the year the Government had broken up 349 cells and committees; arrested 473 members and detained 289.

after being told by Lennox-Boyd in reply to their proposals for more seats that the present constitution was the final increase in communal representation. They were persuaded to return by the promise of constitutional talks and discussion on the conditions necessary for the transfer of power to a self-governing Kenya 'well before the Kenya General Election scheduled for 1960'.

At the time of the walk-out a prelude to the promise of constitutional reform, which was not made public, took place at a private conference in Britain of the Governors of Kenya, Tanganyika and Uganda with Lennox-Boyd in the chair and attended by senior Colonial Office officials 'to discuss the whole future of the East African territories and their orderly development towards self-government'. The reason for holding the conference was said to be the mounting pressure by Julius Nyerere and the Tanganyika African National Union for immediate independence, and the anxieties of the Governor, Sir Richard Turnbull, at being unable to contain this pressure with his inadequate security forces and without affecting the political situation in the neighbouring East African territories. Turnbull, a former Chief Secretary and Minister for Internal Security in Kenya, knew the consequences of denying Africans what they considered to be their rights.

The British Government, still recovering from the Suez débâcle and endeavouring to overcome a difficult balance of payments situation, was faced with a world-wide loss in prestige. The appalling costs of the Kenya Emergency had made it understandably reluctant to become embroiled militarily and economically in East Africa. Another factor was the influence of events in Kenya on the political situation in Britain. The Conservatives were faced with a general election and the Labour Opposition, short of political ammunition in the affluent society of the time, again concentrated on the Emergency and its aftermath as a line of attack. The 'Hola Affair' and its implications of a complete breakdown in justice was all that was needed to create a political storm and 'deep disquiet in the United Kingdom'.

In March 1959, it was symptomatic of the sensitivity of British politicians on Kenya that the death of eleven obscure convicts in a remote part of the Coast province should be the subject of a full-scale debate in the House of Commons. The convicts were among a party of fanatical and intransigent Mau Mau who had been sent to the Special Detention Camp at Hola in the hot, dry country of the

Tana basin. A plan had been made to employ them in the near-by
irrigation settlement for ex-Mau Mau detainees, working their way
back to a normal life; but this had proved difficult. The recalcitrant
convicts refused to do any work as they considered it a violation of
their Mau Mau oath: they would rather die, they said, than co-
operate. It was the original intention to mix them with a group of
more co-operative detainees in small, easily controlled parties but
owing to a misunderstanding of the agreed plan by the officer-in-
charge, a large party of 119 detainees, including the eighty-five
hard-core Mau Mau, was taken to work on the morning of 3 March
without adequate supervision.[1]

The warders were under instructions to use the minimum amount
of force to persuade the non co-operative convicts to work if they
refused, but when the majority of them proved troublesome there
were extensive beatings. In a confused situation with convicts
passively resisting work and being beaten by the African warders —
the sole European officer-in-charge was absent when most of the
beatings took place — eleven of the working party were left dead and
twenty-two injured. The remoteness of Hola made subsequent
inquiries into the deaths difficult and, because of insufficient information, a Government Press handout from Nairobi gave the impression that the cause of the deaths was excessive drinking of water in
the heat of the morning and not violence, as was eventually proved.
The radio, owing to the distances involved in Kenya, was used
extensively by the police and prisons and, as most of the messages
were in plain language, the radio service was a useful source of
unofficial information for the Press. It was not long before the full
story of Hola leaked out and was flashed round the world, for the
international Press was still well-represented in Nairobi. The
Government's apparent suppression of the truth about the affair was
also given wide coverage and although the misunderstanding caused
by the original Press handout was soon cleared up, the damage had
been done.

Hola became as much of a household word as Mau Mau and just
as damaging to Kenya's reputation. The record of proceedings of the
inquest into the deaths and the subsequent Government inquiry
were laid before the British Parliament as White Papers. The affair
resulted in 'deep expressions of concern' (also published as White

[1] Further documents relating to the deaths of eleven Mau Mau detainees
at Hola Camp in Kenya, *Cmnd. 816*, p. 28.

Papers) by the Colonial Secretary and the Governor, and promises that 'every possible step should be taken to ensure that never again is there the risk of such a tragedy occurring'. Hola to Baring was what Mau Mau was to Mitchell. It raised again the whole question of the application of British justice in Kenya and the criticisms that in suppressing Mau Mau the Kenya Government had been unduly repressive and violent in its methods. However true or untrue this accusation, the fact remains that because of the political implications both on the home front and internationally, the Conservative Government in Britain changed its attitude towards Kenya and the policy of a gradual, multi-racial approach to independence.

Lennox-Boyd in a policy statement to the House of Commons on 22 April had refused to fix a date for responsible government or modify his general programme for Kenya.[1] He maintained that the necessary conditions had not yet been realised: 'a sufficient understanding of political institutions, sufficient sense of responsibility in public affairs, understanding and co-operation between the different communities, and a reasonable prospect that the Government to which power was transferred would be able to ensure a fair standing of living in an expanding economy.' But by the end of the year the British Government was giving every indication that it would accede to African demands.

There were a number of other changes in the latter half of the year which influenced the fateful Constitutional Conference now arranged to be held in London at Lancaster House in January 1960. Baring departed on retirement under the cloud of the Hola affair, having completed seven years as Governor, and his place was taken by Sir Patrick Renison, a career colonial servant.[2] There was also a new Colonial Secretary in Iain Macleod who replaced Lennox-Boyd after the October General Election. Macleod, a radical Tory with a practical view of the events taking place in Africa, had no patience with those who saw the future in terms of the *status quo*: the Africans were on the march and it was up to Britain to get out of Africa as quickly and as decently as she could. Assurances by previous administrations were scrapped as Macleod, with the support of his Cabinet colleagues, opened the door and let the winds of

[1] The East African Governors at their January Conference were said to have suggested independence for Tanganyika and Uganda in 1970; and Kenya in 1975. Blundell, op. cit.

[2] One of Baring's last personal acts in Kenya was at Malindi where he rescued an Asian girl from drowning at the risk of his own life.

change blow Kenya and her neighbours to independence. The door to the future was the first Lancaster House Constitutional Conference and as the delegates from Kenya of all shades of opinion and colour prepared to leave for London, Renison, on 12 January 1960, signed a proclamation formally bringing the State of Emergency to an end. Kenya had finished with the 'dark forces of the past' and was now on the threshold of true nationhood.

Part Four

# ROAD TO INDEPENDENCE

## Chapter 13

# Advance of the Black Hordes

---

THE DELEGATES to the Lancaster House Conference, which was restricted to elected members of the Kenya Legislative Council and the Colonial Office, were lined up in a number of opposing racial groups and parties: the Kenya Independence Movement, the extremist Africa party; the Kenya National Party, formed the previous November to represent tribal groups other than the Kikuyu and Luo; the New Kenya Group, the multi-racialists; the United Party, an amalgamation of the Briggs Independent Group and the extremist settlers' Federal Independence Party; and an Asian group representing the Kenya Indian Congress, the Kenya Muslim League and the coastal Arabs. By the time the Conference opened, the two African groups had resolved their differences and combined as a solid front with the Giriama Ronald Ngala as Leader and Tom Mboya as Secretary. The very start of the Conference was threatened by their first move – a boycott of the opening plenary session. All delegate groups were allowed to have with them a constitutional adviser, but although the African delegation already had one in the person of Dr Thurgood Marshall, an American Negro lawyer, they insisted on a second adviser and chose Peter Mbiyu Koinange, the exiled associate of Kenyatta and after him the man held most responsible for Mau Mau. This was unacceptable to the British Government and the other delegations: it was only after a delay of five days that a face-saving compromise was reached and Koinange was allowed into Lancaster House, but not into the Conference itself. The affair was a first show of strength by the Africans and they were able to claim a moral victory. Public opinion was on their side, for as Koinange was 'free to go anywhere in Great Britain' it was difficult to see why he could not enter Lancaster House. The United Party, who had strongly resented the presence of Koinange within the building, had to be content with a token absence of an afternoon from the Conference committee discussions. In the event, their policy of a colonial government in federal form with entrenched European rights was discredited and they played little part in the Conference deliberations. The main clash was between the African delegation and the New Kenya Group.

Macleod's plan was for an elected African majority in the Legislative Council and a widening of the franchise to bring in a million and a half voters. This favoured the African viewpoint, but was completely opposed to the views of the New Kenya Group who wanted a constitution that would enable all races to think nationally rather than sectionally and include a common electoral roll with selective qualifications so that no one race could predominate. On the other hand, except for conceding the principle of a Bill of Rights to protect racial minorities, the African delegation were adamant on a policy of 'undiluted democracy' and one man one vote. Following talks which lasted a month, the expected compromise was reached, the European members of the New Kenya Group, the key figures to the Conference, agreeing reluctantly, knowing full well the storm that awaited them on their return to Kenya.[1] There would be in the Legislative Council 33 open seats for Africans; 20 seats reserved for minority communities on a Common Roll, but with primary elections so that candidates had support within their respective communities; 12 national seats to be voted by the elected members of the Legislative Council.[2]

Although the Lancaster House constitution gave the Africans a clear majority over the other racial groups, it was a long way from the responsible self-government they were seeking. The British Government despite an acceleration of the timetable for African rule in Kenya also insisted on an element of Colonial Office control to allow for the orderly hand-over of power. Under the new constitution the Governor was allowed to retain his right of nomination to ensure a Government majority in the Legislative Council and the appointment of official Ministers; but the number of officials in the Council of Ministers was cut from seven to four, European Ministers from four to three, Asians from two to one, and the Africans going up from one to four. The delegates returned to a Kenya that was in a state of trepidation: the African people deliriously happy at the

[1] The N.K.G. agreed provided the African elected members were willing to work in a new Government and that the British Government made available adequate funds for education and the purchase and development of land in Kenya. After some argument with the Colonial Office a promise of £5 million in aid was given. Blundell, op. cit., p. 276.

[2] Cmnd. 960.

near prospect of independence and the end of European domination; the Asians bewildered at the turn of events and the effect on their traditional position as middlemen; and the Europeans shocked, bitter and angry at their virtual elimination as a political force.

As the settlers of all shades of political opinion united under Cavendish-Bentinck[1] in a new party, the Kenya Coalition, to fight a rearguard action, the Africans in their hour of triumph split once more into a number of rival factions. There were the moderates represented by the Baluyha Masinde Muliro, the founder of the Kenya National Party, who advocated co-operation with the Government and acceptance of the three new Ministries; and the extremists such as Mboya who declared that 'our struggle is still to be won' and that the Lancaster House constitution was already out of date. In March, the Kenya African National Union was formed as the 'Uhuru Party' with Kenyatta as President and the party colours those of the proscribed K.A.U. But the Government stepped in and announced that the new party could not be registered if Kenyatta, who was still under restriction, was made its nominal head. So James Gichuru, a close associate of Kenyatta in the K.A.U. days, became President, on the understanding that he would step down when Kenyatta was released. The outspoken and revolutionary-minded Oginga Odinga was made Vice-President and his rival Mboya the Party Secretary. Afraid that their views would be swamped by this concentration of African political power and by the numerically superior Luo and Kikuyu, the other tribal groups, representative in the main of the pastoral and more backward peoples, formed the Kenya African Democratic Union with Ngala as Leader and Muliro as Deputy Leader.

As the Africans lined up their forces for the general elections to be held in early 1961, an increasing number of Europeans came forward to support the Kenya Coalition. Cavendish-Bentinck, while blaming Macleod and the British Government for the 'harsh and dishonourable' imposition of the Lancaster House constitution, had after the first shock recognised that African interests in Kenya were paramount. The only hope for the future lay in fighting for minority safeguards in a Bill of Rights and, in view of the assurances by past

---

[1] Cavendish-Bentinck resigned as Speaker of the Legislative Council in protest at the Lancaster House constitution. A former champion of the settlers, he felt he could no longer retain a neutral position. He was succeeded by the multi-racialist Humphrey Slade.

British Governments, in adequate compensation for settlers if they should be forced to leave their farms. Pressure by the Kenya Coalition built up as in the course of the year generous compensation terms were announced for Europeans in the Colonial Service if, and when, their posts were 'Africanised'.

The British Government, now that it had taken the decision to absolve itself of responsibilities in East Africa, was determined to extend the principle of Africanisation as widely as possible; but it was, and remained, reluctant to buy out the settlers. The official view was that while the settlers might feel uncertain about their future, so were other people in other countries: Britain was also 'a poor country'.[1] Figures mentioned as compensation for the outright purchase of the White Highlands for settlement of landless Africans ranged from £30 to £50 million – an unrealistic demand in view of the British Government's attitude but, nevertheless, a fair indication of the value of the settler farms as many of them were intensively developed.

The disasters in the neighbouring Congo following the Declaration of Independence from the Belgians on 30 June, and the complete breakdown in law and order when Europeans were forced to flee for their lives from the rampaging Congolese soldiery, had a profound effect on the attitude of the settlers and strengthened their case with the British Government. Many of the refugees from the Congo passed through Kenya and apprehension by Europeans at the political turn of events was replaced by fear for their own safety when British rule ended. Possibly for the first time, the settlers realised that their position in the past had been upheld by British might. Now, as Britain declined as a world power and her economy went from crisis to crisis, that support was no longer available. The Kenya settlers were on their own and they had to come to terms with the African majority or 'scram out of Africa'. Nonetheless, there were some who felt that a strong, united white community, however small in numbers compared with the other races, could have continued to rule Kenya by taking a more militant stand

---

[1] The British Prime Minister Harold Macmillan during a conversation with Blundell at No. 10 Downing Street, London. Macmillan had recently returned from a tour of Africa during which on 4 February he delivered his famous Winds of Change speech while addressing the South African parliament. '. . . The strength of African nationalism is blowing the winds of change through the Continent.'

against the advance of the 'black hordes'. The man with the gun, as had been proved on countless occasions in British colonial history, had the ultimate power and some settlers in Kenya were prepared to use that power. Blundell and his European supporters in the New Kenya Group were therefore vilified for having given way to the Africans and to the Colonial Office, thereby destroying any hope of settler unity. This the settlers could never forgive.[1]

The events in the Congo during the latter half of 1960 also held a lesson for the Kenya African political leaders locked in a struggle for power. The nationalists of K.A.N.U. with their cry of *uhuru* (freedom) were at odds with the separatists of K.A.D.U. with their cry of *majimbo* (regionalism). In the Congo, where the ejection of the Europeans was only a by-product of the fratricidal struggle between rival groups, the same issues were at stake. In Tanganyika the move towards independence was by comparison with Kenya going smoothly and well ahead of schedule because of the single-party system. The lesson in each case was obvious. Continued strife by the two evenly-matched political parties in Kenya could at the best lead to a slow-down in the movement towards independence: at the worst, a series of Congo-type disasters. Providentially for Kenya, the worst did not happen: the Europeans were still integrated politically and socially with the life of the country. White power still held the gun and the general elections in February 1961 passed without any serious outbreak of violence.

The first elections were the Primaries for the reserved European and Asian seats. Owing to the unpopularity of the New Kenya Group policies, Blundell and the majority of his European colleagues only got through by the narrowest of margins over the laid-down minimum of 25 per cent of the total number of votes cast.[2] Blundell, who had decided to contest the Rift Valley constituency again, was himself heavily defeated in votes by his formidable opponent Cavendish-Bentinck; but was allowed to go through to the subsequent Common Roll elections on his total of 26.68 per cent of the votes cast. The vastly superior number of African voters in the constituency then swept Blundell back into Legislative Council and

[1] When Blundell returned to Nairobi after the Lancaster House Conference, he was met by a group of angry settlers: one of them threw a handful of silver 50-cent pieces at his feet crying 'Judas, you have betrayed and left us.'

[2] The European members of the Group fought the election as the New Kenya Party.

rejected Cavendish-Bentinck. It was a good example of the elections under the new constitution and of the control the African voter had over the seats reserved for other communities.

Voting in the open-seat elections was less straightforward, both official parties having official and unofficial candidates: eighty-four candidates stood for the twenty-seven contested seats, the contest being between the Kenya African National Union (Official and party Independent); Kenya African Democratic Union (Official and party Independent); Baluyha Political Union; Shungwaya Freedom Party; and African Independents. In the event, K.A.N.U. won the election with a majority over all other parties and groups.[1] The release of Kenyatta had been a major demand in the K.A.N.U. campaign and immediately after the results of the elections were made known, the leaders announced that they would only form an administration if Kenyatta was released from restriction. The Government refused and Renison, who had once described Kenyatta as the 'leader to darkness and death', made arrangements to rule by decree. But discussions continued with the other political groups and the Government relented, and allowed some of the African leaders to visit Kenyatta in exile to obtain his advice. Eventually, Ngala of K.A.D.U. agreed after two months of deadlock to become Leader of Government Business. He formed a Government in association with the New Kenya Party, the Kenya Indian Congress, Independents and one member of K.A.N.U., the Meru Bernard Mate. At one time, it looked as if there might have been a coalition between the two main parties, but Mboya and Odinga, despite their rivalries,[2] rallied behind Gichuru on the policy 'no Kenyatta, no Government'. K.A.D.U., even with the support of members nominated by Renison on the Government side, had the narrowest of majorities in the Legislative Council and it was obvious that with a powerful and, for the time being, united K.A.N.U. in opposition the new Government could only be a caretaker administration.

[1] Candidates standing on the K.A.N.U. party ticket had 67.4 per cent of the votes (19 seats) and controlled the major tribes, i.e. Kikuyu (including Embu and Meru), Luo, Kamba and Kisii; K.A.D.U., the Masai, Kalenjin, Giriama and several of the smaller tribes, 16.4 per cent (11 seats); the Baluyha Union under Musa Amalemba and the biggest, single tribal group, 3.3 per cent (one seat); Shungwaya Freedom Party 0.4 per cent (one seat); and African Independents (one seat).

[2] Odinga with his Communist connections (he had recently visited Russia and China) was a bitter rival of the Western-minded Mboya for power within K.A.N.U. He had even led a campaign against Mboya during the election.

Although they had stood on the sidelines during the deadlock over the Kenyatta issue, K.A.D.U. also recognised him as the future leader of an administration in which the two parties could be united. They shared the general mass of support for his release: the difference was that they were prepared to join the Government first. Ngala, whose motives in undertaking the unpopular task of forming a Government supported by a minority of the electorate were suspect as it seemed that his aim was to play off one rival faction in K.A.N.U. against the other and split the party, soon showed that he could use his new-found power effectively. His first act was to provide Government funds for the building of a new house for Kenyatta when he returned to Kiambu, and he authorised the men tried with Kenyatta at Kapenguria to be released immediately and to be allowed to return to their homes. He received a promise from the British Government for £18½ million in financial aid during the current year; and in June he was able to announce in the Legislative Council that he hoped Kenya would be able to achieve internal self-government by the year's end. The world of colonial Kenya was turning upside down and the anxious settlers, silent spectators of acts that two years previously would have belonged to the world of fantasy, were powerless.

Ngala's hope of self-government by the end of 1961 was not entirely wishful thinking. Although the Lancaster House constitution had been devised as a planned approach to independence for Kenya – first a period of responsible government, then internal self-government – timetables and plans seemed to have been scrapped for the other East African territories. Less advanced countries such as Somaliland and Tanganyika were now self-governing and there was no reason at the time of Ngala's statement why Kenya should lag behind. But the Kenyatta issue, the multi-party system, rivalries within K.A.N.U., and sizeable immigrant communities demanding safeguards were the halters to Kenya's progress towards independence. As it turned out, Kenya was the last of the colonial territories in eastern Africa to become independent.

The release of Kenyatta was not long delayed and as soon as his new Government-built house was finished he left Maralal a free man in August 1961 and returned in triumph to his people.[1] Almost

---

[1] Kenyatta had been moved from his desert bungalow at Lodwar to the forested heights of Maralal which was healthier and more convenient to Nairobi and enabled the African leaders to keep in closer touch with him.

immediately he made it clear that he intended to play an active part in politics and would not be content to relax in glory as the father-figure of the Kenya independence movement. He called a meeting of African elected members of all parties and as chairman issued a statement demanding an immediate round-table conference on the constitution and full independence in 1962. At subsequent talks with the British Government, K.A.D.U. grew restive at what they considered were K.A.N.U.'s dictatorial demands and 'arbitrary attitudes' as the majority party. The new party coalition split and Kenyatta showed where his sympathies lay when in October he accepted the Presidency of K.A.N.U. One of the main reasons for the split was the outright rejection by K.A.N.U. of K.A.D.U.'s suggestions for a federal type of constitution. The arch-nationalists Odinga and Mboya could not accept that regional autonomy was necessary to protect minority interests. To them, regionalism was a dilution of independence and an in-built source of strife. On the other hand, to Ngala and Muliro who drew their support from the minority tribes – some of whom laid greater claim to the White Highlands than the Kikuyu – a federal form of constitution would give their supporters more control over such matters as land, education, the police and the composition of the civil service. For the present, Ngala as Leader of Government Business had the power, but he lacked that popular support which is necessary to all politicians if they are to remain in power. Kenyatta, getting himself acclimatised again to the Kenya political scene, was content to await the outcome of the new Constitutional Conference which, as had been agreed at the talks, should take place at Lancaster House in London the following February.

*Chapter 14*

# Uncertainty and *Uhuru*

WHILE THE POLITICIANS manoeuvred for position, and the respective parties strengthened their organisation, the social and economic life of the country continued as best it could in a period of uncertainty. The first African majority election was not the only event of national importance in 1961. The severest drought and famine in the known history of Kenya was followed by devastating and widespread floods. By the end of the year, the cost of relief to the starving and homeless had risen to £5 million and the new Kenya Government was forced to appeal for outside help. The United States stepped in with supplies valued at £3,206,000 and the United Kingdom with financial help totalling £1,502,000, and the free use of British military forces and transport stationed in Kenya. It was Kenya's first real national disaster and everyone suffered, black, white and brown. As a result, there was a general feeling of mutual help between the various communities and this undoubtedly took a certain amount of heat out of the political controversy raging at the time. But the disaster was a severe setback to the economy, still in a state of shock after the Lancaster House Conference of the previous year. There was a general lack of confidence over the future of land rights and the property market had collapsed. The political uncertainty coming at the same time as the Congo troubles had checked the inflow of capital and there was a widespread reduction of investment in both industry and farming. The drift of Europeans and Asians to other countries had begun – the Government had to introduce a system of clearance certificates to secure payment of tax liabilities. The increasing unemployment had been aggravated by the flow of Africans from the reserves to Nairobi and other urban areas, and wages were rising.[1]

---

[1] The average earnings for Africans in 1961 were Shs. 127/– a month compared with Shs. 105/– the year before Lancaster House; but still well under the average of Shs. 885/– for Asians and Shs. 2,417/– for Europeans.

Nevertheless, there were indications that steps were being taken to bolster the economy against the birth-pangs of independence. Work had begun on the construction of an oil refinery at Mombasa – the first in East Africa – and a start was being made on a solution to the unemployment problem. A Government survey of unemployment had stated that the solution lay in the full economic development of the African land units. The swift development in African agriculture under the Swynnerton Plan of 1954[1] had shown its full potential and so the International Bank for Reconstruction and Development had readily offered a loan of £2 million for this purpose. A Land Development and Settlement Board had also been set up with the object of stabilising prices for European-owned farms and offering credit facilities to Africans to purchase land in the White Highlands: financial help totalling £13½ million was given by the British Government, the World Bank and the Colonial Development Corporation, sufficient to settle 20,000 African farmers and buy up a substantial acreage of settler land.

The second Lancaster House Conference met under the chairmanship of Mr Reginald Maudling who had succeeded Macleod as Colonial Secretary. On this occasion, the N.K.P. multi-racialists and the few racial elected members for the reserved European and Asian seats were virtually observers with little influence on the proceedings and concerned mainly outside the Conference with campaigning to safeguard the rights of the minorities in Kenya. The Conference was dominated by the two major parties, the main issue being whether nationalism or regionalism was the best policy for an independent Kenya. For seven weeks the struggle went on between Kenyatta, who had now been elected to Legislative Council through a Nairobi by-election, and Ngala. The result was the usual compromise suggested by the Colonial Office and, by the nature of the divided views of K.A.N.U. and K.A.D.U., a complicated one. There would be a Parliament with an Upper and Lower House – a House of Elected Representatives and a Senate; and six Regional Assemblies. The Senate would be elected from an agreed number of districts and the Regional Assemblies would have rights entrenched in the constitution for which any changes would have to be approved by a 90 per cent vote in the Senate. Both parties agreed to form a

---

[1] The Plan was named after its originator, Mr R. J. M. Swynnerton, an Assistant Director of Agriculture, and aimed at an expenditure of £10.5 million on the intensification of African agricultural development.

coalition to work out the details and present them to a general election in May 1963. On their return to Kenya, K.A.N.U. and K.A.D.U. both claimed victory for their ideas. The complicated constitution possibly favoured K.A.D.U.; but as events in Ghana were proving, constitutions in post-independent countries could be scrapped as easily as they were made and K.A.N.U. were no doubt confident that if they could increase their majority at the forthcoming elections they could form a central government so strong that the Regional Assemblies would be reduced to the level of county councils. As for the Senate, which nobody seemed to like, it would become a servant of the House of Representatives.

The coalition Government in the year that followed the second Lancaster House Conference was an uneasy affair. Kenyatta was made Minister of State for Constitutional Affairs and Economic Planning; and Ngala Minister of State for Constitutional Affairs and Administration. The two rivals were in effect joint leaders and as the portfolios in the Council of Ministers were evenly shared between their supporters, there was a stalemate, and the task of working the Government lay mainly with Renison and his deputy Mr E. N. (later Sir Eric) Griffith-Jones. But at least the two leaders were able to concentrate on organising their parties for the forthcoming elections. Their task was not an easy one. Personal and tribal rivalries were threatening to split both parties and over the country as a whole the people were in a restless mood because of the worsening of the unemployment situation and the delays in handing over of power, while next door both Tanganyika and Uganda were already beginning to enjoy the fruits of independence.

Within K.A.N.U. Kenyatta had yet to establish his complete authority over the party. His personal and almost mystic powers of domination, which he had used with such good effect on the Kikuyu people, were not readily accepted within a party of such conflicting tribal traditions and loyalties. He had to use all his skill as a politician to hold it together, for there was a growing feeling that the Kikuyu were again becoming too dominant. The formation of the underground Kikuyu Land and Freedom Army certainly lent strength to this belief and the Luo, the second largest tribe in the party, threatened to hive off on a political movement of their own. Only by the intervention of Mboya in reaffirming his loyalty to Kenyatta and his belief that the non-tribal approach to nationalism was the sole hope for Kenya's future was the threatened break between the Kikuyu and the Luo avoided. There was, however, a break with an important minority in K.A.N.U., when the Kamba Paul Ngei, one of Kenyatta's former lieutenants who had shared his trial and detention, broke away and formed the African People's Party. The new party had a large measure of support from the Kamba, many of whom shared Ngei's view that K.A.N.U. was for the Kikuyu and the other tribes were only drawn in to give it a national appearance and provide funds.

While K.A.N.U. was able through Kenyatta's leadership and Mboya's organisational ability and flair for public relations to overcome internal squabbles and maintain a national front, K.A.D.U. was less successful in consolidating its position as a ruling party. The Commission appointed after the Lancaster House Conference to delimit the regional and constituency boundaries had exposed rival tribal claims to land and also differences over the choice of regional 'capitals'. Traditional enmities were revived and Ngala's organisation was not strong enough to overcome the disputes between K.A.D.U.'s autonomous tribal associations. As a result, he was unable to find a sufficient number of candidates to stand on a party ticket for all the seats at the election on 28 May.

The elections were a resounding triumph for K.A.N.U. and showed that a national rather than a regional approach was the only way to victory.[1] Despite doubts that the new constituencies favoured K.A.D.U.'s associations, Kenyatta's party and supporters won a clear majority over all other parties and independents as well as two-thirds of the total vote. It swept to power in Nairobi and all the towns except Mombasa and even gained two of the ten Kamba seats from the breakaway A.P.P. The biggest single tribal party, the Baluyha Political Union, was wiped out and its leader, the moderate Musa Amalemba, lost his deposit. Only at the Coast and in the Rift Valley among the pastoral Kalenjin and Masai did K.A.D.U. receive any solid measure of support. But while conceding defeat, Ngala

[1] Results of the elections: to the House of Representatives, K.A.N.U. 67 seats, K.A.D.U. 32 seats, A.P.P. 8 seats and Independents 5 seats; to the Senate, K.A.N.U. 20 seats, K.A.D.U. and A.P.P. 18 seats. In the Regional Assembly elections K.A.N.U. won control of the Central, Nyanza and Eastern regions and K.A.D.U. control of the Coast, Rift Valley and Western regions. There was a total boycott in the North-Eastern region for the 5 seats allocated to it in the House of Representatives and for the elections to the Regional Assembly; this was because of the movement to secede from Kenya and join the newly independent Somalia.

claimed that his party had sufficient seats to maintain the provisions for regionalism in the constitution.

On 1 June 1963, Kenyatta became Kenya's first Prime Minister and was asked to form an administration. The country was now poised for independence with a single-party central Government receiving its strength from a wide measure of popular support. Constitutional devices such as senates and regional assemblies had no place in the one-party state of K.A.N.U.; but they would be swept away as the opposition weakened and finally disintegrated. Kenyatta was now in a position of complete power and he could afford to follow the Churchillian concept of being magnanimous to his defeated enemies. His Government was a nice balance between the old guard and the new. He brought into it men with different tribal backgrounds, and even a European, to show that it was not just a Kikuyu–Luo alliance. As the European settlers and Asian middlemen faded from the political scene, the bitterness of racial strife came to an end. The people of Kenya could now concentrate on building up the economy and a new set of institutions to enable their country to become a strong and independent nation.

*Chapter 15*

# *Harambee*

---

THE ELECTIONS in May 1963 gave Kenya an African Government supported by an overwhelming majority in the National Assembly and fully representative of the people.[1] Kenyatta and his Ministers held the reins of power; but it was not the power promised by the slogan of *Uhuru*. Colonial rule in Kenya, especially now that it had the most complex of constitutions, could not be unwound quickly. Despite the assurance of Mr Malcolm Mac-Donald, who had succeeded Renison as Governor, that the grand aim was independence and that no time would be lost in achieving it, the British Government seemed as reluctant to take the final step as its predecessor had been sixty years earlier to take over the protection of that 'sterile region' known as the highway to Uganda. It was believed that the retention of a Governor and British authority over defence and foreign affairs for an indefinite period would give the constitution a chance to work, and time for the new Kenya Government to solve the many internal problems before embarking on ventures outside its capabilities. This was unacceptable to the new leaders, for they were adamant that they and the people would not be satisfied with anything less than an African Government fully responsible for its own affairs at home and abroad.

Active support for an immediate granting of independence came from neighbouring Tanganyika and Uganda. The Prime Ministers of both these newly independent countries had since January been urging the British Government to remove the last remaining colonial ties from Kenya. They claimed that without a fully independent Kenya the East Africa Common Services Organisation could not work effectively and that federation of the three territories would be delayed. Within a few days of the formation of Kenya's new Govern-

---

[1] The Constituency Delimitation Commission had extended the number of seats in the National Assembly to take account of a revised estimate of the total population: 8,676,000 based on a 3 per cent growth since the 1962 census. *Cmnd. 1921* (1963).

ment, Nyerere of Tanganyika and Obote of Uganda had arrived in Nairobi for 'little summit' talks with Kenyatta. In a statement after the meeting, the three Prime Ministers said they had agreed to establish a federation 'this year' and expected the British Government to grant independence to Kenya immediately. They recognised the value of working together within E.A.C.S.O. (East Africa Common Services Organisation) and a common market, and that the scope for 'further joint action' remained wide. A round-table conference would be held in Dar-es-Salaam in August and in the meantime a working party representative of the three territories would work out details.

As Minister for Constitutional Affairs, Mboya was sent to London to press for early independence on the strength of the Nairobi agreement. He expressed on his arrival confidence in the 'rapid formation' of an East Africa Federation. The three Governments could not, he said, ask the Credentials Committee in New York to wait beyond the middle of December, otherwise East Africa would be out of the United Nations for a 'lengthy period'. Following Mboya's visit, the Commonwealth Secretary, Mr Duncan Sandys, who had taken over responsibility for the dwindling number of British colonies, announced in the Commons that Independence Day for Kenya would be 12 December 1963, preceded by a conference in London in September to settle the final form of the constitution. He declared that Her Majesty's Government had chosen these dates having taken into account the intention of the three Governments to set up an East Africa Federation. The British Government supported fully the initiative taken by the East Africa Governments and would do all it could to facilitate the early implementation of this aim.

Sir Geoffrey de Freitas, the British High Commissioner in Ghana, who was appointed High Commissioner to Kenya, remarked on his arrival later in the year that the appointment was 'intended for Federation'. In the event, there was no federation in 1963. Nor was there a conference in Dar-es-Salaam: differences over the siting of a federal capital, the question of a single- or a two-chamber legislature, the granting of East African citizenship and the division of power between the Federal and State Governments in foreign affairs being given as the reasons. Although Obote had declared publicly in London 'we want an understandably East African policy', there had been evidence of apprehension almost from the beginning of the discussions on federation. Obote was having trouble enough of his own in trying to forge a unified nation out of his four autonomous kingdoms which were opposed to federalism in any form, though in effect they were federal states under the new Uganda constitution. He was also in a weak parliamentary position in his multi-party National Assembly and, at that time, increasingly under the influence of Ghana's President Nkrumah, who viewed the possibility of an East Africa Federation with Kenyatta at its head as a threat to his own self-appointed position as the leader of the Pan-Africa movement. Nyerere was also said to be having second thoughts, and so once more the plans for closer union were put on the shelf indefinitely.

Nevertheless, the federation campaign, in so far as Kenya was concerned, had served its purpose in forcing the British Government to grant independence sooner than was intended. Although it was subsequently denied as misleading, a report of a speech by Kenyatta confirmed the impression that the pace of the campaign had been deliberately forced by Obote and Nyerere to help their neighbour to achieve independence that year. Kenyatta was reported to have said to a rally at Kisumi that the call for federation by the end of 1963 had been purely a ruse to speed Kenya's independence and that 'we are now proceeding without haste'. It was not till August 1964 that there was any outward sign of British disapproval. De Freitas resigned because, he said, of East Africa's failure to form a federation. However important and interesting the job of High Commissioner to Kenya was, it was not the one he had come out to do.

The first few months of self-governing Kenya were a testing time for Kenyatta. He had to prove that he was not only a skilful politician, but also a leader who could weld his team of comparatively inexperienced Ministers into an effective Government. His younger colleagues were enthusiastic and filled with fervour for the cause of African nationalism, but this was no substitute for the expertise and experience required of the sophisticated Government machine they had inherited. Kenyatta showed that he was well aware of this when he told an audience of 400 European settlers at Nakuru that what the Kenya Government most needed was experience, and that he would 'grab it with both hands from whatever quarter it came'.

This meeting in the 'capital' of the former White Highlands was presided over by Lord Delamere, the farming son of Kenya's most illustrious settler. It took place in a hall which had been the setting for many a gathering of angry settlers. Now, it was providing a platform for the settlers' 'arch-enemy'. At the start Kenyatta's audience was silent and suspicious, but they warmed to him when he declared that like them he was a farmer and had a feeling for the land. He appealed for mutual forgiveness for past wrongs and he was frank, showing none of the ambivalence of previous years when addressing public meetings: 'Ask me any questions you like. Don't worry about embarrassing Kenyatta.' He told the packed meeting that white, black and brown must work together to make Kenya great and, addressing himself directly to his audience, he said, 'We want you to stay and co-operate with us. Let us join hands and work together for the betterment of Kenya.' Although the farmers rose to Kenyatta and gave him a standing ovation with shouts of *Harambee! Harambee!*, they were under no illusions.[1] Kenyatta was no multi-racialist and his conciliatory mood was no sign of weakness. Like all Kikuyu he was essentially a realist, and he knew that for the present, and for some years to come, he could not run the economy without the European farmers and businessmen. Kenyatta's authority over the country was unquestioned, but he had behind him men who were still bitter and for whom Kenya was a country for black Africans and for nobody else. Kenyatta was strong enough to trounce his own back-benchers in the National Assembly and tell them that he would keep his white officials as long as they were efficient and competent Africans were lacking; yet a time would come when pressure for complete Africanisation in government, land and business would be too great even for Kenyatta to withstand.

For the time being, the European settler was absolutely essential to the economy as Kenya's wealth was wholly agricultural. Rainfall and soil conditions allowed intensive production over a fifth of the country—about 41,600 square miles. African agriculture occupied 34,000 sq. miles, the rest was farmed by Europeans. The settler produced 80 per cent of Kenya's exports, which in 1962 were worth £38 million, and disbursed about £10 million in wages. Kenyatta knew that he could not upset the balance of an already shaky economy. He also knew that even if he had the money to buy out all the settlers, the fact that each square mile of European farming produced £4,150 as against £1,180 from African farming would

[1] *Harambee!* is the Swahili word for 'togetherness' and had become Kenyatta's rallying call to the people of Kenya to work together to build a new nation.

have been enough to deter him from forcing any sudden change in
the settlers' position. Europeans were leaving Kenya at the rate of
700 a month and the country could not for long afford such a drain
on its management manpower and capital resources. Hence, Kenyatta's mood of conciliation was based on economic good sense: the
settlers had lost their political power, but as long as they were able
to remain on their farms they were part of Kenya's future. They
had to be protected and although sceptical after the Nakuru meeting
the settlers in turn knew that in Kenyatta they had, surprisingly, a
powerful ally and protector.

Kenya was in a difficult economic position during the change-
over to internal self-government. The Finance Minister James
Gichuru showed that he was fully aware of the problems and did
not mince his words when he declared that Kenya was bankrupt.
There was a deficit in the Budget of £2,500,000 and the prospect of
an increase in public expenditure by the same amount over the next
two years. Steps had been taken, however, to put the country in a
better financial position. The Economy Commission had produced
recommendations which were expected to cut Central Government
expenditure and save some £7 million over three years. Britain, still
the main source of economic aid, had promised £8 million for
general development and more financial help for the million-acre
settlement scheme to bring it up to £20 million. Nevertheless, Kenya
was desperately short of capital and it was going to take some time
before there was sufficient confidence in the new African Government for overseas investors to renew their interest in the country.
A mission from the International Bank for Reconstruction and
Development, which had spent three months in Kenya studying the
economy, said in its report that £56 million must be spent in economic development over the next four years.[1] The mission reaffirmed
that Kenya would still have to depend on its agriculture, but was
doubtful about its future and called for a considerable effort to be
put in to prevent a rundown in the economy. They advocated a
clear statement towards private investment, including reassurances
about interference by the State with private undertakings, and freedom to transfer earnings and repatriate original capital.

Self-governing Kenya had the powers to deal with the economic

[1] The Economic Development of Kenya: Report of an Economic Survey
Commission of the International Bank for Reconstruction and Development
(Oxford University Press, 1963).

problems of the change-over from colonial to home rule, but the nature of the new constitution prevented Kenyatta from dealing with a problem which threatened the security of his country's north-east frontier and a large proportion of its total land area. The North-Eastern region – the seventh of the new regions – was formed out of the old Northern Frontier District and covers 102,000 square miles: it has a population of about 200,000, mostly groups of wandering, pastoral tribes. The border with Somalia and Ethiopia is the arbitrary line drawn by the Great Powers in the scramble for Africa in the late nineteenth century and bears little relation to traditional tribal grazing areas. There is constant movement across this frontier which, because of the semi-desert nature of the country and complete lack of roads, is practically impossible to administer. The whole region has been a closed area for some years in view of the continual inter-tribal lawlessness and, as such, has been insulated from the rest of Kenya. But when the movement towards self-government was showing signs of success, there were first heard demands for secession of the N.F.D. from Kenya; and for the region to have a period under British authority in which to build up a machinery of government so that it could join with the neighbouring Somali Republic as a self-governing unit. In December 1962, a Commission of Inquiry reported that the people in the area adjoining the Somali border were unanimously in favour of secession: the rest in the other areas wished to remain part of Kenya and to participate in its constitutional development. Although the Commission found in the course of the inquiry that the various ethnological types of people in the region were 'consistently courteous and good-humoured' in the great interest they showed, feelings between the rival parties ran high.[1] The Somali and half-Somalis who supported secession made up 62 per cent of the total population and were the most vociferous in their demands. They had engineered a boycott of the May elections and as a result, no representatives were elected to the National and Regional Assemblies. The attack by several hundred Somalis on the polling booth at the administrative headquarters at Isiolo, in which several people were killed when the police opened fire, was the only sign of serious trouble in the country as a whole during the elections. Later, thirty-three Somali chiefs resigned their appointments and the stage was set for a head-on clash between the secessionists and the new Government.

[1] *Cmnd. 1900* (1962).

Kenyatta had made it clear that 'not an inch' of Kenya would be given up to Somalia, but during the protracted discussions on the secession issue his Government was barred from any direct approach to the Somali Republic, which was actively supporting the secessionists. Until Kenya attained full independence, defence and foreign affairs were matters for the British Government. The situation was complicated further by Somalia breaking off diplomatic relations with Britain over the issue. This did not, however, prevent talks taking place on neutral ground in Rome, although the Kenya representatives were in the anomalous position of being observers. The talks failed and the Somali chiefs, together with the secessionist Northern Province People's Progressive Party, threatened to take the law into their own hands if demands for secession were not met. The situation deteriorated rapidly and in December a State of Emergency was declared throughout the Northern region. A prohibited zone five miles wide was proclaimed along the 400-mile border with Somalia to stop raiders invading Kenya territory and a defence pact signed with Ethiopia as a further barrier to the Greater Somalia movement. The defence of the Northern region from Somali aggression would occupy a substantial part of Kenya's military resources as Kenyatta had declared himself willing to go to any lengths to protect Kenya's northern frontier, even if it was a legacy of the imperial past. The Northern region is a geographical barrier of great strategic importance to Kenya, and the possibility of finding oil and other natural resources within its desert waste can never be discounted.

The Somali separatist movement in the north was time-consuming and created defence problems for the new Kenya Government, but more serious from the point of view of political security were the activities of the K.A.D.U. Opposition. Although K.A.N.U. had received confirmation of its wide support by victories in the local government elections in September, Ngala's party was still a formidable political force and had taken advantage of every opportunity to harass the Government. Kenyatta was therefore obliged to issue a firm warning that negative and destructive tactics could quickly lead to the destruction of rights and privileges of the Opposition itself. This statement confirmed in Ngala's mind that the Government was intent on destroying his party, but Kenyatta's warning did not deter him from walking out of preliminary constitutional talks in Nairobi and refusing to discuss basic changes to the agreements

made at the second Lancaster House Conference. His argument was
that there had been adequate discussions at the Conference and if
further changes were needed then negotiations would have to begin
all over again. But Sandys and Kenyatta had both agreed that there
should be another conference to settle the final form of Kenya's
constitution before independence, and Ngala, who was no longer in
a position to dictate events, was forced to attend in the knowledge
that Kenyatta had made no pretence that he did not like the present
constitution and would do everything possible to amend it to the
'requirements of a unitary state'. The third and final Lancaster
House Conference opened therefore in London in September 1963
on an 'acrimonious and belligerent note'.

The complex nature of the Kenya constitution, which was neither
unitary nor federal, was, as Sandys pointed out to the Conference,
the result of inter-party bargaining rather than of any objective
planning, and seven long weeks of crisis and threats of breakdown
followed the opening plenary session as the Kenya Government
and its Opposition faced each other in a bitter clash of ideals. The
Government based its case for amendments on the section of the
constitution which said 'there should be a strong and effective
Central Government'. On the other hand, the Opposition based
their case on the section which said 'there should be the maximum
possible decentralisation of the powers of Government to effective
authorities capable of a life and significance of their own'. However,
Sandys no doubt recognised that although the Opposition K.A.D.U.
party had about equal strength with K.A.N.U. in the regions, the
Government party had a two-thirds majority in the House of
Representatives and was firmly in control at the centre.[1] As a result,

---

[1] Controlling parties in Regional Assemblies and estimated populations:

| K.A.N.U. | | K.A.D.U. | |
|---|---|---|---|
| Eastern: | 1,560,000 | Coast: | 1,020,000 |
| Central: | 1,334,000 | Western: | 1,010,000 |
| Nyanza: | 1,638,000 | Rift Valley: | 1,776,000 |
| | 4,532,000 | | 3,806,000 |

In the National Assembly 11 of the 12 specially elected members supported
K.A.N.U. Ngei had rejoined K.A.N.U. taking with him the eight seats of his
African People's Party; so at the time of the constitutional talks in September
the line-up of the parties in the National Assembly was as follows:

| K.A.N.U. | | K.A.D.U. | |
|---|---|---|---|
| House of Representatives: | 91 | House of Representatives: | 32 |
| Senate: | 20 | Senate: | 16 |

Kenyatta's views prevailed and the constitutional amendments eventually proposed were much in line with K.A.N.U.'s demands.

The framework of the 1962 constitution had set out in elaborate detail distribution of police control between the central Government and the regions. Now, the whole system was to be simplified with centralised power over staffing and operations exercised by a National Security Council through its chief executive, the Inspector-General of Police. Further, instead of eight separate Public Service Commissions for each region and Nairobi, there would only be one Commission applying common qualifications and standards throughout Kenya, thereby avoiding any question of local patronage in Government employment. The constitution could also be altered by a two-thirds majority in a nation-wide referendum if the National Assembly failed to obtain that majority at the second and third readings of a Bill. This latter amendment was the most controversial, as except for some basic entrenched rights which still needed a 75 per cent majority in the House of Representatives and 90 per cent in the Senate, the Government, with its overwhelming popular support, could change the whole character of the constitution if it so wished.

Ngala showed his feelings about the proposed amendments when he threatened to go back to Kenya and form a separate, breakaway state out of the Rift Valley, Western and Coast regions. But wisely he stayed on in London and by leading his delegation in a boycott of the final plenary session of the Conference was able to register his protest in a constitutional manner. He maintained that the British Government had gone back on previous assurances and he accused Sandys of dishonesty: 'The British Government will have to use their arms in Kenya to uphold their dishonour.' The greater control of the police by the central Government was seen by him as a means of 'destroying the Opposition'.

By contrast, Kenyatta was at his most conciliatory. Although his dislike of regionalism had not changed, he promised to transfer to the Regional Assemblies 'with all possible speed' the departments and services still remaining to be handed over under the terms of the constitution. Kenyatta also gave an assurance on Arab rights in return for a pronouncement by the Sultan of Zanzibar that he would renounce all claims to financial compensation and would relinquish sovereignty over the coastal strip from the date of independence. When he addressed a huge welcoming crowd of 150,000 after his return to Nairobi from the Conference, Kenyatta appealed to the

Opposition for a united front against the 'real enemies' of poverty, disease and ignorance. He said K.A.N.U. had not been struggling at Lancaster House 'one African against another', but to 'redeem our country from the yoke of colonialism and imperialism and to be able to build a Kenya that Africans could be proud of'.

It was an indication of the unpredictability of Kenya politics that at this last of the Constitutional Conferences, the four Europeans, representatives of a once-powerful settler community, should have supported K.A.N.U. throughout and that their leader, the reactionary Mr L. R. MacConochie Welwood, a former Minister and Kenya Coalition supporter, should have paid tribute to the 'good work' being done by Kenyatta: 'Many Europeans who had thought of leaving Kenya were now deciding to stay.'

Ngala, who had by now given up all thoughts of a separatist K.A.D.U. Republic, announced on his return that from henceforth he would rely on the Government's promise to implement the regional constitution. He denied that his party would join the Government, though shortly after the Conference two K.A.D.U. members crossed the floor of the House of Representatives, thereby indicating that the collapse of the two-party system in Kenya had begun.

As Kenya prepared for Independence Day, the London *Times* reported on 31 October that with independence six weeks away one of the sacred *mugumo* (fig) trees of the Kikuyu seemed doomed. The tribe's most famous witch doctor, Mugo Kibiru, had prophesied seventy years ago that the tree, which stood near the settler town of Thika, would fall down on the day of their independence. According to the *Times* correspondent, the tree was already rotting and showed every sign of falling down.[1] Seven years earlier another sacred fig tree is reported to have fallen of its own accord shortly after the capture of the Mau Mau leader Dedan Kimathi.[2]

The tattered remnants of Kimathi's 'Parliament Forces' had chosen to remain in the forest after his capture and were absorbed into the resurgent 'Kikuyu Land Freedom Army'. This body of outlaws was a potential threat to whatever Government was in

[1] Mugo Kibiru is also credited with having prophesied the coming of the railway: 'The iron snake with many legs like an earthworm.'

[2] Ian Henderson, Kimathi's captor, records a conversation in April 1956 with Kingori, Mau Mau's leading witch doctor, in which he said Kimathi would be captured in the 'tenth month before the rains for the millet planting begin'. Kimathi's favourite prayer-tree fell the following October after his capture. Henderson and Goodhart, *The Hunt for Kimathi*, p. 115.

power and Kenyatta, in accordance with his policy of conciliation, offered an amnesty and promise that their leaders would be given an honoured place at the Independence Day celebrations. A formal surrender was therefore held at Nyeri, attended by Kenyatta and all his Ministers, and as the 'freedom fighters' came out of the forest to offer their allegiance to the new African Government of Kenya they were given a 'heroes' welcome'.[1] Kenyatta had also promised an amnesty for 5,000 political and criminal prisoners, including leaders of the banned Land Freedom Army and hard-core Mau Mau. This acceptance of Mau Mau as heroes shocked the European community, resigned as they now were to most of the changes taking place in Kenya; but their views were of little account. The Government showed its disregard for the feelings of settlers on the eve of Independence Day when Delamere's statue was removed from the centre of Nairobi and when Delamere Avenue, the city's main thoroughfare, was renamed Kenyatta Avenue.

Heavy rains threatened to mar the Independence Day celebrations, but nothing could have dampened the enthusiasm of the 250,000 crowd which packed the specially-built stadium on the outskirts of Nairobi to witness the end of colonial rule. The Union Jack which had flown over Kenya for sixty-eight years was lowered at midnight on 11 December 1963 and a great roar of joy went up as the black, red and green flag of Kenya was raised in its place. Distinguished representatives from all over the world, including Russia, China and the United States, were at the ceremony and as the Duke of Edinburgh on behalf of Queen Elizabeth II handed over to Kenyatta the constitutional instruments of independence, Kenya became a full independent member of the British Commonwealth of Nations.[2]

Colonialism in Kenya had now come to an end, and Kenyatta was generous in his tributes to the former overlords:

'We do not forget the assistance and guidance we have received through the years from people of British stock. Administrators,

[1] Although it was estimated that before the Nyeri ceremony, which had been well publicised, 500 freedom fighters remained in the forest, 1,500 had surrendered by the end of the year. There were suspicions that the generous compensation terms and grants of land offered had persuaded a number of Kikuyu to enter the forest and re-emerge as freedom fighters.

[2] The Royal Lodge, built by Mitchell as a wedding present for the Queen and the Duke of Edinburgh, was returned to Kenya in the form of an Independence gift to Kenyatta.

businessmen, farmers, missionaries and many others. Our law, our
system of government and many other aspects of our daily lives
are founded on British principles and justice and the ties between
our two countries now that we move into a new relationship as
two sovereign countries within the Commonwealth will be
strengthened.'[1]

Kenyatta did not, however, let the opportunity of world-wide
interest in Kenya independence go by without an appeal for help
from overseas. Nation-building, he said, was not an easy task and
Kenya needed co-operation from overseas investors and technicians
to help build a stronger and more prosperous economy: 'To our
overseas friends we offer a stable political environment and expanding market in Kenya and East Africa.' But it was Kenyatta the
politician speaking when he declared at the ceremony that Kenya
would not really be free until the whole of Africa was liberated. It
would be Kenya's duty to help with the liberation of South Africa
and the Portuguese territories in every possible way. And he had a
warning for his own people: 'The fact that the Imperialist Government is dead does not mean that the people can do as they please.
There will still be police and there will still be prisoners.'[2]

[1] *The Times*, 12 December 1963.
[2] A story current in Kenya at this time is a good indication of what independence meant to the less worldly Kenya citizen. African lorry drivers are
noted for their carefree driving and are constantly in trouble with the police.
When one of them was asked by an overseas reporter what independence
meant to him he replied: 'Oh, now I can drive on any side of the road I
like!'

*Chapter 16*

# Independence and Unity

---

THE FIRST MONTHS of independent Kenya could have seen the end of Kenyatta and of parliamentary rule. In 1964, Africa was in a ferment. All over the continent a mood of reaction was setting in: newly-independent peoples were becoming restless under the autocratic rule of their new Governments; and the call for Pan-African unity was being ignored in the struggle for power among the new nations. The first hint of trouble came from Zanzibar where a force of 600 revolutionaries under the command of 'Field-Marshal' John Okello, a Uganda-born Mau Mau fighter from Kenya, overthrew the Government in a lightning revolution. The Sultan and Prime Minister were forced to flee the island and later 400 Arabs were packed on to dhows and sent back to Arabia. Members of the new revolutionary Government had been Communist-trained, and from the recent activities of the Russian and Chinese embassies in the East African territories it seemed that this sudden revolution was aimed at procuring a Communist foothold in Africa and for the Island of Zanzibar to become another Cuba.

Across on the mainland the spirit of unrest had spread to Tanganyika where two battalions of the once-proud King's African Rifles mutinied against their officers and for two anxious days it seemed that Nyerere's Government was in danger of being overthrown. But although there were riots and looting in Dar-es-Salaam, leaving twelve dead and 100 wounded, Nyerere, who had disappeared during the trouble, succeeded in restoring calm by appealing to the country to eliminate the 'national disgrace' caused by the mutinous soldiers. There was, however, a chain reaction to the mutiny throughout East Africa. The King's African Rifles had been disbanded and the territorial battalions for Kenya, Uganda and Tanganyika formed into national armies, but there remained a strong feeling of unity among the African soldiers. Up to now they had been spectators of the advance of their respective countries

182

towards independence, and when around them they saw others, mainly the politicians, benefiting from the newly-won power, there was a natural feeling of resentment that the army had been forgotten. The mutiny therefore spread to Uganda and then to Kenya, and only the intervention of British troops, who had been called in by Obote and Kenyatta, prevented a revolt and the overthrow of their Governments. It was fortunate that the mutinies were inept affairs, for the African soldier, though highly trained, had still to learn to act without his British officers. Political agitators were alleged to have sparked off the mutinies, but it seems that the reasons for them were mainly dissatisfaction at the low level of pay and conditions, and a desire for a share in the fruits of *Uhuru*. The mutinies were, however, a warning, and immediate steps were taken to introduce better conditions and prospects for promotion within the national armies and police forces. The three East African Governments had the political power, but they had yet to learn to control the power of the gun on which depended their security and the strength with which to govern. British troops would not always be so conveniently at hand or be willing to intervene. Neither could the newly-independent Governments afford, as Nyerere put it, the national humiliation of using outside forces to suppress their own people. Kenyatta was not quite so reluctant as his neighbours to accept outside help and in March he signed a defence agreement with Britain.

Kenya's security continued to be threatened by the troubles along the Somalia border. Relations with the Somalia Republic had deteriorated and in February 1964 the State of Emergency in the Northern region was extended. Politically, the region was quiet. Three members had been returned unopposed to the National Assembly in a voteless election after the Government had promised to provide £300,000 for development, but Somalia had stepped up the raids across the frontier to establish her rights to the region. Kenya was, in effect, at war with Somalia and most of the army was stationed along the frontier. Britain, which was also in a state of conflict with Somalia, helped Kenya with supporting forces and services, but the cost of the campaign, together with the promised development programme, was an added strain to an already burdened economy. The region was impossible to defend in any depth and raids by guerilla forces from across the frontier reached as far south as Marsabit, Isiolo and Lamu. A Northern Frontier Liberation movement was formed in Somalia and daily from Mogadishu there poured out a continuous stream of hate against Kenya. There were demands by the Kenya National Assembly for invasion and a direct confrontation with Somalia; but Kenyatta, the leading voice of Pan-African unity, resisted pressure to extend the war beyond Kenya's frontiers. He still believed in a peaceful solution and on 12 December 1965 he met the Somalia President, Adan Abdulla Osman, in Arusha. Nyerere acted as mediator, but although the raids continued. By the following year it was estimated that 1,700 Somalis had been killed and that the dispute was costing Kenya £3 million a year. A second attempt was made, therefore, to end the dispute, this time by the Organisation of African Unity with President Kaunda of Zambia as mediator. The attempt was successful and on 29 October 1967 President Kenyatta of Kenya and Prime Minister Ibrahim Egal of Somalia signed a memorandum of agreement to cease fighting, resume diplomatic relations and encourage trade. They also agreed to the gradual suspension of emergency regulations on both sides and to the establishment of a committee comprising Kenya, Somalia and Zambia to 'seek satisfactory solutions of the differences between the two nations'.

As with the Somalia dispute, the federation of the East African territories was a recurrent theme in the years following independence. When the Duke of Edinburgh delivered the speech from the throne at the State Opening of Kenya's first independent Parliament, he declared that the immediate aim of the Government was political union with Uganda, Tanganyika and Zanzibar as a major step towards African unity. The issue blew hot and cold as Nyerere, who had formed on 27 April 1964 his own federation of Tanzania, the United Republic of Tanganyika and Zanzibar, announced that he wanted to withdraw from E.A.C.S.O. Nyerere threatened to impose tariff barriers as he claimed that Tanzania was suffering economic disadvantages because of the uncertainty created by the long talks, and that a bigger share of foreign aid and new investment was going to Kenya and Uganda. The relations between the three countries were not improved when a convoy of lorries from Tanzania, and loaded with Chinese arms, was intercepted as it entered south-west Kenya *en route* to Uganda. The personnel were arrested and Kenyatta declared that the incident was a violation of territorial integrity. Tanzania and Uganda members walked out of a meeting of the Central Legislative Assembly in protest, but after

Obote had flown to Nairobi with two of his Ministers to apologise personally to Kenyatta, the incident was closed and the convoy was released to continue its journey to Uganda.

Despite the evidence that all three countries were preparing to go their own ways, talks continued in Kampala, Nairobi and Dar-es-Salaam. Agreement was reached on the geographical siting of new industries common to the three territories through a permanent committee and the three Premiers were apparently still thinking in terms of closer union and Pan-African Unity when they invited President Kaunda of Zambia to join them in talks on an extension of the East African Common Market. But by June 1965 Nyerere had lost patience and, reiterating his concern about Tanzania's economic difficulties, imposed exchange and import controls and set up his own central bank and currency: Kenya and Uganda were forced to follow with their own monetary systems and controls. This was seen as the virtual end to the hopes for closer union, yet two months later the East African Presidents were meeting again in Kampala. Although they emerged from the meeting 'happy and smiling' and declaring that they still desired stronger links with each other, no decisions were taken and the talks were adjourned for ten days. It was then announced on 1 September that a nine-member Commission of Ministers from Kenya, Uganda and Tanzania would inquire into the whole future of the East African Common Market. There would be an independent chairman and the Heads of State had agreed to abide by the Commission's recommendations.[1] By the end of 1966, the Commission's report, which it was agreed should not be made public, was still under discussion and a final meeting of Ministers in Dar-es-Salaam failed to agree on a treaty for submission to their Governments. Thus it appeared that Kenya, Uganda and Tanzania would continue to go their own political and economic ways, and that the prospect of an East African Federation was very remote. But on 6 June 1967, with little warning, the three Presidents were in Kampala putting their signatures to a 15-year treaty of economic co-operation.[2] There was, however, no mention of political federation.

Kenya's internal difficulties were not lessened by the Act of Independence and the introduction of a workable constitution.

[1] The Chairman appointed was Professor Kjeld Philip, a Danish economist from the United Nations.
[2] Appendix 1: East Africa Common Services.

Confidence in the ability of the new Government to govern and to
find a solution to the acute economic problems had yet to be earned.
In February 1964, unemployment had risen to such a high level –
10 per cent of the total labour force of 500,000 – that the Government was forced to take the initiative. After a tripartite agreement
with the parties concerned, legislation was introduced to enable the
Government to take up 15 per cent more labour in return for a
10 per cent increase by employers in their labour force, and a
guarantee by the trade unions on a strike ban and the acceptance of
a wage freeze. Although it was estimated that the new agreement
would find work for 50,000 more employees, the employment situation deteriorated and in September there were mass demonstrations
of unemployed in Nairobi. Kenyatta spoke again of a return to the
land as a solution of the unemployment problem, though the settlement of landless Africans in the former White Highlands was proceeding slowly.

At the end of 1964, two and a half million acres of the Highlands
remained to be settled, but the first million-acre settlement scheme
had not been a great success and agricultural production from the
land taken over had fallen. The Government now had proof that too
great a fragmentation of the land would disrupt the farming
economy and that the need was for sizeable and efficiently-run
farming units. There was also a shortage of capital for settlement
and so a brake was applied to the various ambitious schemes that
had been put forward. Furthermore there was the political problem
of the thousands of illegal Kikuyu squatters who had settled on
European-owned farms and whose lack of respect for the law had
created a security risk. The Government promised to evict them to
make way for the official settlement schemes, and this aggravated
the problems of satisfying the hunger for land that is inherent in the
character of all African people. Kenya has a low density population
to the square mile and theoretically each head of the African population could have something in the region of ten acres of land. But
over half the total land area is semi-desert and practically unin-
habitable, and the usable land is concentrated in a comparatively
small area of the country where population pressures are acute: the
density is as high as 792 to the square mile in the most populated
part of the Central province. Wholesale grants of land can never be
a solution to the unemployment problem in Kenya. The only answer
is the more productive use of the land and the industrialisation of

the economy. For this Kenya needs a substantial flow of investment from overseas.

An attempt to solve the conflicting political and economic problems facing Kenya was made in the Government White Paper *African Socialism and its Application to Planning in Kenya* published on 27 April 1965. It was presented by Mboya as Minister of Economic Planning and the policies outlined were based on his highly individual interpretation of African socialism. He endeavoured to apply to economic planning what was 'relevant and good' in African customs. Communal or co-operative ownership of land was preferable to outright nationalisation, though this did not prevent direct Government ownership where necessary in the national interest. Nor did it prevent private investment provided it was encouraged and 'to some extent' guided by the Government. In all, the theme of African socialism as interpreted by Mboya is one of moderation and advocates a course half-way between the demands of the Kenya nationalist for undiluted black power and the requirements of the overseas investor for stable economic conditions.

Kenya was now a republic and a one-party state. The 1963 constitution had lasted exactly a year and its end was the result of a complete change in the political picture. Kenyatta's Government had, despite the many problems it faced, adapted itself very quickly to the needs of the country. As Kenyatta himself said, the faint hearts who had forecast internal strife soon after independence had failed to understand the energy and self-reliance that would emerge 'once the talents and ambitions of the people had been unshackled'. It was noticeable in the National Assembly that the K.A.D.U. Opposition had changed feelings about the Government as members began to trickle across the floor of the house. In June, Kenyatta had announced that Kenya would become a republic at the end of the year and that the regional constitution would be scrapped. This caused Ngala to accuse Kenyatta of setting up a dictatorship more worthy of the Middle Ages than twentieth-century Africa; but five months later he was to dissolve K.A.D.U. and join the Government party thereby losing his position as paid leader of the Opposition. The cynics said that if Ngala had not taken this step he would have found himself the only man in his party left on the Opposition benches of the House of Representatives, for the trickle of his supporters crossing the floor had turned into a flood. Nevertheless,

Ngala's announcement on 10 November was greeted with great jubilation and he was carried shoulder-high across the floor of the House to the Government benches. Asked to explain his change of heart he said, 'This is one of the times when we must be prepared to sacrifice our political dignity for the peace and harmony of Kenya.' It was indeed an admission that the 'dictatorship' of the one-party state is perhaps the only way of harnessing the people of a developing country like Kenya to the national effort and that the Westminster pattern of parliamentary government with a paid Opposition is out of place in present-day Africa.

Kenya was declared a Republic within the Commonwealth at midnight on 11 December 1964 on the first anniversary of independence and in the same vast stadium on the outskirts of Nairobi. Kenyatta, now President of a one-party unitary State and supported by an executive Cabinet responsible to Parliament, had carried out his promise of scrapping the regional constitution and had created Provincial Councils out of the Regional Assemblies: he had now reached the pinnacle of his ambitions. He told the crowd of many thousands at the Republic Day celebrations that the kind of unity that had been built in Kenya could offer a new philosophy and 'a practical challenge to a world wrapped in deadlock and whose proudest boast was to annihilate mankind'. But within his own party, among his closest associates, ideological differences were already threatening the unity that Kenya had achieved so quickly.

The differences arose out of the old rivalries between Odinga and Mboya, and their interpretation of African socialism.[1] Odinga, with his Communist background, favoured outright nationalisation in economic planning and revolutionary methods of attaining it. He had little patience with Mboya's moderation and for the need to retain the confidence of foreign investors. He did not attempt to hide his Communist beliefs: 'Communism is food for me' he was to declare. Nor did he hide the strengths of his contacts with Russia and China. As Minister for Home Affairs he had not hesitated to deport well-known Kenya Europeans as part of his 'clearing-out

[1] Another cause of rivalry between the two men was their separate campaigns to send Kenya students overseas for university training. Odinga received substantial Communist funds to send students to Eastern Europe and China. Mboya was African Director of the Afro-American Students Foundation and in 1959 received 100,000 dollars from the Kennedy Foundation, the first of many gifts to airlift Kenya students to America.

process of ill-intentioned imperialist remnants'. Not only was he at odds with Mboya on the tenets of African socialism, but his publicly-expressed sympathies were also at odds with Kenyatta's strict policy of positive neutrality and non-alignment with nations outside Africa.

When Odinga was appointed the new Republic's Vice-President, Kenyatta was said to have failed to grasp the nettle, for in the eyes of the people Odinga was heir-apparent and only second in importance to Kenyatta himself. But Odinga carried great weight within the party. His position among the powerful Luo was, apparently, unassailable and although Kenyatta was now finding Odinga more than an embarrassment he could not afford to demote him or fail to give him a position of prestige. So he made Odinga his deputy. It was, however, a post with little executive power. Odinga lost his influential department of Home Affairs and was made responsible for the National Assembly, Africanisation, training, elections, public holidays, reception of visitors, the National Fund and terms of service for Ministers. For Odinga this was a heavy blow as he had used his former office to advance his own interests in the country at the expense of his close rivals Mboya and Gichuru. Yet he did not rest on his disappointment and with no department to run he had more time for intrigue.

The Lumumba Institute for African Socialism, built in Nairobi with Russian money to train K.A.N.U. party workers, taught Communist doctrines and was run by Bildad Kaggia, one of Kenyatta's lieutenants in the old K.A.U. days, but now an ardent supporter of Odinga. Achieng Oneko, the Minister of Information, was another supporter and through these two men Odinga was able to make his influence felt. There were rumours of a discovery by the Government of an arms-smuggling ring inspired by Odinga and financed by Communist sources. Nothing was ever publicly admitted and the Government was reluctant to give any information except to say that the reports were false. But speculation increased when on 29 April Kenyatta turned back a shipload of arms – a gift from Russia – on the grounds that the arms were out of date and of little use to the Kenya army. In May, concern was expressed in the National Assembly at the activities of the Lumumba Institute, and the Government introduced legislation to bring it under control. In June, Kenyatta declared publicly that Kenya would 'not have communism' and replaced Odinga as head of the Kenya delegation

to the Commonwealth Prime Ministers' Conference by the Foreign
Minister Joseph Murumbi. In July, former students of the
Lumumba Institute, which was now threatened with closure because
of lack of funds, marched on the K.A.N.U. offices in Nairobi and
after breaking their way in demanded replacement of all party
officers except Kenyatta and Odinga. The ringleaders were arrested
and at the trial the affair was alleged to have been an attempted
*coup d'état*. Again Odinga was seen as the master-mind, but nothing
was ever proved. More serious was the circulation of a pamphlet
published by the 'Peoples' Front of East Africa', a Communist
organisation based in Dar-es-Salaam. It bitterly attacked Kenyatta
and accused his Government of being fascist and dishonest. Only
Odinga, Oneko and Kaggia escaped criticism in the long list of
Ministers mentioned in the pamphlet, which also alleged that the
Kenya Government was tottering.

As a national political party, K.A.N.U. had almost ceased to
function. It was heavily in debt and its officers unpaid; but there
was little it could do now in a one-party state where the National
Assembly and the Provincial Councils had become the main forums
of public opinion. However, K.A.N.U. still went through the motions
of a political party and the annual conference in March 1966 was
used by the Government to remove Odinga from power. His opponents had not been inactive during the previous year and they had
successfully built up resistance to his pro-Communist views. When
the principal office-bearers came up for election Odinga was voted
off the Council and replaced as Deputy President of the party by
eight new Vice-Presidents, one from each province. But confident
that he had the support of a majority of the Luo and the left-wing
elements among the Kikuyu, Odinga decided to make an issue of his
differences with Kenyatta and the moderates. He resigned as Vice-
President of the Republic, complaining that Kenya was now being
controlled by an 'invisible Government', and he left K.A.N.U.,
taking with him Oneko and Kaggia, the men who had shared Kenyatta's trial at Kapenguria. All together, twenty-eight elected
members of the National Assembly followed Odinga out of the party
to set up a new Opposition.

Although Kenya was officially a one-party state there was nothing
in the Republic's constitution to prevent the setting up of political
parties. Odinga therefore formed the Kenya People's Union as a
Luo-Kikuyu alliance to break the weakened K.A.N.U. and to bring

down the Government.[1] With strong financial backing from both
Russia and China, alleged later by the Government to have totalled
£500,000, and the potential support of the extreme elements of
Kenya's two most numerous and powerful tribes, Odinga seemed
poised to become the first Communist President in Africa. But he
underestimated the prestige and the political skills of Kenyatta, who
although now in his mid-seventies showed that he could act
decisively with any threat to his position.

Kenyatta was conscious that he had to deal with Odinga constitu-
tionally in order to preserve the image of Kenya as a politically-
stable and united country. He also knew that he could not rule
without the support of the people and Parliament. So he suspended
all the dissident Senators and Representatives and called by-elections
for the vacant seats. He also introduced a Public Security Act which
gave the Government powers of detention without trial, censorship
and control over aliens. However, Kenyatta was confident that when
it came to a choice, a majority of the people would reject Odinga's
Communist-backed party. Events proved Kenyatta right: the 'little
general election' in June 1966 was a vote of confidence in him and
his Government. Although Odinga retained the Central Nyanza
seat and the size of the majority indicated that he had lost none of
his personal popularity in his home province, only a minority who
stood on a K.P.U. ticket were elected.[2] Kenyatta was now in a much
stronger position and this was recognised by Parliament who nominated him Life President. At the end of the year a Bill was passed
abolishing the Senate and postponing the next general election from
1968 to 1970. Support for Odinga's dream of revolutionary power
dwindled with defections from his K.P.U. party and so the country
settled down to a period of political peace and consolidation of the
achievements since independence.

The unity which Kenyatta and a new generation of African
leaders have brought to Kenya has so far stood the test of those
social, racial and economic stresses which rack many of the new, and
some of the old, nations of the modern world. Looking back over
the centuries it can be seen that Kenya has had a turbulent history

[1] K.P.U. was registered as an official party on 27 May, thus making Kenya
a two-party state once more.
[2] Results of Little General Election:

| K.A.N.U. | | K.P.U. | |
|---|---|---|---|
| Lower House | 21 | Lower House | 7 |
| Senate | 8 | Senate | 2 |

from the earliest times. The warring ideologies of East and West
seem to meet in this small country on the Equator, in a continent
which has yet to emerge fully from the depths of man's beginnings.
That Kenya has been able to change so much, and so quickly, in
recent years and yet be able to find its own national identity is a
tribute to the citizens of different race, tribe and colour who despite
their differences have shared a loyalty to a country of great natural
beauty and spirit. The unity which is now so much a part of the new
Kenya could well offer a lesson to 'that other world wrapped in
deadlock and whose proudest boast is to annihilate mankind'.

# Some Facts and Figures about Kenya

## GEOGRAPHY

*Position*: Kenya lies astride the Equator on the eastern coast of Africa between latitudes 4 degrees North and 4 degrees South, and from longitude 34 degrees to 41 degrees East. The northern frontier borders with Sudan, Ethiopia, and Somalia; the western frontier with Uganda and Lake Victoria; and the southern frontier with Tanzania. The eastern shore is bounded by the Indian Ocean.

*Land*: Kenya has a total area of 224,960 sq. miles, including 5,171 sq. miles of inland water – the Kavirondo Gulf, part of Lake Natron, Lakes Magadi, Naivasha, Nakuru, Baringo and Rudolph. There are eight administrative provinces: Rift Valley, Central, Nyanza, Coast, Western, Eastern, North-Eastern and Nairobi (extra-provincial area). Principal towns are Nairobi (capital and commercial centre), Mombasa (main port), Nakuru (provincial headquarters and agricultural centre), Kisumu (lake port), Eldoret (agricultural and educational centre), Kitale (agricultural centre), Nyeri (provincial headquarters and agricultural centre), Kericho (tea and industrial centre), Meru (agricultural centre), Malindi (coastal resort) and Thika (plantation and industrial centre). Only two major rivers, the Tana and the Athi/Galana/Sabaki, cross the dry plateau from the central highlands to the sea.

*Climate*: because of the latitude temperatures have only a small variation. There are no seasons equivalent to the summer and winter of temperate regions. But changes in humidity and cloudiness can create cool or warm weather. Moderation of temperatures is caused by changes in altitude. At Mombasa, the average temperature at sea-level is 80 degrees F, and the temperature is reduced by about 3 degrees F for each 1,000 feet in altitude. This means that at 5,000 to 9,000 feet there is a temperate climate. Over 9,000 feet at the small township of Equator, the highest railway station in Africa, it is cool with a mean temperature of 56 degrees F. Glaciers are found on Mount Kenya down to 15,000 feet. The seasons in Kenya are marked by rainfall rather than changes in temperature. The Coast receives most of its rainfall from the south-east monsoon between April and July, and has a pronounced dry season in January and February. The plateaux and highlands of the Central and Eastern provinces have two rainy periods: the long rains between March and May, the short rains between October and December (Nairobi to Garissa). To the west of the Rift Valley there is a continuous rainy season from March to September: some parts of Nyanza province in the vicinity of Lake Victoria have rain all the year round and a total rainfall of 80 inches. Nairobi provides a good example of the Kenya climate away from the tropical Coast: the altitude of 5,495 feet reduces the mean annual air temperature to 67 degrees F. Mid-December to mid-March is the hot, dry season before the onset of the long rains from mid-March to the end of May which account for half the total rainfall. A cool, cloudy but dry season follows before the short rains from mid-October to mid-December. But these seasons vary greatly from year to year: although the rainfall averages 33 inches in a year, it has been as high as 61 inches and as low as 19 inches.

*People*: the 1966 estimate of total population was 9,643,000 based on the 1962 census: Africans, 9,370,000; Indo/Pakistani, 188,000; Europeans, 43,000; Arab, 38,000; Others, 4,000. Annual population growth is put at 2.9 per cent and average density 42 per sq. mile.

Estimate of populations in main towns (1962 census):

| Town | African | Asian and Others | Europeans | Total |
|---|---|---|---|---|
| Nairobi | 156,246 | 89,073 | 21,476 | 266,795 |
| Mombasa | 111,847 | 62,423 | 5,305 | 179,575 |
| Nakuru | 30,189 | 6,578 | 1,414 | 38,181 |
| Kisumu | 14,119 | 8,809 | 598 | 23,526 |
| Eldoret | 15,059 | 3,882 | 664 | 19,605 |
| Thika | 11,352 | 2,079 | 179 | 13,400 |
| Kitale | 7,000 | 2,104 | 238 | 9,342 |
| Nyeri | 6,256 | 1,164 | 437 | 7,857 |
| Nanyuki | 9,625 | 1,021 | 508 | 11,154 |
| Kericho | 5,950 | 1,511 | 231 | 7,692 |

There are forty major African tribes in Kenya and they belong to four ethnic groups: Bantu, Nilotic, Nilo-Hamitic, and Hamitic. The breakdown of main tribes into groups is as follows:

General Bantu: Kikuyu, Embu, Meru, Kamba, Mbere and Tharaka.
Western Bantu: Luhya, Kisii and Kuria.

Coastal Bantu: Mijikenda, Pokomo/Riverine, Taveta, Taita, Swahili/Shirazi, Bajun, Boni/Sanye.
Nilotic: Luo.
Nilo-Hamitic (Kalenjin speaking): Nandi, Kipsigis, Elgeyo, Marakwet, Pokot, Sabaot, Tugen.
Nilo-Hamitic (others): Masai, Samburu, Turkana, Iteso, Nderobo, Njemps.
Western Hamites (Rendille and Galla speaking): Rendille, Boran, Gabbia, Sakuye, Orma.
Eastern Hamites (Somali speaking): Gosha, Hawiya, Ogaden, Ajuman, Gurreh.
The largest main tribes at the time of the 1962 census were: Kikuyu (1,642,000); Luo (1,148,000); Luhya (1,086,000); Kamba (933,000); Kalenjin (898,000); Masai (154,000).

The great majority of Kenya Africans still live and work on the land, though increasing numbers are entering industry, commerce and the professions. Most of the Indo-Pakistani population live in the towns and work as traders or artisans: the Arabs live mainly at the Coast and many of them are engaged in the Indian Ocean dhow trade. Europeans now left in Kenya are farmers, civil servants, missionaries, business and professional men. The principal languages are Swahili and English (which is spoken in Government and commercial circles): there are a number of African vernacular languages relative to the main tribal groups; and Gujerati, Hindustani and Arabic are spoken by the respective Asian communities. The indigenous population traditionally believe in God in Judaic forms. The Roman Catholic Church under an Archbishop in Nairobi is the strongest of the Christian religions with 1,170,000 adherents. The Protestant Churches under the National Christian Council of Kenya have 936,200 adherents. Kenya is also an Anglican Province with an Archbishop in Nairobi. The Arabs are Moslem, and Islam has spread to the Hamitic tribes in the north-east and to the coastal tribes. About two-thirds of the Asians are Hindu: the rest are Moslem with the exception of Goans who are Roman Catholic.

# CONSTITUTION

Kenya is a sovereign Republic and a member of the Commonwealth of Nations. The constitution is contained in Schedule 2 of the Kenya Independence Order in Council 1963 as amended by the Constitution (Amendment) Acts Nos. 28 and 38 of 1964, No. 14 of 1965, and Nos. 16, 17 and 18 of 1966.

*Rights and Safeguards*: the constitution defines Kenya citizenship; makes provisions for the protection of fundamental rights and freedom of the individual, and safeguards the judiciary, the rule of law and land held under trust. The areas of land which were formerly Crown Land were vested in the Government in 1964. Land in the Special Areas (the former African tribal land units or reserves) together with certain Special Reserves is vested in the County Councils in whose areas the land lies, to hold in trust for the benefit of the people resident in County Council areas. A Commissioner of Lands administers both Government and County Council land to ensure uniformity of policy and procedure. The constitution recognises all estates, interests or rights in land which were extant immediately before the establishment of a Republic.

*Parliament*: the constitution can be altered by a 65 per cent majority in the National Assembly. The Senate was abolished in December 1966 and amalgamated with the House of Representatives, creating 58 new seats of which 41 were taken up by former senators and 17 in by-elections. The new National Assembly comprises a Speaker, Deputy-Speaker, the Attorney-General *ex officio*, 175 constituency members elected by adult suffrage, and 12 special members elected by the National Assembly sitting as an electoral college. The President must be a Member of Parliament and not less than thirty-five years of age. He is Head of State, Commander-in-Chief of the Armed Forces and while in office is immune from civil and criminal proceedings. The President is also Head of Cabinet, appointing Ministers from the National Assembly. He also appoints the Vice-President, Chief Justice, Chief Commissioner of Police and most senior civil servants. The Vice-President is principal assistant to the President and acts as President when the President is absent; but he has no automatic rights of succession. Under the constitution, election of the President follows the dissolution of Parliament which must be dissolved every five years or sooner by the President. At the general election, every candidate must declare his choice of President. The presidential candidate who receives the support of an outright majority of successful M.P.'s is declared President. Parliament is constituted by the President and the National Assembly. In the constitution, executive and legislative powers are divided so as to give effect to the three main principles guiding the Republic: that strong national leadership should exist and be apparent to the people; that the President and his Cabinet should be collectively responsible to Parliament; and that Parliament should be supreme. The strength of national leadership is assured by the election of an executive President who with the Cabinet governs with the support of a majority in Parliament. The supremacy of Parliament is assured in that the President must resign or dissolve Parliament if he cannot command support. Parliament is the only law-making body and controls public finance. There are eighteen executive Ministers in the Cabinet: Finance, Economic Planning and Development, Defence, Agriculture and Animal Husbandry, Health, Local Government, Works, Power and Communications, Labour, Tourism and Wild Life, Lands and Settlement, Housing, Information and Broadcasting, Natural Resources, Co-operative and Social Services, Commerce and Industry, Education.

*Judiciary*: the courts of justice are centred on the High Court in Nairobi. A Chief Justice and eleven Puisne Judges sit continuously at Nairobi, Mombasa, Nakuru and Kisumu: sessions are held at Eldoret, Nyeri, Meru, Kitale, Kisii and Kericho. Resident magistrates preside over subordinate courts in the main provincial centres and sit on criminal cases throughout the year; but on civilian cases only during the High Court terms. Laymen preside over about 100 courts dealing with cases brought before them according to African customary law. There are also Moslem subordinate courts in areas where the population is predominantly Moslem. They are presided over by Khadis and have limited jurisdiction over matters governed by Mohammedan law. The East Africa Court of Appeal in Nairobi is the final court of appeal for Kenya courts.

*Defence*: the Kenya Army with a Brigadier as Chief-of-Staff consists of three battalions and a paratroop company, and has a strength of 4,200 men. There is a small Navy of four coastal vessels. An Air Force is in the process of being built up with a strength (in 1966) of six Chipmunk primary trainers, one Caribou twin-engined transport, and several single-engined Beavers for transport and security purposes.

*Education*: about £4 million a year is spent by the Government on education for maintained and assisted schools. In 1965, there were 5,078 Primary Schools with 1,010,889 children attending the seven-year course: 641,088 boys and 369,801 girls. In 1966, there were 336 Secondary Schools with a total enrolment of 47,976: boys, 34,720 and girls, 13,256. After four years of secondary schooling, pupils take the Cambridge Overseas School Certificate Examination and the Higher School Certificate after a further two years. There is also a Kenya Junior Secondary Examination after two years of secondary schooling. A number of institutions offer technical education: the Kenya Polytechnic in Nairobi (1,500 students), the Mombasa Technical Institute, technical high schools in Nairobi and Mombasa, a secondary technical school at Nakuru, five other technical schools and two secondary trade schools. In 1966, at Teachers' Training Colleges, 5,061 students were being trained for primary schools and 413 for secondary schools: Kenyatta College and the Kenya Science Teachers College in Nairobi are the principal teacher-training establishments. For higher education, there is the University of East Africa constituted in Makerere University College in Kampala; University College in Nairobi; and University College in Dar-es-Salaam. The three colleges are supported jointly by Kenya, Uganda and Tanzania, and the Chancellor is President Julius Nyerere. The United States Agency for International Development has given £4 million for expanding University College in Nairobi as a forty-year loan at one per cent interest for a grace period of ten years and 2½ per cent thereafter. The University of East Africa provides courses in the Arts, Sciences, Engineering, Agriculture, Medicine, Art, Architecture, Education, Veterinary Science, Law and Domestic Science. In 1966, some 5,000 Kenya students were at college in East Africa (1,000 at University College, Nairobi).

*Health*: the Government provides hospitals in the urban areas and in all district headquarters: these facilities are augmented by a number of mission and private hospitals in various parts of the country. In 1965, there were 12,490 hospital beds at Government hospitals. In-patients numbered 156,690 and out-patients 3,207,756 in 1964. At the end of 1965 there were 167 health centres in operation and mobile clinics in the sparsely populated pastoral areas among the nomadic peoples. A free medical service for children and out-patients was introduced in 1965. Total Government expenditure on health in that year was £3,312,419.

*Labour*: the total number of persons in wage-earning employment in 1965 was 594,005 (6½ per cent of the population); and of this figure 209,478 were employed in large-scale agriculture, forestry and fishing; 206,495 in private industries and commerce; and 178,032 in the public services. The wage bill was estimated at £115.7 million, being made up of £12.7 million for agriculture, forestry and fishing employment; £56.4 million for private industries and commerce; and £46.6 million for the public services. There are no statistical figures available, but estimates indicated that in 1965 the number of self-employed and wage-earners in the monetary economy was about 800,000. A National Security Fund was set up in December 1965 to cover 15,000 employers and 400,000 employees in full-time employment. There were 61 registered trade unions of which 45 were employee unions and 16 employer unions.

# THE ECONOMY

*Development and Planning*: Kenya's economic policy is embodied in the Five-year Development Plan 1966–70. The aim of the Plan is an integrated economy and a 7.1 per cent growth in the gross domestic product to bring it up to an annual figure of £405 million at the end of the period. The Plan is based on a total population of 10,850,000 and on a total of 1,100,000 wage-earners in the monetary economy by 1970. It budgets for a total capital expenditure of £324.6 million (or £200 per family) made up as follows:

| In the private sector | £ million | | £ million |
|---|---|---|---|
| Agriculture | 48.2 | | |
| Manufacturing Industries | 61.5 | | |
| Electricity | 24.0 | | |
| Transport | 15.0 | | |
| Housing | 11.1 | Privately financed | 180.0 |
| Private Cars | 25.0 | Government finance (contributions) | 25.7 |
| Others | 20.9 | | |
| | 205.7 | | 205.7 |

| In the public sector | £ million |
|---|---|
| Central Government Development Estimates | 64.5 |
| Central Government (other) | 7.5 |
| Local Authorities | 20.0 |
| East African Common Services | 22.8 |
| University College, Nairobi | 4.1 |
| | 118.9 |

In 1966, budgeted development expenditure for the year was £22 million of which £7 million was expected to come from local sources and the rest in foreign aid. This dependence on foreign aid and the realisation that overseas capital is necessary to the Development Plan have led Kenya to reject nationalisation as followed by neighbouring Tanzania. The Foreign Investment Protection Act, favourable treatment for local industries through tariff protection, refunds

of customs duties, a low level of taxation, and political stability have
created a steady rate of economic growth. In 1966, capital formation
reached £51 million, in money terms the highest figure on record.
Balance of payments surplus and foreign exchange assets of the
Central Bank of Kenya increased to £24 million.

*Budget*: approved estimates of expenditure for the financial year
ending 30 June 1966 were:

    £52.3 million on Recurrent Account
    £15.7 million on Development Account

Estimated Revenue:

    £48.9 million on Recurrent Account
    £11.6 million on Development Account

The overall Public Debt stood at £95.4 million. Of the budgeted
expenditure, £7 million was for interest and redemption on loans
and £5.4 million for pensions and gratuities, mainly to pensioners
resident in the United Kingdom.

*Trade*: the volume of external trade in 1966 was £174.7 million:
imports, £112.4 million and exports, £62.3 million. The apparently
unfavourable trading account was balanced by re-routing of imports
to neighbouring territories in the E.A. Common Market, re-exports,
invisible exports, e.g. tourism, and the proportion of capital goods in
the import bill. The bulk of imports came from the United Kingdom
(33.6 per cent), United States of America (10 per cent), West Germany (7.3 per cent). Japan is normally Kenya's second largest
country of origin for imports but there has been a partial ban to
redress a trade imbalance. The main destinations for exports were:
United Kingdom (21.2 per cent), West Germany (14 per cent),
United States of America (9.1 per cent).

*Agriculture*: Kenya is predominantly an agricultural economy with
two-thirds of the population deriving its living from the land. Gross
farm revenue in the monetary sector was £58.5 million in 1966.
Together with forestry, fishing and horticulture the agricultural
industry provided 42 per cent of the National Output in 1965. There
are three systems of agriculture in Kenya: plantation crops such as
coffee, sisal, tea and wattle grown on a large scale and involving
considerable capital investment; mixed farming of cereals, pyrethrum, livestock and sometimes small areas of coffee; ranching of
beef and sheep for meat and wool. There are 30,400 sq. miles of
high potential Class I land with rainfall of 35 inches and over; and
12,100 sq. miles of medium potential land in the 20–35-inch rainfall
zone. In 1965, the total number of registered holdings was 250,000

and this is expected to double by 1970. It is envisaged that when Class I or Class II land is developed it will provide an annual gross farm income of £230 million. The remainder of the total land area with less than 25 inches of rain is best suited to sisal and livestock ranching; but it is thought unlikely to produce more than £20 million in gross farm income. However, development of irrigation in the Nile Basin and along the lower and upper reaches of the Tana could produce a substantial increase in agricultural revenue from the lower rainfall areas.

Small-scale or semi-peasant farming takes up three-quarters of the high potential land in Kenya, but produces only a quarter of the production of exportable crops. The planned growth in agriculture will therefore be concentrated in this sector. Government policy aims to consolidate these small farms into larger, more economic units: it is hoped to complete the consolidation and registration of 27 million acres of land by the end of 1976. The million-acre settlement scheme in the former White Highlands cost by the middle of 1965 a total of £23 million and it is estimated that another £7 million will be spent on the scheme between July 1965 and 1968. Although 25,000 families were settled in the Highlands, the Government has abandoned plans for further large-scale settlement. The Agricultural Development Corporation was set up in 1965, charged specifically with the organisation of farming units during the transitional stage between European and African ownership. The Corporation is financed by the Agricultural Finance Corporation and the Land Bank of Kenya. The International Development Association, an agency of the World Bank, has granted £3.2 million for rural development in Kenya, including £1.4 million to increase productivity on small farms. In addition, Britain has made available in loans and grants a total of £33.4 million for agricultural settlement and development since 1963. There is a full range of agricultural and veterinary research and advisory services in Kenya. The headquarters of the East Africa Agriculture and Forestry Research Organisation and the East Africa Veterinary Research Organisation are at Muguga on the outskirts of Nairobi. The principal cash crops are coffee, tea, sisal, pyrethrum, maize, wheat, barley and oats. Cotton, pineapple and rice are being developed as potential export crops. The sugar-cane industry is also being developed to make Kenya self-sufficient in sugar and a possible exporter of the refined product. The livestock industry is also expanding. Much of the country is suitable for beef ranching and the cooler, wetter Highlands for intensive dairying. Butter, cheese, milk and ghee are exported to Uganda and Tanzania, and also overseas. The wool industry provides wool for local

manufacture and export. The pig industry provides local requirements for a wide range of pig products and also a surplus for export.
Agricultural exports in 1965 were valued at:

|                                     | £ million |
|-------------------------------------|-----------|
| Coffee                              | 14.0      |
| Tea                                 | 6.0       |
| Sisal                               | 4.5       |
| Meat and Meat Preparations          | 2.4       |
| Pyrethrum and Pyrethrum Extract     | 2.2       |
| Hides and Skins                     | 1.7       |
| Wattle Bark and Wattle Extract      | .8        |
| Tinned Pineapples                   | .7        |
| Raw Cotton                          | .7        |
| Wool                                | .5        |
| Timber Products                     | .5        |
| Cashew Nuts                         | .4        |
| Beans, Peas and Lentils             | .4        |

*Industry*: manufacturing accounted for 10 per cent of the National
Output in 1965. The principal manufacturing industries in order of
size are food processing, beverages and tobacco; metal products;
wood, paper and printing; textiles, clothing and footwear; non-
metallic mineral production, i.e. cement. Industry is centred mainly
at Nairobi and Mombasa, although there are a number of factories
at Thika, Eldoret and Nakuru. New manufacturing projects include
the production of electric lamps, torch-cell batteries, suitcases, paper
and pulp. There are also a number of engineering and vehicle
assembly workshops, and shipping repair facilities exist at Mombasa
and Kisumu. The most rapidly expanding industries have been
petroleum products, cement, clothing and textiles. The designed
capacity of the new oil refinery at Mombasa is two million metric
tons: in 1965 imports of oil fuels and spirits totalled £9.2 million;
and exports of petroleum products £4.5 million. Two major industrial projects were under way in 1966: the first £6 million stage of
the Tana River Hydro-Electric Scheme which will give Kenya an
ample supply of electricity from its own resources; and a £3.5 million rayon textile factory at Thika. Final negotiations were also
being reached on the establishment of a £6 million fertiliser factory
on the Coast. The Kenya Development Finance Corporation, in
which the Government has a substantial interest, and the Industrial
and Commercial Development Corporation have been formed to
promote new industries.
*Mining*: about three-quarters of the Kenya land area has been geo-

logically surveyed and mapped. At the end of 1965, two special oil licences covering 31,510 sq. miles were extant. A joint United Nations-Kenya team was investigating mineral resources in western Kenya and the Annual Report of the Kenya Mines and Geological Department noted that there was growing interest among prospectors and private mining companies in Kenya's mineral resources. The contribution of mining to the National Output was .2 per cent. Total value of mineral exports was £6.5 million: the main exports were Soda Ash, Copper, Gold, Limestone, Diatomite, Carbon Dioxide, Crude Salt, Refined Salt, Crushed Sodium and Silver.

*Power*: hydro-electric schemes utilising river flows are the main source of Kenya's power. The other sources of power are thermal generating stations using light and heavy fuel oils. Bulk supplies of electricity are imported by overhead lines from the Owen Falls of Lake Victoria in Uganda and serve west Kenya and Nairobi. The East Africa Power and Lighting Company, a commercial concern, has stations at Nairobi, Mombasa, Nakuru, Kisumu, Eldoret, Kitale, Nyeri, Nanyuki, Machakos, Gilgil, Naivasha, Kericho, Thomson's Falls, Malindi, Embu, Kakamega and Meru. The Mombasa system is supplied from an oil-fired steam generating station. The Company is also exploring the possibility of harnessing geothermal steam jets found in numerous places along the floor of the Rift Valley.

*Tourism*: eight per cent of the National Output comes from tourism which is Kenya's second largest industry after agriculture. More than 81,000 tourists came to Kenya during 1965; including 44,000 from Europe and 1,350 from America. The Minister of Tourism and Wild Life is responsible for the industry through the official Kenya Tourist Corporation, the Tourist Advisory Board and the Central Hotel Authority. Kenya's main tourist attractions are its wild life, scenery and climate. There are eight National Parks covering some 8,532 sq. miles, five of them being set aside for game watching: Nairobi, Tsavo, Aberdare, Mount Kenya and Lake Nakuru. Gedi and Fort Jesus on the Coast are scheduled as national parks of historic interest and Olorgesailie in the Rift Valley of prehistoric interest. Tsavo is the biggest of the National Parks and extends over the 8,000 sq. miles of bush country between Nairobi and Mombasa. It contains a large number of elephant and other big game. The Nairobi National Park is within five miles of the city centre and attracts about 150,000 visitors annually to see the wide variety of wild animals, including lion, in their natural habitat. There are also four game reserves run by local authorities: Masai (Amboseli), Masai (Mara), Samburu (Uaso Nyiro) and Meru County Council.

*Communications*: Kenya has 26,000 miles of public roads of which 1,340 miles are bitumen-surfaced. There are 3,871 miles of all-weather main roads and where they are not bitumenised they are gravel-surfaced. Of the 6,657 miles of secondary roads, 740 miles are bitumenised; the remainder mainly gravel-surfaced but subject to closure in heavy rains. The Development Plan provides for an expenditure of £21.5 million on roads: £11.9 million for trunk roads and £9.6 million for secondary roads. The railways are operated by the East African Railways and Harbours in Kenya and cover 1,270 route miles. Steam and diesel locomotives are used, the former being oil burning. The railways also own Kisumu Port and its shipping facilities. A number of branch lines connect the country districts with the main line which runs north-westwards from Mombasa to Nairobi (330 miles); Nakuru (442 miles); Eldoret (567 miles) and on into Uganda to Kampala (823 miles). A line from Nakuru to Kisumu (131 miles) connects the Highlands with Lake Victoria. The line from Voi to Moshi (94 miles) connects the Kenya and Uganda main line with the Tanzania lines. Mombasa is the largest port in East Africa and serves Kenya, Uganda and northern Tanzania. There are thirteen deep-water berths together with an oil berth and a new oil jetty for large modern tankers. In 1965, over 1,500 ships called and a total deadweight tonnage of 4.5 million tons of cargo was handled at the port. Nairobi Airport is classified as an international airport. The runway at Embakasi, eight miles from the city centre, is two and a half miles long and can take the largest jets in service. Aircraft movements in and out of Nairobi average 1,200 a month with 46,000 passengers and 750,000 kilograms of freight. The East African Airways Corporation, which is a service of the East Africa Common Services Organisation, operates on international air routes and on a network of domestic routes linking Kenya with Uganda and Tanzania. Wilson Airport on the Nairobi city boundary, and the municipal airports at Mombasa and Kisumu, deal with the smaller aircraft serving the domestic routes.

# MISCELLANEOUS

*Cinemas*: there are 36 cinemas in Kenya.
*Citizens*: by December 1965 some 6,000 Britons had renounced British citizenship and applied for Kenya citizenship since independence. In the same period, some 70,000 people, mainly Asians, had applied for British passports.

*Clothing*: summer-weight clothing can be worn in many parts of Kenya and at most times of the year. In the higher altitudes (above 6,000 feet) and during July and August, woollens are advised. Lightweight tropical clothing is essential at the Coast.

*Cost of Living*: the rise between 1960 and 1966 was 16 points (1960 = 100). Living costs are much the same as they are in the United Kingdom. Fresh food is readily available and cheaper, but imported processed foods come in over high tariffs and are expensive. A monthly food bill, based on European standards, would normally be about £30 a month for a family of three. Clothing is expensive as materials have to be imported. A servant costs £8 a month in wages and an unfurnished European-type house £35–£45 a month to rent. A three-bedroomed house would cost £5,000 to buy. Lack of public transport makes a car essential away from the towns (*1967 prices*).

*Currency*: the standard coin is the Kenya Shilling which is divided into 100 cents. There are 20 shillings to the Kenya Pound and to the pound sterling. Notes: 5, 10, 20, 50 and 100 shillings. Coins: 1 shilling, 5, 10, 50 cents.

*Distances*: Nairobi is 4,000 miles by air from London: Mombasa is 6,800 nautical miles by sea via Suez from London.

*Domestic Product*: the gross product at constant prices for 1964 showing the planned product for 1970 in brackets:

| *Monetary sector* | *£ million* |
| --- | --- |
| Agriculture and Livestock | 46.22 (66.25) |
| Manufacturing | 29.38 (46.60) |
| Construction | 4.38 (12.00) |
| Transport, Communications | 26.30 (39.50) |
| Wholesale and Retail Trade | 34.06 (48.30) |
| Central Government | 34.11 (51.20) |
| Other Activities | 38.34 (57.90) |
| | 212.79 (321.75) |
| Subsistence Product | 68.53 (83.10) |
| | 281.32 (404.85) |

*Electricity Supply*: 240 volts, 50 cycles A.C.

*Health*: Kenya falls within the yellow fever area, but there has not been an outbreak for many years. Risk of malaria varies from place to place, depending on the altitude and climate and being greater near the Coast. Dysentery is a common risk.

*Hours of Business*: Government offices and business houses: 8.30–
12.30 p.m.: 2–4.30 p.m. (Monday to Friday); 8.30–12.30 p.m.
(Saturday).

*Income Tax*: Shs. 2/50 in the pound; surtax of Shs. 3/– on second
£1,000, Shs. 5/– on third £1,000, Shs. 7/– on fourth £1,000, thereafter rising Sh. 1/– per £1,000 to Shs. 12/– in the pound. P.A.Y.E.
has been introduced at a flat rate of Shs. 2/50 in the pound (*1967*).

*National Flag*: horizontal tricolour of black, red and green separated
with white stripes and with a shield and crossed spears in the centre.

*Official Holidays*: New Year's Day; Good Friday; Easter Monday;
Labour Day (1 May); Madaraka Day (1 June); August Bank Holi-
day; Kenyatta Day (20 October); *Uhuru/Jamhuri* Day (12 December); Christmas Day; Boxing Day.

*Overseas Representatives*: Kenya has its own representatives, at
ambassadorial level, abroad in Britain, France, West Germany,
Nigeria, United Arab Republic, United States of America and the
Vatican. In Britain and Nigeria they are High Commissioners; in
other countries Ambassadors.

*Press*: there are three daily newspapers: two in English, one in
Swahili. Circulations range from 17,000 to 48,000. There are also
three English-language weekly papers, two in Swahili, one in
Gujerati, one in Luo and with circulations from 12,000 to 25,000. In
addition, there is a fortnightly English-language news magazine
with a circulation of 10,000. A wide variety of trade and technical
journals are also published, most of them monthly.

*Purchasing Power*: about one in seven of the adult population in
Kenya is in regular employment. *Per capita* income in 1966 was
estimated to be Shs. 600/– (£30).

*Pyrethrum*: Kenya supplies the bulk of the world's pyrethrum
requirements.

*Social Custom*: in the towns European customs and manners are
followed. The country districts are less civilised, but perhaps more
friendly and hospitable towards strangers. Most hotels and restaurants in the towns add a 10 per cent service charge, but additional
rewards are always appreciated: hotel porters. Sh. 1/– for carrying
a bag; room servants, Shs. 5/– a week; dining-room staff, about Shs.
2/– a meal; restaurants, Shs. 1/50–Shs. 2/50 per person; bars, 50
cents–Shs. 3/– per person at the end of the evening; taxi drivers,
50 cents or Sh. 1/– on a Shs. 5/– fare, but not more than Shs. 2/–
in town. Cloakroom attendants, 50 cents or Sh. 1/–; railway
porters, Sh. 1/– or Shs. 2/–, and if trolley is used, Shs. 1/50 each
plus Sh. 1/– for use of trolley (*1967*).

*Weights and Measures*: the Kenya legislation for weights and

measures is identical with that of Britain, but the introduction of
the metric system is being considered.

# EAST AFRICA COMMON SERVICES

The general administration of services common to Kenya, Uganda
and Tanzania by the East Africa High Commission in pre-independence days was taken over by the East Africa Common Services
Organisation in 1962. Policy was controlled by the Premiers of the
three states sitting as the East Africa Common Services Authority.
There were five committees of three Ministers, one from each territory, to control the five groups of services: *Communications* (railways, harbours, posts and telecommunications, civil aviation and
meteorology); *Finance* (income tax, customs and excise collection,
and administration of the General Fund for the various services);
*Commercial and Industrial Co-ordination*; *Social and Research
Sciences*; *Industrial Relations and Co-ordination of Labour*. The
Central Legislative Assembly, responsible for passing the legislation
for the administration of the common services, consists of a Speaker,
15 Ministers (five from each state), 27 members (nine from each
state and elected by their legislatures), and two official members (the
Secretary-General and the Legal Secretary).

On 6 June 1967 in Kampala, President Kenyatta (Kenya), President Obote (Uganda) and President Nyerere (Tanzania) signed a
15-year treaty of economic co-operation which came into force on 1
December 1967. Under the treaty, there will be an East Africa
Development Bank, inter-territorial tariffs on goods originating in
one state and exported to another, replacement of the ministerial
committees, decentralisation of E.A.C.S.O., and the organisation of
an East Africa Economic Community of 25 million people.

The Development Bank will promote financial and technical
assistance to industrial projects. Priority will be given to raising the
industrial level of Uganda and Tanzania on a par with Kenya. Each
state will contribute an initial £2 million each and it is hoped to
raise £4 million overseas. The directors can call up a further £10
million over consecutive five-year periods. Tanzania and Uganda
will each get 38¾ per cent of the Bank's total investment while Kenya
will receive 22½ per cent.

A 'transfer tax system' will allow a state that has a trading deficit with its partners to impose transfer taxes on goods originating
in these countries, up to the amount of the deficit, but only if similar
goods are manufactured, or are expected to be, within three months

in the tax-imposing country. The protected industry will also have a capacity to at least 15 per cent of domestic consumption or to a value of £100,000, whichever is the less. The tax will not exceed 50 per cent of the tariff on goods originating outside East Africa, nor can it be imposed for more than eight years. Its aim will be to favour Tanzania and allow her to compete freely with Kenya and Uganda with which she had trade deficits.

The ministerial committee system for E.A.C.S.O. will be replaced by a Minister for East Africa from each state, permanently based at E.A.C.S.O which will be moved from Nairobi to Arusha in northern Tanzania. The Development Bank and postal headquarters will be in Kampala; East African Railways and East African Airways in Nairobi; and the Harbour headquarters in Dar-es-Salaam.

The three Presidents will retain their authority as the controlling body of the East Africa Economic Community; a Common Market Council will handle the Community's day-to-day affairs; and a tribunal will be created as a judicial body. Provision will also be made for the association or active participation by Zambia, Burundi, Ethiopia and other interested countries in the East Africa Common Market.

*Appendix 2*

# Memorandum Submitted by the Kenya African Union to the Rt. Honourable James Griffiths, P.C., M.P., Secretary of State for the Colonies, on 17 May 1951

W E, THE KENYA AFRICAN UNION, on behalf of the African people of Kenya generally, greatly appreciate your short visit to our country. We are particularly pleased that you have been able to find an opportunity to visit this country a few months after your memorable statement which you made in the House of Commons regarding the Constitutional development of Kenya. We broadly welcome your statement.

The following are the main important points which we would like to raise regarding the Constitutional development of Kenya:

1. CONSTITUTIONAL CHANGES

(a) Executive Council: The African people in Kenya have no direct representation on the Executive Council, and we do not see any biological justification for their exclusion in this essential body. We, therefore, strongly request that immediate consideration should be given to the appointment of an African member in the Executive Council.

(b) Kenya Legislative Council: There are at the present moment over five million Africans in Kenya who are represented by only four African Nominated Members in the Kenya Legislative Council. The absurdity of this, admittedly, cannot be overstressed. Each of the four members has at his back a constituency of over one million souls and it is practically and physically impossible to cope with the ever increasing public duty as far as the interests of the Africans are concerned. We, therefore, strongly request that immediate consideration should be given to increasing the African seats from four to twelve on Provincial basis. We recommend as follows:

Central Province:          3 Members
Nairobi:                   1 Member

Coast Province:            2 Members
Rift Valley and Settled
    Areas:                 2 Members
Nyanza Province:           2 Members
Masai and the N.F.D.:      2 Members

(c) East Africa Central Assembly: We favour and support the continuation of the life of the Central Assembly, but we demand that
only capable African Members should be appointed in this important body.

(d) Nairobi City Council: There are over 85,000 Africans residing
in Nairobi. About three-quarters of this number is a permanent
population. They are represented by only two African Nominated
Members in the City Council. It is, therefore, very difficult to know
how to apportion the various work of the City Council which is
principally in form of Committees and Boards and it is impossible
for the two Members to divide themselves up to fit in properly with
the necessary work.

We, therefore, strongly recommend that we should have eight
African Elected Members in the City Council. We also request that
special consideration should be given to the appointment of an
African Member in the Kenya Legislative Council to represent the
interests of the African residents of Nairobi.

(e) Other Government and Municipal Boards and Committees: We
strongly recommend that the Africans should be adequately represented in all local Government and Municipal Boards and Committees. Appointment of African Members on the Transport Licensing Board and Rent Control Board whose duties and functions are at
the moment increasing tremendously as far as African interests are
concerned is a matter of dire necessity. It is our considered opinion
at this juncture to stress that such opportunities will undoubtedly
fall in conformity with your statement in which you expressed the
hope of His Majesty's Government that all persons having concern
with the future of these territories will work together towards that
goal of true partnership on which the future prosperity and happiness
of all in East Africa must depend.

We sincerely appreciate and endorse this statement if it could be
implemented in its true sense.

(f) European Parity: We have given a matured consideration to the
demand for Parity by the European Unofficial Elected Members of
the Kenya Legislative Council, and we have come to our honest conclusion that we cannot under any circumstances give support to this
unreasonable demand.

The following resolution which was passed unanimously by the Kenya African Union and the East African Indian National Congress during their joint meeting on Sunday, 13th May, 1951 in the Kaloleni Hall, Nairobi, indicates our stand against this demand:

'This mass meeting held under the auspices of the Kenya African Union and the East African Indian National Congress on the 13th May, 1951 strongly opposes the demand by the European Elected Members of the Kenya Legislative Council for Parity between European Unofficials on the one hand and all non-European Unofficials on the other.'

We have six points which were passed as a Resolution by the Kenya African Union on the 20th December, 1950, immediately after your statement.

The following are the points:

1. The goal should be a common roll for all races on a basis suitable to circumstances of the Colony.

2. This meeting is totally opposed to nomination of its Members and demands the immediate introduction of elective principles.

3. As a transitional step, until a common roll is introduced the Africans must have on the Legislative Council parity of membership with non-African Unofficial Members as in Uganda with the difference that the elective principles must be introduced.

4. That if equality of unofficial representation for the Africans with each of the two major immigrant communities is proposed, African public opinion must be consulted before accepting any such proposals.

5. That on one account any African representatives accept parity of Unofficial representation for Europeans with the other races combined.

6. There should be not less African Members on the Executive Council than are allowed to any other community.

## 2. DISCRIMINATION AND COLOUR BAR

One of the things which have created considerable amount of suspicion among the African subjects in this Colony towards the British Administration, is the discriminatory policies which are not only practised by some individual Europeans and Asians, but are supported and encouraged by certain laws governing the country.

There are discriminatory laws relating to the issue of Trade Licences, deciding price for foodstuffs grown and produced by Africans and there is intensive discrimination in Hotels and Restaurants, etc.

We strongly appeal that all racial discriminatory laws including the Penal Code Section 159 and other most irritating laws should be completely abolished as soon as the new charges come into force.

We appeal to the British Government in the United Kingdom, through you, Sir, to take a serious view towards stamping out the Colour Bar in all her Colonies, Dominions, etc., by enforcing a special legislation. This fact will definitely increase and consolidate the degree of confidence among the African subject which has now been badly shaken by the present situation.

## 3. EDUCATION

Education is the key to progress. We, therefore, request that the British Government should give more aid to African education in Kenya. General and Technical Education should be given in parallel to both African boys and girls. We again appeal strongly to the Government to pay particular attention to this matter.

## 4. AGRICULTURE AND ECONOMICS

We attach particular importance on the question of land for which a Petition has been addressed to you under separate cover. Land is the only Social Security that the African has. We entirely agree that preservation of our soil is a matter which should receive drastic attention by both Government and the African people. Tremendous improvement is required in Agricultural Education among the Africans, and State financial aid to African farmers and livestock keepers is of the utmost importance.

We recommend that every possible encouragement and facilities should be provided for Africans economically in order to build up a self-supporting community.

## 5. CIVIL SERVICE

At the moment the Africans are not appointed to higher posts in the Civil Service. We see no reason why posts in the Secretariat should not be created for capable Africans such as Assistant Secretary and Deputy Chief Native Commissioner.

## 6. FREEDOM OF ASSEMBLY AND FREEDOM OF MOVEMENT

Freedom of Assembly and Freedom of Movement are not what they should be in Kenya. In certain parts of Kenya Africans cannot hold meetings to discuss their social and political problems. In certain districts in Kenya Africans are not allowed to visit each other without a pass from the D.C.

We would strongly recommend total abolition of the Native

Authority Ordinance which empowers District Commissioners and the Local Chiefs to disallow people to meet. This, as a matter of fact, has been responsible for encouraging some Africans in certain Provinces to organise secret societies.

This does not in any way mean that Law and Order should not be maintained.

## 7. TRADE UNION MOVEMENT

We strongly recommend that Trade Union movement should be allowed to function in Kenya the same as it does in other advanced countries without unnecessary interference.

## 8. CONCLUSIONS

We hope and trust that you will give these and other points your sympathetic attention, and we request you, Sir, to convey our loyal greetings to H.M. Government and to the people of Great Britain.

# Historiography

---

600 B.C.: It is probable that Hindus were trading with East Africa about this time and settling on the Coast.

A.D. 67: Hippalus informs the Western world of the existence of the monsoon trade winds.

A.D. 80: Graeco-Roman ships from Berenice recorded as visiting East Africa.

A.D. 400: The Aksum empire extends trade routes into the country now known as Kenya.

A.D. 800: East Africa coastlands come under the influence of Islam and the Arabs.

A.D. 1000: East Africa known to the Chinese as Po Pa Li: extensive trade between Mo Lin (Malindi) and Canton.

A.D. 1300: Indian system of weights and Maldive cowrie-shell currency widespread in coastal regions of eastern Africa.

A.D. 1400: Arabs established along the Coast at trading ports and at the peak of their power in East Africa.

1498: Vasco da Gama, the Portuguese sea-explorer, becomes the first European recorded as having visited Mombasa.

1565: East Africa declared a Portuguese territory.

1588: East African Arabs with the help of the Turks rise in revolt against the Portuguese.

1589: Mombasa sacked by the Portuguese with the assistance of the Zimba tribe from the south.

1593: Portuguese build the citadel of Fort Jesus at Mombasa with labour from Malindi and India: Mombasa becomes the military and administrative headquarters for the Portuguese conquest of the East African Coast from Barawa to Cape Delgado.

1631: Second revolt of the Arabs against the Portuguese who are driven out of Mombasa.

1632: Portuguese reconquer Mombasa.

1660: The Omani Arabs from the Persian Gulf raid Mombasa and capture the town, but not Fort Jesus. Arabs now in control of the East African Coast.

1678: Portuguese re-establish their authority on the East African Coast.

1696: Omanis besiege Fort Jesus at the beginning of the year.

1698: The thirty-three-month siege ends on 12 December when the Omani Arabs overrun Fort Jesus. A Portuguese naval squadron carrying reinforcements from Goa finds the red flag of the Oman flying over the citadel and retires.

1728: Portuguese recapture Mombasa.

1730: The Omani Arabs expel the Portuguese from Mombasa for the last time.

1741: Mombasa Arabs under the leadership of the Mazrui family renounce allegiance to Oman.

1798: On 18 December a British naval reconnaissance squadron anchors off the Juba River. Six days later on Christmas Eve a landing party from the ships is attacked and wiped out by the local inhabitants. This is the first record of contact between the British and the East Africans.

1799; On 12 January, the British naval reconnaissance squadron anchors off Mombasa for the night. No landing is made as 'the Moorish Colours' are seen flying over Fort Jesus. But this is the first recorded visit of the British to Mombasa.

1822: Seyidd Said, Sultan of Oman and Zanzibar, signs Moresby Treaty banning traffic of slaves on the East African Coast. The treaty implies British recognition of the Sultan's overlordship of East Africa.

1823: The Mazrui rulers of Mombasa appeal to the British for protection.

1824: British Protectorate established at Mombasa on 9 February by Captain William Owen, R.N., of H.M.S. *Leven*. British flag hoisted over Fort Jesus.

1826: Owen's Protectorate ended by Captain Arland, R.N., of H.M.S. *Helicon* and the British flag hauled down at Mombasa.

1828: Peace treaty signed on 11 January between Seyidd Said and Mazrui chiefs of Mombasa after first expedition by Omanis against the island. Said occupies Fort Jesus.

1828: In December, the Omani governor of Mombasa is forced to surrender Fort Jesus to the Mazrui. Mombasa once again independent.

1830: Second peace treaty signed between the Mazrui chiefs of Mombasa and Seyidd Said after second expedition by Omanis against the island.

1833: Third Omani expedition against Mombasa repulsed by Mazrui defenders.

1837: Seyidd Said sends a final expedition against Mombasa and takes possession of Fort Jesus after negotiations with the Mazrui.

1840: Seyidd Said moves his court from Muscat to Zanzibar which becomes the centre of his East Africa 'dominion'.

1841: Captain Atkins Hamerton appointed British consul to Zanzibar and first official representative of Britain in East Africa.

1845: Sultan of Zanzibar signs treaty with Britain banning exports of slaves from East Africa.

1870: First steamships arrive from Europe via the Suez Canal (opened in 1869).

1877: Sir William Mackinnon proposes the formation of a commercial company to exploit the mainland of East Africa.

1885: Anglo-German agreement signed in London in October defining British and German spheres of influence in East Africa. The British East Africa Association formed by Sir William Mackinnon to operate in the British sphere.

1888: Royal Charter awarded in September to Mackinnon's Association which becomes the Imperial British East Africa Company.

1890: Britain and Germany sign the Heligoland treaty under which Germany recognises Uganda as a British Protectorate and abandons all claims to Witu and Zanzibar. Captain (later Lord) Lugard establishes trading post for the Imperial British East Africa Company at Dagoretti.

1892: General Act of Brussels Conference lays down rules for development of East Africa and the suppression of slavery.

1893: British Protectorate declared over Uganda (which includes the present Nyanza and Rift Valley provinces of Kenya). British Foreign Office takes over the Imperial British East Africa Company's interests.

1895: The British East Africa Protectorate (what is now a major part of Kenya) declared on 15 June.

1896: Sir Charles Hardinge appointed first Commissioner to the British East Africa Protectorate. British Government approves loan of £3 million to build a railway from Mombasa to Lake Victoria. The Kedong Massacre takes place on 28 November.

1897: Sultan of Zanzibar abolishes legal status of slavery in East Africa.

1901: Kenya to Uganda railway completed.

1902: Uganda boundary re-adjusted and the British East Africa Protectorate becomes the governing power for all the upland areas lying between the sea and Lake Victoria. King's African Rifles formed.

1903: Hut and Poll Tax for Africans introduced. Sir Charles Eliot appointed Commissioner to the British East Africa Protectorate.

1904: Mombasa Arabs revolt against British authorities. First Masai agreement signed. Sir Donald Stewart appointed Protectorate Commissioner.

1905: British East Africa Protectorate comes under British Colonial Office. Commissioner renamed Governor: Executive and Legislative Councils introduced. Sir James Hayes-Sadler appointed Governor.

1907: Winston Churchill visits Kenya as Under-Secretary of State for the Colonies.

1908: Sir Percy Girouard appointed Governor.

1910: Masters and Servants Ordinance introduced.

1912: Native Authority Ordinance introduced to regulate African administration. Sir Henry Belfield appointed Governor.

1913: Second Masai agreement signed: Masai concentrated in one large reserve of 15,000 sq. miles south of the railway.

1914: British forces in British East Africa Protectorate in a state of war with German forces in Tanganyika.

1915: Land Ordinance passed to give 999-year leases and individual rights over land occupied by European settlers. Native Registration Ordinance passed to provide registration certificates for all Africans employed outside the African areas.

1916: War Council formed to co-ordinate the war effort against the Germans in Tanganyika.

1917: Sir Charles Bowring appointed Acting Governor of British East Africa Protectorate. Economic Commission set up to report on economy.

1918: End of hostilities with Germans in Tanganyika. Year of drought, famine and rinderpest.

1919: Major-General Sir Edward Northey appointed Governor. War Council dissolved. Europeans granted franchise. Ainsworth circular outlines Government policy on African labour.

1920: First communal (European) elections held in January. Kenya becomes a Crown Colony in July. The East African rupee stabilised at Shs. 2/-. Income Tax proposed but rejected by European community.

1921: Harry Thuku forms Young Kikuyu Association.

1922: The East African shilling introduced at the rate of Shs. 20/- to the East African pound and pound sterling. The Nairobi Riot: police open fire on demonstrators outside Nairobi jail where Harry Thuku has been imprisoned. Sir Robert Coryndon appointed Governor.

1923: European Convention of Associations propose a 33 per cent cut in African farm wages. Devonshire White Paper published: outlines British policy on 'paramountcy of native interests' in Kenya.

1924: General (communal) election held for European, Indian and Arab seats in the Legislative Council. Legally appointed Local Native Councils introduced. Royal (Ormsby-Gore) Commission appointed to examine social and economic developments in East Africa.

1925: Sir Edward Grigg appointed Governor.

1928: Special (Hilton Young) Commission appointed to examine closer union between the East African territories.

1929: Board of Agriculture established to administer European farming. Hilton Young Report published. First locust invasion for 30 years.

1930: British Labour Government publishes its policy on closer union and relationships with native population: the 'Black Papers'.

1931: Report published of the inquiry into East African affairs by the Joint Select Committee of the British Houses of Parliament. Sir Joseph Byrne appointed Governor. General elections held: Indian candidates pledge themselves not to take up seats in Legislative Council. Jomo Kenyatta, General Secretary of the Kikuyu Central Association, leaves Kenya for Europe.

1932: Poll Tax for Europeans and Asians introduced. Lord Rayne, Special Commissioner, reports on Kenya taxation.

1933: Kakamega 'gold rush'.

1934: Report published of Kenya (Carter) Land Commission to inquire into land rights and to define African and European settled areas.

1935: Report of the Economic Development Committee published. Native Land Board set up.

1936: Income Tax introduced to Kenya.

1937: Air Chief Marshal Sir Robert Brooke-Popham appointed Governor.

1938: Kamba tribesmen march on Government House, Nairobi, to protest at Government's de-stocking policies.

1939: First recorded labour stike by dock workers in Mombasa. Kenya at war with Germany. Sir Henry Moore appointed Governor.

1940: Kenya Central Association banned and leaders detained.

1941: Kenya soldiers of the East African Brigade lead British forces across Kenya frontier into Italian-held territory in Somaliland and Ethiopia.

1942: Last Italian stronghold in Ethiopia surrenders to East African forces in February. 11th East African Division sails for India and Burma to join Allied forces in the fight against Japan. East African

APPENDIX 3                                     219

troops invade Madagascar and capture island from the Vichy
French.
1943: Former leaders of K.C.A. released from detention.
1944: First African (J. W. Mathu) nominated a Member of Legislative Council. Kenya African Union formed. Sir Philip Mitchell
appointed Governor.
1945: End of hostilities with Germany and Japan.
1946: East African Division returns from successful campaign in
Burma. Jomo Kenyatta returns to Kenya from Europe: takes over as
President of the K.A.U.
1947: East Africa High Commission and Central Legislative Assembly established with headquarters in Nairobi.
1948: Mau Mau proscribed as an illegal society.
1949: Kenya police take over responsibility for policing African
reserves.
1950: British Government announces that official policy will be to
guide the people of the colonial territories to responsible self-government.
1950: Nairobi achieves city status.
1951: Central Committee of the K.A.U. approves adoption of Kenya
flag.
1952: Communal fine of £2,500 imposed on 8 April on the Aguthi
and Thegenge locations of Nyeri district as punishment for outbreaks of arson. Sir Philip Mitchell retires as Governor on 21 June.
First mass K.A.U. meeting held at Nyeri on 26 July. Kikuyu and
Meru tribesmen sentenced on 6 October for attacks on cattle and
farm buildings at Timau. Senior Chief Waruihu assassinated on 7
October. Sir Evelyn Baring sworn in as Governor on 19 October.
State of Emergency declared 20 October: Jomo Kenyatta and other
leaders arrested in Operation 'Jock Scott'. Trial of K.A.U. leaders
opens at Kapenguria on 25 November.
1953: Jomo Kenyatta sentenced to seven years' hard labour for
managing Mau Mau. Lari Massacre and raid on Naivasha Police
Station on 26 March. British forces launch forest offensive against
Mau Mau in June. K.A.U. proscribed 8 June.
1954: Privy Council turns down Kenyatta's appeal against sentence.
Operation 'Anvil' clears Mau Mau suspects from Nairobi. 'General
China' captured and first surrender talks open. War Council formed.
Lyttelton constitution introduced.
1955: Second forest offensive launched in January. Second surrender
talks open. Hunt for Kimathi begins.
1956: Kimathi captured and executed. General election for European, Indian and Arab seats in Legislative Council held in October.

1957: First African general election held in May. Lennox-Boyd Constitution introduced.

1958: Six additional African members elected to Legislative Council. All African members announce boycott of Council proceedings, but persuaded to return by promise of constitutional talks.

1959: New Kenya Group formed. Sir Patrick Renison appointed Governor.

1960: First Lancaster House constitutional talks held in January. Kenya African National Union and the Kenya Coalition formed.

1961: Primary and general elections under Lancaster House constitution held in February. Ronald Ngala forms multi-racial Government in April. Jomo Kenyatta released from detention in August and accepts presidency of K.A.N.U. Severe floods follow drought and cause famine: National Disaster declared.

1962: Second Lancaster House constitutional conference held in London in February. K.A.N.U. and K.A.D.U. Coalition Government formed.

1963: General elections under second Lancaster House constitution held in May. K.A.N.U. wins sweeping victory and Jomo Kenyatta becomes Kenya's first Prime Minister. Independence Conference held at Lancaster House in London in October. Kenya becomes an independent state on 12 December. State of Emergency declared in the Northern Frontier District.

1964: Army units mutiny in Tanzania, Kenya and Uganda. Kenya declared a Sovereign Republic on the first anniversary of independence: Jomo Kenyatta becomes Kenya's first President.

1965: Kenya Government publishes its views on African socialism and its application to planning in Kenya.

1966: Vice-President Oginga Odinga resigns and forms Kenya People's Union. 'Little General Election' held in June. K.A.N.U. wins overwhelming majority. Senate abolished and amalgamated with House of Representatives.

# Bibliography

J. Hawkes and Sir L. Woolley, *Prehistory and the Beginnings of Civilisation*: Vol. 1: *History of Mankind* (UNESCO, 1963).
Sonia Cole, *The Prehistory of East Africa* (Penguin Books, 1954).
J. A. Gregory, *The Rift Valley and Geology of East Africa* (Seeley Service, 1921).
Bailey Willis, *East Africa Plateaus and Rift Valleys* (Carnegie Institute, 1936).
L. S. B. Leakey, *The Stone Age Races of Kenya* (Oxford University Press, 1935).
W. H. Schoff, *Periplus of the Erythraean Sea: Travel and Trade in the Indian Ocean by a Merchant of the First Century* (Longmans, Green, 1912).
Z. Marsh and G. W. Kingsnorth, *Introduction to the History of East Africa* (Oxford University Press, 1956).
*History of East Africa*: Vol. I, edited by Roland Oliver and Gervase Mathew (Oxford University Press, 1963).
*History of East Africa*: Vol. II, edited by J. Harlow, E. M. Chiver and A. Smith (Oxford University Press, 1965).
R. Coupland, *East Africa and its Invaders* (Oxford University Press, 1956).
R. Coupland, *The Exploitation of East Africa* (Oxford University Press, 1939).
J. L. Krapf, *Travels, Researches and Missionary Labours during 18 Years' Residence in Eastern Africa* (Kegan Paul, 1860).
Lord Lugard, *The Dual Mandate in British Tropical Africa* (Blackwood and Sons, 3rd edn., 1926).
Lord Lugard, *The Rise of our East African Empire* (Blackwood and Sons, 1893).
Margery Perham, *Lugard: The Years of Adventure* (Collins, 1956).
Roland Oliver, *The Missionary Factor in East Africa* (Longmans, Green, 1952).
Joseph Thomson, *Through Masailand* (Sampson Low, 1885).
Sir Charles Eliot, *The East Africa Protectorate* (Arnold, 1905).
Vere Hodge, *The Imperial British East Africa Company* (Macmillan, 1959).

Sir Frederick Jackson, *Early Days in East Africa* (Arnold, 1930).

C. W. Hobley, *Kenya: from Chartered Company to Crown Colony* (Witherby, 1929).

W. M. Ross, *Kenya from Within* (Allen and Unwin, 1927).

M. F. Hill, *Permanent Way* (E.A. Railways and Harbours, 1950).

L. W. Hollingsworth, *The Asians in East Africa* (Macmillan, 1960).

G. Delf, *The Asians in East Africa* (Oxford University Press, 1963).

A. M. O'Connor, *An Economic Geography of East Africa* (G. Bell and Sons, 1966).

Elspeth Huxley, *White Man's Country: Lord Delamere and the Makings of Kenya* (two volumes) (Chatto and Windus; Praeger, 1968).

Julian Huxley, *African View* (Chatto and Windus, 1931).

Lord Altrincham, *Kenya's Opportunity* (Faber and Faber, 1955).

Sir Philip Mitchell, *African Afterthoughts* (Hutchinson, 1954).

G. Bennett, *Kenya: a Political History* (Oxford University Press, 1963).

Sir Michael Blundell, *So Rough a Wind* (Weidenfeld and Nicolson, 1964).

Elspeth Huxley and Margery Perham, *Race and Politics in Kenya* (Faber and Faber, 1956).

G. Delf, *Jomo Kenyatta* (Gollancz, 1961).

Montagu Slater, *The Trial of Jomo Kenyatta* (Secker and Warburg, 1955).

G. Bennett and C. Rosberg, *The Kenyatta Election* (Oxford University Press, 1961).

Tom Mboya, *Freedom and After* (André Deutsch; Little, Brown, 1963).

Ian Henderson and Philip Goodhart, *The Hunt for Kimathi* (Hamish Hamilton, 1958).

Donald L. Barnett and Karari Njama, *Mau Mau from Within* (*Monthly Review*, 1965; MacGibbon and Kee, 1966).

D. H. Rawcliffe, *The Struggle for Kenya* (Gollancz, 1954).

Susan Wood, *Tensions of Progress* (Oxford University Press, 1962).

*Federation in East Africa: Opportunities and Problems*, edited by Colin Leys and Peter Robson (Oxford University Press, 1965).

*The Economic Development of Kenya: Report of an Economic Survey Mission of the International Bank for Reconstruction and Development* (Oxford University Press, 1963).

*Kenya: an Economic Survey* (Barclays D.C.O., 1966).

Carl G. Rosberg, Jr., and John Nottingham, *Nationalism in Kenya* (Praeger, 1966).

OFFICIAL DOCUMENTS

*Report of the East African Commission* (Cmnd. 2387/1925).

*Report of the Special Commission to East Africa* (Cmnd. 3378/1929).

*Report of the Joint Select Committee on Closer Union* (Commons 156/1931).

*Report by the Financial Commissioner (Lord Moyne) on Certain Questions in Kenya* (Cmnd. 4093/1932).

*Report of the Kenya Land (Carter) Commission* (Cmnd. 4556/1934).

*British Territories in East and Central Africa* (Cmnd. 7987/1950).

*Report by Parliamentary Delegation to Kenya* (Cmnd. 9081/1954).

*East Africa Royal Commission Report* (Cmnd. 9475/1955).

*Record of Proceedings and Evidence in the Inquiry into the Deaths of Eleven Mau Mau Detainees at Hola Camp in Kenya* (Cmnd. 795/1959).

*Further Documents Relating to the Deaths of Eleven Mau Mau Detainees at Hola Camp in Kenya* (Cmnd. 816/1959).

*Historical Survey of Origins and Growth of Mau Mau* by F. D. Corfield (Cmnd. 1030/1960).

*Report of Kenya Constitutional Conference, London* (Cmnd. 960/1960).

*East Africa: Report of the Economic and Fiscal Commission* (Cmnd. 1279/1961).

*Kenya: Report of the Kenya Constitutional Conference, London* (Cmnd. 1700/1962).

*Kenya: Report of the Kenya Coastal Strip Conference* (Cmnd. 1701/1962).

*Kenya: Report of the Northern Frontier District Commission* (Cmnd. 1900/1962).

*Kenya: Report of the Regional Boundaries Commission* (Cmnd. 1899/1962).

*Kenya: Report of the Independence Conference* (Cmnd. 2156/1963).

*Kenya: Report of the Delimitation Commission* (Cmnd. 1921/1963).

*Kenya: Summary of Proposed Constitution for Internal Self-Government* (Cmnd. 1970/1963).

*Development Plan for the Period 1965/66–1969/70* (Government Printer, Nairobi, 1966).

*Statistical Abstracts* (Ministry of Economic Planning and Development, Nairobi).

*Economic and Statistical Review* (East Africa Statistical Department).

# INDEX

# Index

East African Indian National Congress, *see* Indian National Congress

East African Mounted Rifles, 57
East African Syndicate, 50
Economic Commission (1917), 61
Economics and Finance Committee, 75
Economy Commission, 174
Edinburgh, Prince Philip, duke of, 113, 180, 184
Egal, Ibrahim, Prime Minister of Somalia, 184
Egypt, 22, 26, 34, 37, 48
Eldama Ravine, 46
Eldoret, 54
Electors' Union, 101
Elgumi, tribe, 45
Eliot, Sir Charles, Commissioner to British East Africa Protectorate, 49–50, 55
Elizabeth, Princess, *see* Elizabeth II
Elizabeth II, Queen, 113, 180
Embu Reserve, 125
Embu tribe, 45, 125
Emergency, the, 107, 115, 119, 125–6, 130, 134, 137, 139, 145, 151; cost of, 135
Entebbe, 45
Equator, 25, 192
Erskine, General Sir George, 133–4
Ethiopia, 19, 25, 46, 142, 175
Europe, 26, 30–31, 36, 48, 56–8, 61
European Elected Members Organisation, 135, 147
European Invaders, 28
European settlement, 53; *see also* White settlement
European settlers, 35, 49; *see also* Settlers
European types, 21
Europeans in Kenya, 49, 51–2, 55, 60–61, 72, 74, 78–9, 84–5, 96, 102, 105, 110, 114, 129, 132, 134, 146, 160–61, 165, 174; plot to murder, 118; march on Government House, 130; killed by Mau Mau, 143

Executive Council (Kenya), 51, 72, 74, 87, 90, 97, 100, 107

Far East, 26–7
Federal Independence Party, 146, 148–9, 157
Fiji, 97
First World War, 53, 56, 88, 93
Foreign Office, British, 38, 40, 50, 55
Fort Hall, 45–6
Fort Jesus, 28
Fort Smith, 44
Forty Group, 108
France, 29, 31, 34
Freitas, Sir Geoffrey de, 171–2
French, the, 31, 37, 93

German East Africa, 51, 58
Germans, 34, 37, 57–8
Germany, 32, 34–6; aggressive policies of, 38; and the Berlin Act of 1885, 57; threatens Kenya's security, 89
Ghana, 147, 167
Gichuru, James, 159, 174, 189
Girouard, Sir Percy, Governor of Kenya, 53–4, 56, 76
Githunguri Teachers' Training College, 102–3
Gloucester, Prince Henry, duke of, 104
Goa, 28, 127
Gondar, 93
Government, *see* Kenya Government
Government departments, 47
Government House, 130
Governors' Conference, 95, 98; *see also* East African Governors' Conference
Gowers, Sir William, Governor of Uganda, 77
Graeco-Roman ships, 25
Great Lakes, 35
Great Powers, 36
Great Rift Valley, 20
Greeks, 19, 21
Griffith-Jones, E. N. (later Sir Eric), 167

Kenya Land and Freedom Armies,
126, 129, 132–4, 137–8, 141–3
Kenya Land Commission, 89; see
also Carter Commission
Kenya Masai, 51
Kenya Muslim League, 157
Kenya National Party, 157, 159
Kenya Peoples' Union, 190–91
Kenya Police, 131, 136
Kenya Police Reserve, 126
Kenya Province, 44; see also
Kikuyuland
Kenya Regiment, 92, 126
Kenya Riigi, 142
Kenyatta, Johnston (later Jomo):
General Secretary, Kikuyu Central
Association, 85; escapes arrest, 95;
returns to Kenya, 101; launches
*Uhuru* campaign, 102, 103; pre-
sents memorandum to Colonial
Secretary, 107; strengthens hold
on K.A.U., 108; features in
intelligence report, 109; personal
magnetism, 115; addresses Kiambu
meeting, 117; arrested, 121;
brought to trial, 127; trial of, 128;
nominated leader of K.A.N.U.,
159; release and return, 162–3,
164; struggle with Ngala, 166;
becomes Minister of State, 167,
168; becomes Prime Minister, 169;
talks to European farmers, 173;
ally and protector, 174; on
Somalia dispute, 175; agrees constitutional conference, 177;
assures Arabs, 178; receives
European tribute, 179; offers
amnesty, 180; appeals for overseas help, 181; faces army mutiny,
182; calls in British troops, 183;
holds talks with Somalia, 185;
speaks on unemployment, 186;
announces Republic, 187; becomes President, 188; relations
with Odinga, 189; attacked by
Communists, 190; deals with
Odinga, 191; other references to,
114, 116, 129, 137, 140, 142–3,

150, 157, 170, 172
Kericho, 45–6
Ketosh tribe, 45
Khartoum, 22
Kiambu, 50, 103, 113, 117, 162
Kikuyu, tribe and people, 23–4, 40,
50, 86, 89, 95, 107; association
with Mau Mau, 109, 110, 112,
114–17, 132, 138–9, 141, 150, 159,
167–8, 173
Kikuyu Association, 84
Kikuyu Central Association (K.C.A.),
85–6, 95–6, 108, 110
Kikuyu Christians, 119
Kikuyu (Home) Guard, 129, 132–3,
141; see also Home Guard
Kikuyuland, 44, 50, 54, 86, 89, 107,
126, 131–2, 139
Kikuyu Land and Freedom Army,
167, 179–80
Kikuyu Provincial Association, 86,
95–6
Kikuyu Registration Ordinance, 132
Kikuyu Reserve, 125, 134
Kilimanjaro, 24, 77
Kilindini (Port of Mombasa), 54
Kimathi, Dedan, 129, 131, 141–2,
179; capture and execution, 143
King's African Rifles, 57, 71, 92,
126, 182
Kipsigis tribe, 45
Kirichwa River, 113
Kisumu, 46, 49, 54, 57
Kitchener, Colonel Horatio (later
Lord), 36
Koinange, Chief, 84
Koinange, Peter Mbiyu, 157

Labouchere, Henry, 41
Labour Government (British), 77, 80
Labour Opposition (British), 136,
151
Labour Trade Union, 91
Laikipia District, 51, 125
Laikipia Plains, 50
Lamu, island of, 36, 183
Lancaster House (conferences), 153,
157–9, 163–8, 177, 179

PRINTED IN GREAT BRITAIN BY
WESTERN PRINTING SERVICES LTD., BRISTOL